FORENSIC NEUROPSYCHOLOGY

FORENSIC NEUROPSYCHOLOGY
Legal and Scientific Bases

HANS O. DOERR
ALBERT S. CARLIN
Editors

THE GUILFORD PRESS
New York • London

© **1991 The Guilford Press**
A Division of Guilford Publications, Inc.
72 Spring Street, New York, NY 10012

Printed in the United States of America

This book is printed on acid-free paper.

Last digit is print number: 9   8   7   6   5   4   3   2

Library of Congress Cataloging-in-Publication Data

Forensic neuropsychology : legal and scientific bases / Hans O. Doerr,
    Albert S. Carlin, editors.
        p.   cm.
    Includes bibliographical references and index.
    ISBN 0-89862-770-2
    1. Forensic neuropsychology.   I. Doerr, Hans O.   II. Carlin,
Albert S.
    [DNLM: 1. Forensic Psychiatry.   2. Neuropsychology.
    W 740 F7145]
RA1147.5.F67   1991
614'.1—dc20
DNLM/DLC
for Library of Congress   91-16389
                                                                     CIP

Contributors

G. Andrew H. Benjamin, J.D., Ph.D. Member: American Bar Association, American Psychological Association, Arizona Bar Association, Washington State Psychological Association. Acting Assistant Professor, University of Washington. Outpatient Psychiatry, University of Washington Medical Center, Seattle, Washington.

Daniel R. Bird, Ph.D. McMaster University. Department of Psychology, St. Joseph's Hospital, Hamilton, Ontario.

Albert S. Carlin, Ph.D. Associate Professor, Psychiatry and Behavioral Sciences, University of Washington. Outpatient Psychiatry, University of Washington Medical Center, Seattle, Washington.

C. Munro Cullum, Ph.D. Assistant Professor, Department of Psychiatry, University of Colorado. Neuropsychology Laboratory, Health Science Center, University of Colorado, Denver, Colorado.

Hans O. Doerr, Ph.D. Professor, Psychiatry and Behavioral Sciences, University of Washington. Outpatient Psychiatry, University of Washington Medical Center, Seattle, Washington.

M. Alan J. Finlayson, Ph.D. Professor, Department of Psychiatry, McMaster University. Department of Psychology, Rehabilitation Unit, Chedoke-McMaster Hospital, Hamilton, Ontario.

David J. Fordyce, Ph.D. Adjunct Clinical Faculty, Rehabilitation Medicine, University of Washington. Physical Medicine and Rehabilitation, Virginia Mason Clinic, Seattle, Washington.

Lee Glass, M.D., J.D. Practicing attorney, Mercer Island, Washington.

Igor Grant, M.D. Professor and Acting Chair, Department of Psychiatry, University of San Diego School of Medicine, La Jolla, California. Assistant Chief of Psychiatry, Veterans Administration Hospital, San Diego, California.

v

Robert K. Heaton, Ph.D. Professor of Psychiatry, School of Medicine, University of California, San Diego, California.

Alfred W. Kaszniak, Ph.D. Professor, Department of Psychiatry, University of Arizona School of Medicine, Tucson, Arizona.

David R. Knowles, Ph.D. Associate Professor of Economics, Albers School of Business and Economics, Seattle University, Seattle, Washington.

Jan E. Leestma, M.D. Neuropathologist and Associate Medical Director, Chicago Neurosurgical Center, Columbus Hospital. Executive Director, Chicago Institute of NeuroSurgery and NeuroResearch, Columbus-Cabrini Medical Center. Consulting Neuropathologist, Children's Memorial Hospital, McGaw Medical Center, Chicago, Illinois.

Vernon Neppe, M.D., Ph.D. Associate Professor and Director, Division of Neuropsychiatry, Department of Psychiatry and Behavioral Sciences, University of Washington. Psychiatry and Behavioral Sciences, University of Washington Hospital, Seattle, Washington.

Glenn T. Stebbins, Ph.D. Department of Neurological Sciences and Department of Psychology and Social Sciences, Rush-Presbyterian-St. Luke's Medical Center, Chicago, Illinois.

Gary Tucker, M.D. Professor and Chairman, Department of Psychiatry and Behavioral Sciences, University of Washington. Psychiatry and Behavioral Sciences, University of Washington Hospital, Seattle, Washington.

Margaret A. West, M.S.W., Ph.D. Research Assistant Professor, Department of Social Work, University of Washington. Clinical Training Unit, Child Development and Mental Retardation Center, University of Washington, Seattle, Washington.

Robert S. Wilson, Ph.D. Associate Professor, Department of Neurological Sciences and Department of Psychology and Social Sciences, Rush Alzheimer's Disease Center, Chicago, Illinois.

Along with the explosive growth of neuropsychology there has been dramatic increase in the use of neuropsychological expertise in legal proceedings. As attorneys have become more sophisticated in appreciating the potential impact of brain impairment on behavior—ranging from subtle to catastrophic—they have turned to psychologists for the documentation, quantification, causative attribution, prognosis, and everyday meaning of deficit. Psychologists who engage in assessment may find their data, their reports, and themselves suddenly (or not so suddenly, as legal wheels grind slowly) thrust into the legal system.

This book was written for practicing behavioral and clinical neuropsychologists, but may also be useful to trial attorneys who seek familiarity with the language and the reasoning process of neuropsychology. Clinical neuropsychologists, first and foremost, have to be schooled both in the scientific and in the clinical understanding of the complexities of human behavior. In addition, they have to appreciate the role and operations of the physiological organ of behavior—the brain—in both health and disease. They must also have a thorough understanding of the psychometric properties, strengths and limitations of the measurement tools they employ. Finally, they must be sensitive to the psychological reality and motivational world of the agent of behavior, the person, and be able to place and think about the person's performance within the appropriate historical, cultural, and psychosocial contexts. When neuropsychologists become participants in forensic issues, these obligations remain, as does professional responsibility to the patient and allegiance to one's data. However, there are additional complexities: multiple client relationships (attorney vs. patient), legal standards of proof, restrictions on confidentiality. The legal arena can be bewildering to one trained in the seminar, the laboratory, and the clinic. The courtroom has a choreography of its own, and the participants in the process are expected to follow the steps.

Most psychologists are somewhat familiar with the role of educator, but now they have to condense a mass of complicated data into a time span of an hour or so, translate the language of findings from comfortable jargon to plain English, and accomplish all this following not their outlines but the lawyers' scripts.

Our goal is to provide a map, an itinerary, and a list of important landmarks to the professional who is called upon to enter the legal forum. The first two chapters address the structure and process of the forensic arena. Glass discusses the basic assumptions underlying the legal resolution of differences and gives us an outline of the entities that society has set up for this purpose. Benjamin and Kaszniak describe the complex rules and rites that govern the introduction of expert testimony into the decision process. The third chapter by Doerr describes the point at which attorney and neuropsychologist meet and develop ground rules. This is also when the psychologist identifies the basic parameters of the expert testimony: questions asked by the attorney or trier of fact, background materials needed to address these questions, and the selection of neuropsychological tools.

The following two chapters (4 and 5) are written by experts in neurology, neuropsychiatry, and neurophysiology, the medical fields most closely concerned with brain function and dysfunction and whose data are most likely to be encountered by the neuropsychologist in the perusal of medical background records. Leestma gives a thorough description of the physical processes and resulting pathophysiology of head trauma and toxicity. Tucker and Neppe provide an introduction to neurological, neuroradiological, and neuropsychiatric assessment.

The next four chapters address crucial issues in interpretation that arise once the assessment data set has been assembled. Wilson and Stebbins deal with the construction of a valid baseline against which the impact of new trauma or illness can be measured. Carlin focuses on the neuropsychological effects of current and past use of psychoactive drugs and alcohol that may be primary or coexist with other causes of impairment. Finlayson and Bird discuss the impact of psychological pathology on cognitive function. Finally, Cullum, Heaton, and Grant address issues in the significance and detection of volitional and nonvolitional attempts to fake or exaggerate impairment.

The concluding two chapters lead beyond the initial assessment of impairment and causation to prognosis, rehabilitation, and cost of impairment. Fordyce reviews the growing field of remediation, including cognitive rehabilitation, and writes on the long-term outcome of brain impairment. West and Knowles introduce methods and procedures to estimate the economic significance of a reduction in neuropsychological functions.

Commonly asked questions in forensic neuropsychological testimony are presented in the Appendix. They are culled from actual deposition and trial testimony transcripts originating from or reviewed by the editors.

This book has benefited greatly from the generous assistance of many. Sharon Panulla, our publishing senior editor, never flagged in her support and faith in this enterprise. Nancy Monahan, Jim Pruess, and Tracy Cranick provided invaluable service in the preparation of the manuscript. Finally, we owe a deep gratitude to our contributors, who gave so much of their time and interest to turn this book from concept to reality.

HANS O. DOERR
ALBERT S. CARLIN

Contents

PART III. INTERPRETING THE FINDINGS

PART IV. PROGNOSIS, REMEDIATION, AND COST

PART I

Neuropsychology and the Law:
Structure and Process

chapter 1

The Legal Base in Forensic Neuropsychology

LEE S. GLASS

The U.S. judicial system is a marketplace of a very special sort. Business is transacted within its walls that cannot be transacted anywhere else. A criminal court calendar will proceed in a fashion reminiscent of a Middle Eastern bazaar. In a steamy courtroom reeking of tobacco, sweat, and alcohol, it can be hard to hear the proceedings over the rumbling ebb and flow of an often forlorn and hostile humanity. The haggling, however, is over duration of imprisonment, not the price of a carpet from Istanbul. In comparison, a pretrial conference in a large civil case may remind one more of a Sotheby auction. Convivial and urbane proxies may intermix social amenities with their bidding. Nobody involved ever forgets, though, that they have been brought together by a lawsuit, which each seeks to resolve at his or her client's desired price.

The market deals in only one item—controversy. Through the kaleidoscope of litigation, that single item becomes an infinitely variable image of dazzling, shifting colors and shapes. Were we to gaze for a sufficient time, we would see that its crystalline scenes span our continent, cross our globe, and pierce to the depths of outer space. They involve our young and our elderly. They involve children not yet born, and legal fictions that will never be born. They concern the lowering of our salaries, the raising of our taxes, the widening of our liabilities, and the narrowing of our civil rights. They show our boardrooms and our barrooms and our bedrooms. They display virtually every facet of our complex society. We might observe, as Walt Kelly's Pogo concluded, that "we have met the enemy, and he is us."

Neuropsychologists can figure prominently in the adjudication process because a large number of cases involve questions of the mental status of one or another party to the proceedings. Neuropsychologists are trained

3

in investigative techniques that produce objective, quantifiable data. Such data are viewed favorably by many triers of fact, precisely because of their objectivity.

This chapter provides the interested neuropsychologist with an overview of certain aspects of the adjudicative process in the United States. After some further introductory remarks, I explore features of both the state and federal court systems, and then investigate aspects of criminal law that commonly involve neuropsychological expertise. At the end of the chapter, I examine issues of civil law that are of interest to the forensic neuropsychologist.

OVERVIEW OF THE ADJUDICATIVE PROCESS

Persuasion is the uniform currency of our adjudicative marketplace. The power of ideas, the strengths of arguments, and the apparent wisdom of a thought decide (or, perhaps, should decide) cases. The strength of an advocate in our system of dispute resolution lies in his or her ability to bring out the necessary factual basis of a controversy, to be convincing about the law that should be applied, and to apply the facts to that law in a way that persuades observers that there is justice in the result sought.

The first step in the resolution of any dispute is the portrayal of the facts from which it is derived. Commonly, the underlying facts will be disputed. When such is the case, there must be a determination made as to the correct version of those facts. Such determinations are made by a "trier of fact." Juries are often used to decide disputed facts, but the resolution of such disputes may be within the province of the judge or hearing officer, depending upon the nature of the case.

In courts, a showing of fact must be based upon the introduction of evidence. Relevant evidence is something that has a tendency in logic to prove or disprove some fact that is of consequence. Evidence can be something tangible, like a fingerprint, or intangible, like an opinion. It can be powerful ("I saw him point the gun and pull the trigger") or weak ("I suppose that is possible"). It can go to a central point in a case, or may be only marginally applicable to something on the periphery. Once something is allowed into evidence, any party can generally argue that it means whatever it might want it to mean. Each side to a dispute will attempt to present evidence sufficient to prove the existence of those facts necessary to win its case. When a party has introduced those facts, it will "rest."

Because "facts" are based on evidence, they may be real only in the minds of the courtroom observers. They may have no other basis in reality. They may be as far from "truth" as Savannah is from San Francisco.

Nevertheless, as long as there is evidence to support them, facts—real or illusory—may be used to support a decision. This is a major imperfection in our system of adjudication, one that is exploited by the less scrupulous participants in the process. A medical expert, for example, may offer an opinion to a judge or jury, but would never give the same opinion to a room full of medical peers, because it lacks a firm scientific basis. Yet opinions are flippantly tossed about daily in our courts and administrative proceedings by those whose concerns are more about business than about professional responsibility. Such conduct is fraught with peril. The wise psychologist will recognize that testimony founded upon strict intellectual honesty best serves the process, as well as the reputation of the expert witness.

In a legal analysis, once the facts to the controversy have been established, the next step is to determine the applicable law. As a practical matter, the determination of law will often be made before the trial or other type of hearing. Questions of law are decided only by judges or hearing officers; they are never decided by juries. In theory, juries decide only questions of fact. In practice, juries are very much involved in the determination of questions of law. If a jury does not feel a particular result is proper, it can deliberately reach a verdict intended to effectuate its notions of justice, even though these notions misconstrue or misapply the law.

Intuitively, it may seem a straightforward matter to determine the law that applies to a given case. Often, however, it is the source of constant wrangling. The law may prescribe vastly different results in a particular case, depending upon a determination of the applicable law.

Questions of law that do not involve disputed facts are resolved by the judge or hearing officer alone. If disputed facts are involved, the matter must also be considered by the trier of fact. For example, a defendant may be guilty of murder if sane at the time of the homicide, but guilty of nothing if insane. In such cases, there must be a vehicle for informing the jury as to the variety of legal results that flow from various determinations of facts. Jury instructions are used for this purpose.

These instructions, usually delivered orally by the judge at the close of the trial, inform the jury in considerable detail about the law in the case. When appropriate, the instructions may provide alternatives. In a hypothetical murder trial, the instructions might be, in part: "If you find the defendant was sane, you shall find the defendant guilty. If you find that the defendant was insane, you shall enter a verdict of 'not guilty by reason of insantiy.'" Jury instructions can be very complex, covering in minutes what it might take a lawyer months to learn. Everyone assumes that juries will understand and properly apply the instructions.

Advocacy in our system requires that the facts be applied to the law, and that the resulting conclusion bear some resemblance to justice or fairness. Most caring adjudicators will not accept a result that seems to work a substantial injustice, although "justice" and "fairness" often depend upon whose ox is getting gored. Generally, to accomplish this, the advocate must be a storyteller. He or she must construct the framework of the story long before trial and must gather the evidence to support each portion of the tale. Each witness and each piece of evidence will presumably add in their own way to the unfolding drama. Ultimately, given those facts, the conclusion the advocate seeks, and its apparent justness should be obvious.

Experts entering this arena find themselves in constant peril of becoming compromised. Too often, advocates are concerned only with storytelling; the search for truth is a distant concern and could lead to the ruin of a perfectly fine fable. Advocates are often fiercely result oriented. An expert who does not make a commitment to professional integrity from the outset may suffer great embarrassment later in the process.

With this general overview of the system in mind, we will briefly explore certain more technical aspects of the U.S. system for conflict resolution.

THE STRUCTURE OF THE DISPUTE RESOLUTION SYSTEM

The Federal Court System

Portions of our judicial system were born before we were a country with a constitution. Those political entities that were colonies before the Revolutionary War became states when the conflict ended. In those days, "states" carried the meaning that we give to "nations" today. Each unit viewed itself as sovereign, and each had its own court systems that were wholly independent of those of even its closest neighbor. Adoption of the Constitution left those existing systems largely intact, but superimposed another judicial authority: the courts of the federal government.

Federal courts are, by constitutional definition, of limited authority. The union formed by the original states was to be held together by a federal government of limited authority. The powers given to the judicial branch of that government were sharply defined. Under the Constitution, federal judges can hear only such cases as may be allowed by the Constitution, or by laws of Congress.

The federal court system was established with two principal purposes in mind: first, to allow federal cases and federal questions to be decided in federal courts in order to avoid potential state court prejudice; and second, to provide citizens of different states a potentially neutral forum in certain types of suits. As a result of these considerations, federal courts are generally involved in cases arising under federal law. They also hear important cases in which the parties are from different states.

The federal court system is organized into three tiers: the trial court level, the first appellate level, and the Supreme Court. Federal trial courts are called "district courts." Each state has at least one federal district, and each district has a court.

More populous states have many districts. Federal cases are generally filed in a district court, where they are first heard. It is at this level that trials are held, witnesses called, and judgments entered. A party dissatisfied with a district court opinion generally may appeal to the circuit court level. There are nine circuits, and each has a court. These courts are appellate bodies; trials do not occur at this level. Rather, these courts review the records from the trial courts and consider the written and oral arguments of attorneys. Issues of public policy are given careful concern at this level of adjudication.

A party dissatisfied with an appellate court decision may attempt to have the decision overturned by the Supreme Court, the highest judicial tribunal in the United States. The Court hears only a select few cases each term. Public policy considerations are paramount at this level: the Supreme Court wants to know why it should reach a certain result. This court has the authority to declare any law of the federal government or any state "unconstitutional." It is not bound by the rulings of any other court and has the authority to ignore or overturn any of its own prior decisions that might be viewed as present impediments. When serving as an appellate body, the Supreme Court considers the material that had previously been submitted to the lower courts, the briefs of counsel for the litigants, and frequently "friend of the court" briefs from interested groups. It is constitutionally authorized to conduct trials in certain cases, but it virtually always appoints "masters" rather than conduct trials itself.

State Courts

State courts are organized in a variety of ways, in keeping with their historical sovereignty. Generally, each county has two levels of trial courts: a district court and a superior court. The names vary from state to state, but the volume of cases generally requires the processing of a large number of somewhat "small" cases and a lesser number of "large" cases. Commonly, "district" courts handle misdemeanor offenses and small civil cases. "Superior" courts adjudicate cases involving felonies, and civil disputes that exceed some statutory minimum amount, such as $10,000. Typically, superior courts consider appeals from district court decisions as well.

Most states have two appellate levels, similar to the federal system. An intermediate appellate court gives a final decision in most cases that are taken up on appeal, with a few cases making it all the way to the state's highest court.

Administrative Agencies

A 20th-century phenomenon has been the growth in the number and scope of administrative agencies at every level of government. As our society has become more complex, the activities of individuals have become increasingly regulated. This regulation is usually first authorized by some statute, then given to an administrative agency for enforcement. A variety of entitlement programs over the past several decades have similarly been delegated to any number of agencies for administration.

When agencies decide cases, they act in a somewhat judicial fashion, and their actions must comport with acceptable standards. Generally, agencies must give adequate notice to the parties involved, appropriately explain various rights and responsibilities, and provide opportunities to confront and cross-examine witnesses.

CRIMINAL LAW

In our legal system, responsibility for the commission of a crime may not attach to the defendant if the state cannot show that he or she had the necessary culpable state of mind. Once charged with a crime, a defendant may keep the prosecutorial wolves from the door if his or her lawyer can show that the defendant is incapable, due to some mental impairment, of participating in the defense of the case. Even after conviction a defendant may be spared the harshness of the court's wrath: Insane convicts may not be executed as long as they are insane.

Culpable State of Mind

In our system of justice, most serious crimes involve a *mens rea*, that is, a culpable mental status. We can think of this roughly as a requirement of "intent." More precisely, to be guilty of a crime, a person must have acted cognitively; actions during fugue states are not sufficient to support a conviction. Thus, a potentially important issue in every criminal case is the mental status of the defendant at the time of the apparently criminal act.

Generally, a person must intend to do something wrong before criminal liability for his or her acts will attach. A person who shoots another but who truly believes he or she is shooting a corpse is not guilty of murder, because that crime includes the requirement of an intent to kill another human being. As the seriousness of the crime diminishes, the strictness of the intent test usually declines as well. Behaving in a reckless manner may be sufficient to sustain a conviction for manslaughter, even if the defendant truly did not intend to injure another person. At the farthest end of the spectrum, no intent needs to be shown for the more trivial offenses: Even a potential candidate for sainthood can be convicted of speeding.

As with most things, there are exceptions to the need to prove a culpable state of mind. A few very serious offenses, such as the adulteration of foods shipped in interstate commerce, have been defined by statute in a fashion that does not require a culpable mental status. These crimes, however, represent only a tiny percentage of the types of criminal misconduct.

Intent must be proven by the prosecutor; it is not the defendant's burden to prove that the intent was lacking. If the prosecutor cannot prove every element of the offense beyond a reasonable doubt, the defendant is entitled to an acquittal. Often it is difficult to prove intent; it frequently must be inferred from the defendant's conduct. On the other hand, an action may be susceptible to a variety of interpretations. A defendant need only raise in the minds of the trier of fact a "reasonable doubt" about the presence of the requisite mental status to be entitled to acquittal.

Diminished Capacity

One way to raise a challenge to the prosecutor's portrayal of intent is to claim "diminished capacity." According to this argument, it takes a relatively properly functioning intellect to formulate a criminal intent. Alcohol, drugs, the heat of passion, abnormal psychiatric status, and a host of other influences may interfere with normal intellect. Under unusual circumstances, actions that are normally the product of criminal intent may occur without any forethought whatever. In such cases, the actors should not be subject to the same punishment as those performing the same deeds with an antisocial intent.

The Insanity Defense

The insanity defense is a humanitarian extension of the concepts that support the doctrine of diminished capacity. If a defendant can prove that he or she was insane at the time of committing an offense, the defendant cannot be found guilty of that offense or any lesser included offense. Support for this rule rests on the following philosophical precept: Persons should not be punished for otherwise antisocial conduct if they are unable to conform to socially acceptable norms. In principle, this doctrine has widespread support; in application, however, it has generated storms of controversy that continue to rage across medical and legal boundaries.

A defendant's mental status is precisely the area in which neuropsychologists are expert. Despite this expertise, the probes available to the forensic practitioner are often crude tools when applied to finely drawn questions of considerable social importance. In the final analysis, the defendant's mental status at the time the offense was committed may be a matter of guesswork. The opinions of the psychologist are often best approximations over which there can be considerable disagreement. This situation is fraught with peril for the psychologist. The unwary expert witness can easily be drawn outside his or her area of expertise by skillful cross-examination. Similarly, an overzealous expert may offer a view that cannot be supported by scientific opinion. At best the situation can cause embarrassment; at worst it can ultimately lead to an unjust verdict. The cautious psychologist will not venture from opinions that can be supported by professionally acceptable data.

Competency to Stand Trial

Before a defendant can be convicted, of course, there must be a trial. But there can be no trial unless the defendant possesses a requisite degree of competency. To be tried, a defendant must be able to understand the nature of the charges and be able to assist in the defense of the case. Issues in these areas are generally much more amenable to definitive neuropsychological inquiry than those involved in diminished capacity and in the insanity defense for at least two reasons. First, the issues concern present capability and do not require retrospective analysis. Second, they concern matters less abstract than the concept of "right and wrong": For example, can the defendant understand that somebody is saying he pointed the gun and pulled the trigger, and that he should go to jail?

Neuropsychological testing can provide objective insight into questions such as those presented above. Deficits in cognition and memory can be probed and mapped. The psychologist can then formulate opinions that will help the court to determine whether a defendant is legally capable of being tried for a criminal offense. If the court finds the defendant unfit to be tried, the process can be repeated at regular intervals until the defendant has the ability to understand the nature of the charges and can participate meaningfully in the defense of the case.

CIVIL LAW

Civil law differs from criminal law in a variety of ways. The chief distinction (to a defendant, at least) is that imprisonment does not result from loss of a case. On the other hand, the burden of proof for the plaintiff is less: Matters need be proved only by a "preponderance of the evidence," which means "more likely than not." The result is that although a litigant cannot go to jail for losing the case, if the trier of fact feels that the other side is more likely correct than not, the litigant may very well lose a job, spouse, bank account, house, child, professional license, anything else of value, or all of the above. Consequently, civil litigation can easily be a big-stakes gamble with a relaxed burden of proof.

DISABILITY DETERMINATIONS

The employment model most Americans are raised with assumes several years in preemployment training (usually childhood and perhaps young adulthood), followed by several decades of employment culminating in retirement. For an unfortunate many, this career pattern may be temporarily or permanently interrupted by illness, trauma, termination, or other causes. Any employment hiatus may spell economic disaster for a family, with devastating ramifications in the areas of food, shelter, clothing, medical care, or education.

To help provide for the necessities of life during periods of unemployment, a variety of insurance programs—public and private—have been established. Some programs, such as Supplemental Security Income (SSI), administered by the Social Security Administration, are available to any person who is disabled, and who falls within certain income guidelines. Other programs have an employment nexus, such as Social Security Disability Insurance (SSDI), which requires a certain period of employment for eligibility. Every state has a workers' compensation program; although the benefits vary from state to state, virtually all provide benefits for employment-related disability, even if that disability occurs within the first minute of employment. A host of private insurance companies offer disability insurance benefits to both groups and individuals; generally, the benefits increase and restrictions decrease with increasing premiums.

The common denominator of every plan is the determination of benefits according to some degree of disability. For many programs, disability is not presumed and will be investigated.

A worker who has lost a limb or an organ of sensation, for example, has an easily identifiable loss. Insurance companies (and their governmental equivalents) can easily rate such disabilities: One need only turn to the appropriate page in the American Medical Association's *Guides to the Evaluation of Permanent Impairment*, find the extent of the loss, and read off the amount of impairment. Rating changes in neuropsychological function is quite a different matter.

For a variety of reasons, many, if not most, of these changes are not appreciated for what they are. First, the vast majority of disability evaluators have little or no training in the recognition of neuropsychological disorders.

Even experienced disability claims evaluators often lack the necessary education. Because the least experienced evaluators in an organization are usually the first to review a claim, an already unclear picture may become even murkier during processing at the lowest level.

Second, physician awareness of the presence of the signs and symptoms of neuropsychological changes is not universally high. Subtle cognitive deficits are often ignored by treating physicians, and alterations in mood are often either overlooked or treated perfunctorily with a medication. Claims evaluators reviewing medical records of persons treated by such physicians see nothing significant to suggest an employment disability.

Third, family awareness of the signs and symptoms observed from day to day is frequently low. Family members, particularly spouses, may recognize that something has changed but, understandably, are unable to appreciate the nature of the alteration. When they present their observations to others involved in the disability determination process, the significance of the information is often lost in the manner of the presentation, which may show considerable frustration or other emotional involvement.

Finally, the claim for disability benefits may arise at a time that legitimately causes evaluators to suspect the accuracy of the claim. Claims occurring just before an announced layoff or soon following any form of termination may be suspect. Claims filed during a period of severe marital turmoil may raise questions as to the legitimacy of the applications. Also, claims filed by people nearing retirement age who have had other health problems may suggest that they are seeking disability benefits for an otherwise noncompensable impairment.

Even after recognition of neuropsychological changes, disability benefits are usually not immediately forthcoming, often for perfectly legitimate reasons. A claims evaluator must determine whether the extent of the changes constitutes a "disability" according to the definition used by the organization considering the claim. For example, no benefits are available under SSDI unless the impairment prevents the claimant from earning about $300 per month in "any job that exists in substantial numbers in the entire national economy," whereas private carriers (for an appropriate premium) may grant benefits if an impairment prevents the insured "from engaging in his or her regular occupation." A neurosurgeon with a minor motor impairment might be totally disabled under the latter definition, but not at all disabled under the former.

Furthermore, the availability of benefits may be conditioned not only upon the presence of a disability, but upon a linkage between that disability and some legally or contractually required event. For example, insurance benefits may be available if—but only if—a disability is caused by a motor vehicle accident. In such cases, the evaluative process contains at least two steps: the identification of a disability (whatever that might mean under the terms of the applicable insurance policy), and the relationship of that disability to a particular motor vehicle accident.

Thus, once a neuropsychological change is suspected, accurate evaluation of the nature and extent of the deficit is of central importance to a determination of disability. The quantifiable nature of neuropsychological testing is of enormous importance in such instances because it provides objective data upon which decisions concerning disability can be based.

In my experience, objective evaluations of neuropsychological impairment have aided greatly in the efficient determination of disability. It is relatively easy to compare the nature and extent of objectively determined impairments to the applicable definition of disability, and reason one's way to a conclusion as to whether benefits are in order. A trustworthy psychologist's report, which fairly and carefully translates the objective data into examples of how the impairment is likely to affect employment, is generally quite acceptable to disability examiners. Such a report greatly facilitates in the comparison of the impairment to the definition of disability, and thus speeds the evaluation process considerably.

Naturally, neuropsychological evaluations are not the final word in the disability determination process. Neuropsychological impairment found following a work-related head injury does not mean that the head injury caused the impairment. It would be important to know that the patient was a 55-year-old alcoholic with a 34-year history of barroom brawling before attributing causation to the work-related injury. Similarly, it would be embarrassing to attribute cognitive deficits to a motor vehicle accident only to find that the deficits continued to worsen over time and were thus more likely related to Alzheimer's disease. Nevertheless, used with appropriate professional caution, neuropsychological evaluations are a powerful tool in the process of disability determination.

Determinations of Competency

Frequently, civil litigation raises questions of mental competency. Adults are generally presumed to be competent to handle their important affairs, but this presumption may be set aside if there is evidence to the contrary. Both the state and private parties may have occasion to question the competency of a particular individual. The state may be interested in a competency determination for purposes of limiting or suspending a professional or other type of license, for example, or to seek confinement of the person for purposes of medical treatment. Individuals may desire a ruling on competency in order to allow a responsible person to administer the financial affairs of another. Rarely (but often flamboyantly), an individual may seek to set aside a will or some other dispositive document because of a perceived entitlement to something of value of which he or she was not made a beneficiary. A common allegation in such circumstances is that the person preparing the document lacked a requisite degree of cognition at the time of its preparation.

In competency determinations, there must first be an analysis of the cognitive, memory, and sensorimotor skills that are required by virtue of the activity in which the individual seeks to engage. An evaluation of the individual's physical and mental status must then be performed, followed by a comparison of requirements and capabilities. Finally, a determination must be made as to whether, given a discrepancy between the two, legal authority exists to restrict some aspect of the individual's behavior.

In proceedings to challenge a person's competency, the burden of proof is generally upon the party bringing the challenge. The party must show, usually by a preponderance of the evidence, that incompetency exists. What constitutes incompetency will depend upon the nature of the proceeding. The restriction or suspension of a professional license may be premised upon an even otherwise minor cognitive impairment that interferes with the professional capabilities of the individual in question. For example, a physician who confabulates because of an anomia involving injectable medications may lose a license to practice medicine. The same impairment in a retired person may not be sufficient grounds for any restriction of the individual's right to conduct his or her daily affairs in whatever manner he or she chooses.

Neuropsychological evaluation has obvious applications in competency determinations. Commonly, the thorniest questions involve opinions concerning an individual's ability to consistently process environmental input and arrive at reasonable, abstract conclusions. Frequently, family members or close associates notice a mental status deficit of some sort, but argue that the deficit does not impair functioning in the disputed area. Neuropsychological testing can nicely demonstrate the presence or absence of deficits in abstract reasoning ability, and can often determine whether there is likely to be impairment in the performance of the activities under question.

Sequelae of Trauma

Personal injury litigation is an industry that generates employment for legions of adjudicative warriors. Camp followers (including expert witnesses of all manner and description, court reporters, illustrators, accountants, actuaries, and a host of others) benefit from the dollars spent by the protagonists in waging their battles. It can take an enormous amount of professional integrity for those caught up in the periphery of the fray to refuse lucrative, repeated business by a clearly stated commitment to strictly honest, professional opinions.

Although the rules of engagement are changing as an increasing number of state legislatures enact "tort reform" legislation, the goals remain the same: Plaintiffs seek to obtain the greatest amount of compensation for damages attributable to the injury, whereas defendants attempt to thwart the plaintiff efforts.

The visible results of trauma have been the foundation upon which plaintiff attorneys have built their cases for damages. Juries can see the result of the injury, and can apply the observations to their own experience to come up with some estimate of the impact of such harm. Juries can contemplate expert testimony as to the loss of earning potential that such injuries may cause, as well as the pain and suffering attributable to the injuries.

With increasing frequency, injured parties are claiming to have damages as the result of closed head injuries, in addition to whatever visible injuries they may have incurred. Presumably, there are two explanations for this phenomenon. The first is legitimate: As knowledge of the signs and symptoms of the sequelae of closed head injuries spreads, attorneys are properly sending trauma victims for evaluation of their neuropsychological status. Greater awareness of applicable signs and symptoms has led to an increased rate of diagnosis. The second is less benign: After an examination, disreputable psychologists can attribute abnormalities to head injury, regardless of their actual cause.

Properly used, neuropsychological testing can be of enormous benefit to triers of fact because the results can go a long way toward proving the presence or absence of deficits that are otherwise difficult to diagnose. Virtually every aspect of higher cerebral functioning can be evaluated, giving the court a clear picture of the plaintiff's neuropsychological profile. If thorough medical, educational, employment, and psychosocial histories are obtained, it may be possible to assess the likelihood that abnormalities found on testing are actually the result of closed head injury. To the extent that such a determination can be made, injured parties can be properly compensated for all damages that resulted from their injuries.

SUMMARY

In a variety of ways, the evaluation of neuropsychological function can play an important role in the adjudicative process. In criminal, civil, and administrative areas, questions frequently arise as to the presence or absence of deficits in cognitive, memory, sensory, and motor capabilities. The skills of the neuropsychologist can provide invaluable assistance to triers of fact in such cases. Any psychologist involved in the process must be acutely aware that compromising strict principles of intellectual honesty may result in harm not only to one or more of the parties in a particular litigation, but also to the system as a whole.

REFERENCES

Braker, S. J. (1975). *Presumption, bias, and incompetency in the criminal process.* Chicago: American Bar Association.

Colen, B. D. (1976). *Karen Ann Quinlin: Dying in the age of eternal life.* New York: Nash Publishers.

Cull, J. G., & Hardy, R. E. (1973). *Understanding disability for social and rehabilitation services.* Springfield, IL: Cha. C. Thomas.

Fingarette, H. (1972). *The meaning of criminal insanity.* Berkeley: University of California Press.

Gerber, R. J. (1984). *The insanity defense.* New York: Associated Faculty Press.

Goldenson, R. M. (Ed.). (1978). *Disability and rehabilitation handbook.* New York: McGraw-Hill.

Morton, D. A. (1983). *Medical proof of Social Security disability.* St. Paul, MN: West.

Nagi, S. Z. (1969). *Disability and rehabilitation: Legal, clinical, and self-concepts and measurement.* Athens: Ohio University Press.

Osterweis, M., et al. (Eds.). (1987). *Pain and disability: Clinical, behavioral and public policy perspectives.* Washington, DC: National Academy Press.

Roesch, R., & Golding, L. (1980). *Competency to stand trial.* Champaign: University of Illinois Press.

chapter 2

The Discovery Process:
Deposition, Trial Testimony, and Hearing Testimony

G. A N D R E W H. B E N J A M I N
and A L F R E D K A S Z N I A K

The purpose of this chapter is to provide the neuropsychologist with guidance in preparation for deposition, trial, and hearing testimony. Following a brief discussion of the role of deposition in the discovery process, we review principles about preparing for the deposition and the trial or hearing. This review covers aspects of both courtroom and hearing testimony that require attention from the neuropsychologist serving as an expert witness.

THE ROLE OF DEPOSITION IN THE DISCOVERY PROCESS

Deposition is one of several discovery methods that a party or potential party in a legal or administrative cause of action may use to obtain information about a particular case, before the cause of action is tried in court or at a hearing. The rules governing discovery differ somewhat from one jurisdiction to another. However, most states have adopted, in their entirety or in a slightly modified version, the Federal Civil Judicial Procedure and Rules (Fed. Civ. J. P. and R. 26 et seq.). In general, cases that arise in either federal or state courts will follow similar discovery procedures (Blinder, 1986; Friendenthal, Kane, & Miller, 1985).

The following discussion of the neuropsychologist as expert witness is based upon the federal rules. The lawyer who employs the neuropsychologist as an expert witness will clarify the procedural nuances of each jurisdiction. Typically, the neuropsychologist will first encounter the legal system during discovery. The expert will be queried from written questions (interrogatories) and/or through oral examination (deposition) before the courtroom trial or formal hearing. Both methods provide a written, authenticated testimonial record about the neuropsychologist's findings. Discovery is the preliminary process for eliminating the least pertinent issues, thereby narrowing the dispute. Deposition is recognized as the most exacting form of discovery. It is the first opportunity to evaluate the opposing case, counsel, and witnesses (Luvera, 1981). Hayslock and Herr (1983) further note that depositions can help lawyers to:

> (1) explore and obtain information from the other side through prepared and spontaneous, flexible follow-up questions; (2) determine what a deponent knows and does not know; (3) pin down a deponent to a particular story; (4) assess the witness's demeanor to determine what type of trial witness that person would be; (5) confront an adversary deponent with damaging information or probe the deponent about weaknesses in the case prior to trial; and (6) preserve testimony to be used later as admissions, impeachment evidence, or for other evidentiary or cross-examination purposes at trial. (p. 87)

In many cases, the results of depositions cause the parties to settle, avoiding the length of time and the costs needed to reach a final adjudication. Depositions are considered "the most deadly weapons in the arsenal of the trial lawyer" (Luvera, 1981).

Preparation for Deposition

Neuropsychologists typically are subject to deposition only after comprehensive interrogatories and/or the production of records based upon an earlier neuropsychological assessment. This preliminary activity allows the opposing counsel to prepare the questions more thoroughly. It also permits the neuropsychologist to anticipate likely questions and provides time to prepare for the deposition. However, the expert will occasionally receive a subpoena to attend a deposition without opposing counsel submitting interrogatories or requesting production of records. In either case, there will be time to attend a preparation conference with the employing lawyer.

At the first conference, the employing lawyer will provide the following background: (a) the nature of the claim and the principal defenses; (b) what information has been produced by discovery to date and what further will be sought; (c) the type of issues that are likely to arise during the deposition; and (d) where the deposition will occur, who may be present, and the likely atmosphere to be encountered (Suplee, 1982).

The neuropsychologist is most frequently called to act as an expert witness in cases involving the behavioral sequelae of head injuries or chronic pain problems. Many medical and perhaps other developmental or psychological records about the plaintiff's injuries will exist. Obtaining information from as many different sources as possible is quite important. Relying just on information edited by the employing counsel is insufficient. The employing attorney may inadvertently edit certain facts that would alter the expert's opinion. A good opposing counsel will discover what facts formed the underlying basis for the opinion in order to impeach the expert's testimony. The employing attorney may also have questioned the opposing counsel's expert during deposition, obtaining the results and opinions about an earlier neuropsychological evaluation. At the first preparation conference, the lawyer should provide much of this information. If the neuropsychologist has little experience, the lawyer also may produce for review a copy of a deposition transcript compiled in a similar case.

The records and notes from the preparation conference will establish a foundation for thoroughly preparing for the deposition. Depending upon the facts of the case, the expert witness will have to explain the various subtleties about the alleged injuries and the assessment results: (a) What childhood, family, and social factors shaped the premorbid history? (b) How has the person changed because of the alleged injuries? (c) How are day-to-day living capabilities affected by the sustained injuries? (d) What is the risk of further morbidity developing? (e) Is the injured person malingering? In preparing responses to the anticipated deposition questioning, the expert should think about how to describe the impairment and the clinical implications of the injuries in plain language. He or she should define all the neuropsychological terms that will be used, provide illustrations of the brain, and detail those assessment results that indicate particular aspects of impairment. The nature of neuropsychological concepts and findings are often technical and complex, often confusing fact finders (either a judge or hearing officer, or jury members). Justifying the assessment conclusions requires cogent explanations that nonspecialists will understand without any difficulty.

Some aspects of the case may remain uncertain because of the limits of expertise and knowledge. The neuropsychologist should identify these uncertainties, as well as any relevant published research that would assist in weighing the facts involved in the case. Finally, the expert should request that at least one other preparation conference be held with the employing lawyer shortly before the deposition occurs. The lawyer can conduct a mock examination while acting as opposing counsel. This will provide practice for the expert in answering accurately and simply. The examination also will highlight possible damaging testimony that might occur due to uncertainties in neuropsychological knowledge or in the particular facts involved in the case. The expert must give special consideration to these uncertainties in order to respond truthfully without lessening his or her credibility as a witness.

Before the deposition, the opposing counsel may seek an informal statement from the expert. These out-of-court statements can be used to impeach the expert's credibility later. Therefore, the expert should decline to make any statements until a subpoena is received and the deposition is held. A subpoena may not be enforced for a number of legal reasons. The expert should consult the employing attorney upon receipt of the subpoena to provide the attorney enough time to present legal arguments to the court. For instance, two of the most common legal obstacles that prevent the expert from being questioned by the opposing counsel during deposition are jurisdictional issues and the need to protect the work product of the attorney (Suplee, 1982). If the employing attorney does not contest the subpoena, the expert must attend the deposition at the appointed time and location unless other arrangements are made. Receiving a subpoena also establishes the neuropsychologist's right to reasonable fees for responding to the opposing counsel's formal discovery demands; the fees cover preparation time, travel time, and time during the deposition.

Considerations of professional liability provide another reason for not making out-of-court statements. As a participant in the discovery process, the expert will decrease the risk of a later negligence lawsuit being filed for breach of confidentiality. Revealing confidences under formal process of the law is one of the exceptions to maintaining client confidences. In addition, the expert further decreases the risk of lawsuit by undergoing an informed consent process with the client (Kovacs, 1985; Waitzkin, 1984). One part of the informed consent process details the limits of confidentiality. Both informed consent and subsequent signed releases of information are practical procedures that mitigate the risk of being sued for breaching confidences, whether or not the case reaches deposition or trial.

The Deposition Process

Generally an expert whose opinion is sought by an employing attorney will be questioned by the opposing counsel during deposition. If the expert's opinions contradict the employing attorney's assertions, the expert will rarely testify. Instead, the employing attorney will prevent the expert from testifying by asserting the work product doctrine. Unless there are exceptional circumstances (Feder, 1985), the attorney could prevent any information obtained by the expert in preparation for the trial from being discovered. The opposing counsel will be unable to discover discussions with experts labeled as the "work product" of the employing attorney in which the attorney's "thought processes" about the case are being developed (Maurer, 1984; Notes, 1982).

The employing attorney will typically not question the expert, if the expert testifies. There is always a chance that the opposing counsel will be unprepared and fail to question the expert before the trial. A deposition by the employing attorney may unnecessarily reveal information about the case before trial.

Considerable controversy exists about what role an expert witness should play during the legal process. Under the Federal Rules of Evidence (Fed. R. Evid. 702) an expert's role is vaguely construed. The expert assists the fact finders in understanding the evidence or a fact in issue. Commentators are split as to whether experts are co-opted, acting more as advocates than educators (Camper & Loftus, 1985; Loftus, 1986; Wasyliw, Cavanaugh, & Rogers, 1985). If the expert adheres to the results of the available data and not to situational demands to become another advocate, he or she can meet ethical responsibilities without sacrificing economic opportunities.

Generally, the people present during the deposition include the opposing counsel, the employing attorney, and a court reporter. The court reporter is also a notary public who will administer the oath. Sometimes the opposing counsel may employ an expert witness to be present. This expert would suggest lines of inquiry based upon an earlier review of the discovery documents or perhaps based upon the expert's answers at the deposition. The opposing counsel's expert also may assist in assessing the qualifications, capabilities, and demeanor of the expert employed by the claimant's attorney.

If an expert learns that the opposing counsel has secured the services of another expert, one option to avoid the "battle of the experts" is to convince the lawyers that all neuropsychological experts should work together. A full disclosure of all pertinent information about the diagnosis and prognosis could occur with a joint report identifying all areas of agreement (Watson, 1978). This disclosure would narrow the scope of any dispute between the experts. Another option is for the court to authorize the appointment of its own expert and charge the expenses to both parties (Fed. R. Evid. 706). In either case, the fact finders may be better served if they focus upon the facts of the case rather than upon the personality differences of the experts.

Under the rules in most jurisdictions, the deposition can proceed in any manner and to whatever extent the two opposing attorneys agree upon (Fed. Civ. J. P. and R. 26). The rules do not limit the number of depositions or the length of a deposition. Also, neuropsychological depositions may occur anytime during a lawsuit. If a deposition is scheduled, it is usually held during business hours in a conference room at the deposing attorney's office or a conference room at the courthouse. Occasionally, if many documents or records are in the possession of the expert, the deposing attorney will suggest conducting the deposition at the deponent's office so that records will be readily available. Regardless of the site, the expert can bring anything that may assist at the deposition, including notes, drawings, reference books, and even refreshments.

Protective orders (Fed. Civ. J. P. and R. 26 (c)(5)) can be used to keep records confidential, to limit discovery to a method other than a deposition, or to provide judicial relief (Fed. Civ. J. P. and R. 37) in unresolved procedural disputes between the opposing sides. However, courts generally allow the "free flow of unbridled depositions, regardless of the inconvenience of the witness" (Johnson, 1984, p. 313). Most disputes about the deposition process will be resolved by the attorneys out of court. An expert's reasonable request to keep certain records confidential, limit discovery or change the planned procedure of the deposition are all negotiable and are often resolved in favor of the expert's choice. If the expert notifies the employing attorney in a timely manner as to any concerns, the attorney will strive to find a solution or a compromise.

At the beginning of the deposition, an oath is administered to the expert and the opposing counsel provides some basic instructions about the process before starting the questioning. Every word uttered becomes part of the record unless both attorneys agree to stop recording the action. Deposition is a formal process with a transcribed record, which is used in an exacting manner as the case moves forward. If applied, the following suggestions will help the expert educate the fact finders without calling into question either credibility or knowledge (Bennet, Bryant, Vanden-Bos, & Greenwood, 1990; Gutheil & Appelbaum, 1982; Luvera, 1981; Pappas, 1987; Watson, 1978):

1. Take time to answer, as this will provide the employing counsel greater opportunity to form appropriate objections—the transcript will not reflect any pauses.
2. Answer questions directly, without volunteering unsolicited information—if a yes or no will suffice, say no more, but if an answer requires qualification, you are not compelled to give a simple response.
3. Respond to understandable questions only—paraphrasing a confusing question may suggest an entirely different matter unknown to the opposing counsel.
4. Wait until after consulting with the employing counsel if an earlier incomplete or incorrect answer requires greater explanation; the lawyer will know when best to return to the line of questioning.
5. Draw reasonable inferences between the data of the case and expert knowledge—this type of opinion evidence is based on reasonable

medical or psychological probability and is not subject to the stringent demands of scientific validity or reliability.

6. Use plain language—explain all technical terms, so that a lay audience would understand, while avoiding extreme adjectives or superlatives.

7. Answer questions about information within any documents or texts only after they are reviewed or the passage in question is read aloud—a refreshed recollection will provide more accurate answers and avoid the opposing counsel's trap of exposing memory deficits when questioning you about the entire document or text.

8. Refrain from stating that any single article or text is authoritative within neuropsychology; otherwise, you will be viewed as having relied explicitly on the document to formulate opinions, and the opposing counsel may use any part of the document to impeach your credibility.

The opposing counsel may skip from one subject to the next in an attempt to keep the expert off balance. At different points in the deposition, the counsel may summarize the expert's testimony inaccurately, expecting the expert to agree with the summaries. He or she may ask compound questions that assume other facts not in evidence. The expert should separate out the unproven assumptions and avoid the taint of speculation. Questions involving time are particularly difficult, and answers (if given) should be labeled as estimates. The expert does not need to define complicated or controversial concepts such as "cure" for the opposing counsel. Watson (1978) recommends that in responding to this type of question the expert turn the question back to the lawyer and ask what the opposing counsel means by "cure." This response anticipates the counsel's next line of questioning, which is to ask about a long list of possible definitions about the concept, all different and all tending to confuse the fact finders.

Generally the employing attorney will ask very few questions during the deposition. The questions will be reserved for the trial to avoid tipping the opposing counsel to another line of inquiry (Suplee, 1982). However, the attorney will be following the opposing counsel's questioning and either instructing the expert not to answer certain questions or objecting to them. The judge will rule on the objections at a later date. The expert should stop talking immediately when the employing attorney interrupts. Argument and contention should be left to the attorneys. At the very least, the interruption can provide the expert time to think carefully and form a more accurate response during the wrangling of the attorneys.

If at any time during the deposition the expert wishes to consult with the employing attorney, the rules do not preclude taking a recess. A break will permit the expert to regain composure as well as a chance to suggest possible areas in the testimony that could be stated more accurately. The attorney may wish to redirect the questioning at the earliest possible occasion after the break so that the responses are included within the record.

The employing attorney will question the expert only if the expert may be unavailable for the trial. If a witness is unavailable, then a deposition can be used as substantive evidence at the trial (Fed. Civ. J. P. and R. 32 (a)(3)). The most common, acceptable excuse for an expert's not being available (McNamara & Sorenson, 1986) is that he or she lives more than 100 miles from the courthouse (Fed. Civ. J. P. and R. 32 (a)(3)(B)). If the expert will be unavailable, then the employing attorney should consider videotaping the deposition. Suplee (1982) suggests that, given the technical content of the expert's testimony, the jury will be much more impressed with a videotaped deposition than with a dry, written transcript.

At the end of the deposition, the opposing counsel will often attempt to foreclose modifications of the record or additional comment by asking something, such as "Is that all?" The expert is advised to leave the door open, perhaps by responding, "To the best of my recollection" (Cook, 1983). Once the deposition is finished, the court reporter will transcribe the expert's testimony and send a copy to read, correct, and sign, vouching for its accuracy.

The expert may change any inaccuracies in the written transcript (Fed. Civ. J. P. and R. 30(2)). In making changes, the expert should state the reason for the change, attach the change as an appendix, and sign the deposition. Videotaped depositions are modified similarly. The modified segments will be edited from the tape after agreement from both lawyers. Under the federal rules, the expert has 30 days after receiving the transcript to make any changes and file them with the court. Otherwise, the court reporter will file the unsigned, uncorrected copy of the deposition with the court.

Occasionally, the employing attorney will mistakenly agree to the opposing counsel's suggestion that the expert waive signing the transcript (Hayslock & Herr, 1983). The expert will not receive, correct, or sign a copy of the transcript, and consequently all misspellings and substantive inaccuracies will remain. An uncorrected transcript provides a greater impeachment opportunity than if the expert has to explain at the trial why the transcript was corrected after the deposition. In addition, the written corrections would be available to the fact finders after the expert has testified if statements made at the deposition became an issue at trial. Most fact finders would have no difficulty with the expert admitting to and correcting mistakes. A well-prepared statement at trial, stating why the changes are necessary, is more convincing than uncorrected testimony in the transcript that varies from the expert's courtroom testimony (Suplee, 1982).

THE TRIAL

At trial, experts may testify by opinion if "scientific, technical, or other specialized knowledge will assist the trier of fact to understand the evidence or to determine a fact in issue" (Fed. R. Evid. 702). In common law, expert testimony was permitted only if the subject matter was beyond lay comprehension (Saltzburg & Redden, 1982). Experts cannot state an opinion of law or an opinion that mixes fact and law, or tell the jury what verdict it should reach (Fed. R. Evid. 704). The experts may base their opinions or inferences about the evidence on relevant data "if of a type reasonably relied upon by experts in the particular field" (Fed. R. Evid. 703). This permits experts to testify about data that would otherwise be inadmissible under certain rules of evidence that apply to other witnesses. Opinions can be based on personal observations or assessment of facts for testimony arising during the deposition (even facts that are not in evidence at the trial), or on any other method depended upon by professionals in the field.

Both at depositions and at trial, lawyers will raise objections about the technicalities of the rules of evidence. The primary reason for objections is to keep irrelevant or immaterial information from being discussed in front of the fact finders. The fact finders must base their verdict solely on the evidence presented at trial. The attorneys will manage the presentation of the evidence, in part, by arguing that certain information should be excluded or included according to their interpretation of the rules of evidence.

The attorneys must persuade the judge as to the proper evidentiary ruling. Some of the argument may occur as the expert is testifying. These objections may feel as if they are addressed to the expert personally. It is the attorney's job to answer objections. The expert should remain uninvolved in the argument and its sometimes associated heated emotions.

The two most common objections that may interrupt the expert's testimony are "no foundation has been laid" for the expert to state an opinion, or "the expert's testimony is irrelevant." The first objection arises when the attorney believes that the expert's opinion is incomplete or inadequate for one of the following reasons: (a) the expert has omitted critical facts before reaching an opinion by failing to review findings from depositions, earlier assessment records, or data about other cases; (b) the expert has relied upon the wrong facts in reaching an opinion, for example, an inadequate assessment; and (c) the expert is providing a response to a misleading hypothetical question that has omitted relevant facts (Baum, 1984).

Relevancy objections arise if the expert's testimony does not directly address the facts or issues in question. For instance, if an attorney has failed to raise a particular issue in the pleadings of the case before trial, no testimony about the particular issue would be allowed during trial. Often, the legal definition of relevance does not necessarily parallel the common-sense definition.

Finally, the form of the question asked by the opposing counsel can become the source of the objection. A question may be termed "argumentative," "complex and confusing," "cumulative," or "already asked and answered." These objections are usually made to protect an expert who is being badgered or harassed by the opposing counsel during cross-examination.

Direct Examination

Testimony will begin with the employing counsel establishing the qualifications of the expert on direct examination (i.e., during the initial testimony). The attorney will ask for a full description of the academic degrees, evidence of specialization, current duties of employment, number and content of publications, and previous practical applications of expertise. However, no particular set of criteria exists to establish whether an expert is qualified to provide neuropsychological testimony. In general, qualification occurs without difficulty if the expert's credentials are commonly accepted among neuropsychological peers as sufficient.

If qualification becomes an issue, the opposing counsel will object that the expert is not qualified and cannot state an opinion. Trial strategy generally calls for inflicting damage to the credibility of the witness as soon as possible. The opposing counsel will ask the court to *voir dire* an expert before proceeding, in an attempt to persuade the judge that the person is not an expert. *Voir dire*, which occurs before the fact finders, is a preliminary examination to determine the competency of an expert or other witness. Even if the judge qualifies the person, the opposing counsel may focus on inadequate credentials or experience in order to dampen the effect of the expert's direct testimony.

Direct examination continues after the expert has been qualified. The expert should assume the position of one interested in justice and a friend of the judge and jury, helping them to arrive at a just verdict (Costello, 1981, p. 24). The questions will be open ended to enable the expert to convey opinions and the rationale behind them. The attorney must not ask leading questions; thus, the expert should discuss in advance with the employing attorney how the testimony should unfold. Parsimonious testimony keeps the fact finders focused upon the issues. The expert should pay attention to the fact finders and notice when their attention has begun to wander. The expert will be addressing an audience who is unfamiliar with neuropsychology. Every aspect of the testimony may appear novel, or else boring or confusing. Thus, the expert must testify clearly, avoiding technical words and assumptions, or concepts that assume the fact finders' knowledge of unstated information.

Lawyers are often unaware of what can be done to enliven the expert's testimony. Much of the testimony will lend itself to summary in charts, graphs, slides, pictures, videotape presentations, and replicas or models of the brain. The more the testimony incorporates demonstrative aids, the more alive and less confusing it will be for the fact finders (Balabanian, 1980; Tigar, 1982). Empirical research has demonstrated how to present graphic material most effectively (Cleveland & McGill, 1985). If exhibits are technically accurate and admissible by the opposing counsel before the trial, or are admitted as exhibits at the trial, the members of the jury, if they desire, will be able to review the exhibits during their deliberations. Nothing better assures the education of the fact finders than well-done demonstrative aids (Whittington, 1983).

The expert is most persuasive during direct examination when taking into account the following suggestions for giving testimony (Brodsky & Robey, 1972; Feder, 1985; Postol, 1987; Tigar, 1982):

1. Appear definite and reasonable by responding deliberately without using qualifying or exaggerating phrases—hesitations and uncertainty in the testimony will raise doubt in the fact finders' minds.
2. Support all opinions with full descriptions of the data, the gathering techniques, and the inferences drawn from the assessment results.
3. Identify all vulnerable portions of the assessment process and analysis of the results.
4. Testify consistently with the earlier reports, interrogatory writings, or depositional statements.

Finally, one commentator summarized how best to present direct testimony: The expert's opinions must appear to be based on adequate knowledge, be expressed in an unbiased manner, and meet "the layperson's test of reasonableness—does it sound right and make sense" (Postol, 1987, p. 24).

Cross-Examination

During cross-examination the expert will often be limited to responding yes or no to the leading questions of the opposing counsel. In this respect, testifying during cross-examination appears easier than during direct examination. However, the expert should be cautious because the opposing counsel—whatever style or manner of questioning is adopted—will be trying to discredit the expert. Postol (1987) suggests:

The opposing attorney will do his best, through his questions, to demonstrate that the expert witness is stupid, ill-informed, did not have all relevant facts necessary to evaluate the situation, was improperly paid off by the attorney who hired him, and provided an analysis which is illogical and contrary to established scientific principles. (p. 25)

Other than contesting the qualifications of the expert, the opposing counsel will ask leading questions about the independence and the thoroughness of the expert. Lack of independence arises as the opposing counsel questions the expert's opinions because of alleged financial bias. Brodsky and Robey (1972) suggest a very direct response to this type of allegation:

Certainly it is possible to be biased in some way about most things. It has been written whose bread I eat, his songs I sing. Being very aware of this, I try to be even more cautious than usual and do my best to be sure that my bias is not interfering with my clinical judgement. (p. 176)

A typical attempt to question the expert's thoroughness occurs when the opposing counsel cites inconsistent testimony. Examples of inconsistent testimony may be presented unfairly by the opposing counsel. If the cross-examiner reads from a deposition transcript to show the inconsistency, the material may be out of context. If the expert responds that the opposing counsel is taking something said out of context, the employing attorney will object. The Federal Civil Judicial Procedure and Rules (32 (a)(4)) require the reading of any other part of a transcript that ought in fairness to be considered with the part introduced. Also, the Federal Rules of Evidence (803 (5)) permit witnesses to refresh their memories by rereading any recollection that was recorded before the trial. Often is is helpful to ask to review the document or deposition before responding to cross-examination questions.

Another way to impeach the expert's credibility is to claim a lack of foundation for the expert's opinion. The opposing counsel may challenge the expert's thoroughness by questioning whether the expert omitted certain facts or relied on the wrong facts in forming opinions or by demonstrating that the expert performed an inadequate assessment that led to unjustified conclusions before considering all the data or other causes of the injury (Baum, 1984). In responding to any of these allegations, the expert should preface the answer by reminding the opposing counsel that he or she raised similar issues during the deposition. Prior consistent statements made by the expert will bolster that expert's credibility with the fact finders. The expert may also point out that the opposing counsel's expert reviewed the same information and that reasonable differences of opinion between experts are possible.

Leading questions can be irritating because they paint black-and-white pictures while leaving little room for explanations. Often, the opposing counsel intends to increase the frustration level of the expert. When the opposing counsel allows the expert to provide a fuller explanation about a particular issue, the purpose is to lead the expert away from the basic facts of the case and give full rein to the expert's pride and wordiness in order to possibly place him or her in a bad light. Behaving as an educator and a disinterested professional can be difficult when being grilled and set up by a good cross-examiner. The best course is to avoid arguing, appear polite and cooperative, and answer all the questions directly and dispassionately.

Redirect Examination

The employing attorney will conduct a redirect examination after the cross-examination. Once again the questions will be open ended, providing the expert an opportunity to explain points raised during the cross-examination that may have left a misleading or incomplete impression because of the expert's brief and simple responses. Often, a recess will occur before redirect examination begins. The employing attorney may have suggestions about what points raised during the earlier testimony require clarification or emphasis. If at all possible, the expert should use the demonstrative aids again while addressing the fact finders.

THE HEARING

It is quite difficult to generalize about the procedures and content of administrative hearings. Pfeiffer (1979) noted that "the qualifications of hearing officers, the degree of formality of the hearing, and the weight given the product of the hearing officer all vary greatly" (p. 12). The nature and procedures of the hearing are also within the discretion of the agency in charge. However, attorneys who practice administrative law will be familiar with the formalities of a particular agency hearing and know how closely the rules of evidence and civil procedure will be followed. The expert should work with the employing attorney to shape the testimony with the particular structure of a hearing in mind. Most administrative or arbitration hearings will allow the employing attorney to ask leading questions during direct examination. This practice, and the fact that the typical atmosphere at hearings is less emotionally charged, makes testimony easier. Furthermore, most expert witnesses are seldom cross-examined. Because discovery is expensive and time consuming, and thus rarely employed, few opposing lawyers are prepared to cross-examine an expert witness and will avoid running the risk of conducting a poor cross-examination.

Our personal experience, as well as discussions with a number of practicing clinical neuropsychologists, suggests that neuropsychological testimony is being increasingly used in disability hearings, such as those conducted by state workers' compensation boards and Social Security Disability Insurance (SSDI) hearing examiners. Although the various principles of deposition and trial testimony, already discussed in this chapter, have relevance for hearing testimony, there are unique aspects of hearings that deserve discussion. (See Glass, this volume, for a description of the legal base of the neuropsychologist's role in disability determinations.)

In compensation hearings, such as those conducted by a state department of economic security, the neuropsychologist is likely to encounter several similarities to, and some departures from, his or her experience in trial testimony. The degree of preparatory interaction with the claimant's attorney tends to vary considerably from one lawyer to the next. The neuropsychologist will rarely be questioned by any opposing attorney, and some neuropsychologists have experienced only the briefest contact with the claimant's counsel, just prior to the scheduled hearing.

Hearing procedures will be similar to those of the courtroom, although the atmosphere may appear less "formal." A court reporter will be present to transcribe the testimony, and the expert witness will be sworn in and have his or her credentials reviewed, in a manner similar to that of the courtroom.

In SSDI appeal hearings, although it is technically acceptable for the expert witness to render an opinion through a written report alone, the neuropsychologist should render live testimony, as it will carry greater weight. In either case, the expert should be as specific as possible in describing the nature, probable duration, and severity of impairment in functional terms. The report or testimony should clearly detail the objective evidence of impairment that has led to the neuropsychologist's conclusions. In disability determinations, the diagnosis of a specific disease or syndrome is less crucial than the specification of how the ability to work may be impaired (Kapp & Bigot, 1985). The ability of the hearing officer, as trier of fact, to consider adequately all of the evidence in making a decision will be hampered by a report or testimony that provides conclusions without sufficient objective observations to justifying them.

Throughout this chapter, we have emphasized the necessity of adequate preparation for the neuropsychologist's role as expert witness, whether in providing deposition, trial, or hearing testimony. Not only must the neuropsychologist acquire expert knowledge of his or her clinical specialty, but also a reasonable understanding of the role that the testimony will play and the nature of the proceedings themselves. We hope that the review

provided here will serve the purpose of alerting the reader to those aspects
of the discovery, trial, and hearing processes critical for fulfilling the forensic
role.

REFERENCES

Balabanian, E. (1980). Medium v. tedium: Video depositions come of age. *Litigation*,
    6, 26–27.
Baum, D. B. (1984). Taking on the opposing expert. *Trial, 20*, 162–166.
Bennet, B. E., Bryant, B. K., VandenBos, G. R., & Greenwood, T. K. (1990).
    Professional Liability and Risk Management, Washington, D.C.: American
    Psychological Association.
Blinder, M. (1986). Psychiatric analysis in personal injury cases. *Trial, 22*, 75–
    77.
Brodsky, S. L., & Robey, A. (1972). On becoming an expert witness: Issues of
    orientation and effectiveness. *Professional Psychology, 3*, 173–176.
Camper, P. M., & Loftus, E. F. (1985). The role of psychologists as expert
    witnesses in the courtroom: No more Daniels in the lion's den. *Law &
    Psychology Review, 9*, 1–13.
Cleveland, W. S., & McGill, R. (1985). Graphical perception and graphical methods
    for analyzing scientific data. *Science, 229*, 828–833.
Cook, E. A. (1983). Preparing your client for deposition. *Barrister, 10*, 45–46.
Costello, J. M. (1981). The direct examination of the expert witness. *For the
    Defense, 23*, 21–24.
Feder, H. A. (1985). The care and feeding of experts. *Trial, 21*, 49–52.
Federal Civil Judicial Procedure and Rules (1991). St. Paul, MN: West.
Federal rules of evidence for United States courts and magistrates. (1975). St. Paul,
    Minn.: West.
Friendenthal, J. H., Kane, M. K., & Miller, A. R. (1985). *Civil procedure*. St. Paul,
    MN: West.
Gutheil, T. G., & Applebaum, P. S. (1982). *Clinical handbook of psychiatry and the
    law*. New York: McGraw-Hill.
Hayslock, R., & Herr, D. (1983). *Discovery: Theory, practice, and problems*. Boston:
    Little, Brown.
Johnson, L. G. (1984). *Deposition guide: A practical handbook for witnesses*. Seattle,
    WA: Forum Press.
Kapp, M. B., & Bigot, A. (1985). *Geriatrics and the law*. New York: Springer
    Press.
Kovacs, A. (1985, May). *Bulletin*. Washington, DC: Division 42, American Psy-
    chological Association.
Loftus, E. F. (1986). Experimental psychologist as advocate or impartial educator.
    Law & Human Behavior, 10, 63–78.
Luvera, P. N. (1981). How to take depositions. *Personal Injury Annual*, 866–
    879.
Maurer, V. G. (1984). Compelling the expert witness: Fairness and utility under
    the federal rules of civil procedure. *Georgia Law Review, 19*, 71–120.

McNamara, T. J., & Sorenson, P. T. (1986). Deposition traps and tactics. *Litigation*, *12*, 22–24.

Notes (1982). Discovery of retained non-testifying experts' identities under the federal rules of civil procedure. *Michigan Law Review*, *80*, 513–523.

Pappas, E. H. (1987). Preparing your witness for deposition. *For the Defense*, *29*, 8–9.

Pfeiffer, G. S. (1979). Representing clients in administrative adjudicative proceedings. *Litigation*, *5*, 12–54.

Postol, L. P. (1987). A legal primer for expert witnesses. *For the Defense*, *29*, 21–25.

Suplee, D. R. (1982). Depositions: Objectives, strategies, tactics, mechanics and problems. *Review of Litigation*, *2*, 255–328.

Tigar, M. E. (1982). Handling the expert like an expert: Back to basics. *National Law Journal*, 13–20.

Waitzkin, H. (1984). Doctor–patient communication. *Journal of the American Medical Association*, *225*, 2441–2446.

Wasyliw, O. E., Cavanaugh, J. L., & Rogers, R. (1985). Beyond scientific limits of expert testimony. *Bulletin American Academy of Psychiatry & the Law*, *13*, 147–158.

Watson, A. S. (1978). On the preparation and use of psychiatric expert testimony: Some suggestions in an ongoing controversy. *Bulletin American Academy of Psychiatry & the Law*, *6*, 226–246.

Whittington, H. G. (1983). Role of the psychiatrist in personal injury litigation. *Journal of Psychiatry & Law*, *10*, 419–440.

chapter 3

Issues in Initial Contact: Neuropsychologist– Attorney–Patient

HANS O. DOERR

WHEN SHOULD AN ATTORNEY CONSIDER CONSULTATION WITH A NEUROPSYCHOLOGIST?

In recent years, there has been a tremendous increase in the use of neuropsychological expertise in legal proceedings, but a decision to consult a specialist should not be taken lightly. Neuropsychological assessment, interpretation, and testimony are time consuming and costly. A referral can conjure up the specter of "brain damage," which may be difficult to erase from the mind of an attorney's client even in the face of subsequent negative findings. There are, however, indicators of possible abnormal neuropsychological functioning that can make the referral decision easier and more informed. These include:

1. Physical findings, such as a penetrating head injury, an intracranial lesion discovered and or produced during brain surgery, an abnormal head computerized axial tomography (CT) scan, abnormal magnetic resonance imaging (MRI) results, abnormal electroencephalogram (EEG) findings, and positive neurological signs such as abnormal reflexes, Battle signs, "Racoon's eyes," and double vision
2. Abnormal findings on a previous neuropsychological examination
3. Loss of consciousness or altered states of consciousness
4. Presence of amnesia for events prior, during, and after trauma

5. Presence of seizures
6. Presence of low scores on neurologic indices of responsiveness, such as the Glasgow Coma Scale (Teasdale & Jennett, 1974)
7. Reports of loss or change in sense of taste and smell
8. Changes in school or vocational achievement
9. Increased frequency of traffic violations and traffic and home accidents
10. Occurrence of or increase in frequency of socially inappropriate behaviors such as violence, off-color language, or questionable sexual conduct
11. Personal or family complaints of memory problems, irritability, explosive temper, moodiness, word-finding problems, and reduced initiative and interests

The presence of these indicators is no assurance that a neuropsychological examination will result in abnormal findings, but their total absence suggests a very low probability of such findings.

HOW TO LOCATE A QUALIFIED NEUROPSYCHOLOGIST

The term "neuropsychologist" is essentially a self-description of a psychologist who offers neuropsychological services. There is as yet no "official" set of qualifications beyond that of license or certification as a psychologist in the state where the services are offered. Members of the American Psychological Association are bound by Principle 2 of the Ethical Principles of Psychologists, which restricts the practice to services and techniques for which a psychologist is qualified by training and experience (American Psychological Association, 1989). State psychology license and certification rules have similar provisions. The Code of Ethics has nothing on the specifics of training, and the training backgrounds of practicing neuropsychologists are quite varied, with doctorates in experimental psychology, educational psychology, counseling psychology, and clinical psychology well represented. A relatively recent voluntary credential is the diploma in clinical neuropsychology from the American Board of Professional Psychology. The holder of the diploma has passed a board examination and has 5 or more years of postdoctoral professional experience in psychology, and 3 or more years of clinical neuropsychological experience. It is likely that this credential will gain in acceptance and importance in the years to come, especially for psychologists in private practice who are not subject to the internal institutional quality control of academic and hospital settings. The future neuropsychologist will probably have a solid grounding in general and clinical psychology as part of the predoctoral training and internship, followed by specialized postdoctoral training in neuropsychology.

Given the recent emergence of neuropsychology as a professional clinical specialty, it is not surprising that standards for subspecialization such as pediatric or geriatric neuropsychology are even less developed. The qualification to work with young or old patients must be based on the individual's background and experience.

A helpful resource in locating credentials of neuropsychologists is the *Directory of the American Psychological Association* (1989). It is published every 4 years and lists membership in three classes. Fellows hold a doctoral degree in psychology, have at least 5 years of professional experience, and have displayed evidence of unusual and outstanding contribution or performance in the field of psychology; members hold a doctoral degree in psychology; associate members have completed at least 2 years of graduate work or hold the master's degree in psychology plus 1 year of professional experience. The listings include membership in the divisions of the organization, including Division 40 (neuropsychology), and the members' own designation of clinical specialties practiced. There is also a listing of holders of diplomas in neuropsychology from the American Board of Professional Psychology. Another helpful reference is the *National Register of Health Service Providers in Psychology* (1989), which is published every 2 years with regular supplements. Criteria for inclusion are current license or certificated by the State Board of Examiners of Psychology at the independent practice level, a doctoral degree in psychology, and 2 years of supervised experience in health services in psychology. The state psychological associations can also be helpful in providing names of licensed or certified psychologists, along with their specialties. Ultimately, one of the best sources of referral is word of mouth. Fellow attorneys will have consulted with neuropsychologists who have qualified as experts in the courts and are recognized as professionally competent and proficient in presenting findings to the trier of fact. Neuropsychologists will be able to assist in evaluating credentials and identifying individuals who have contributed to the field in specialized areas of competence. However, rarely is a neuropsychologist an "expert" on another professional. As with other aspects of neuropsychological practice, evaluation of a colleague's background should be based on objective, verifiable data.

ISSUES FOR DISCUSSION DURING THE INITIAL CONTACT OF ATTORNEY AND NEUROPSYCHOLOGIST

Prior to the discussion of the client and the specific details of the case, the attorney should confirm that the neuropsychologist is available for consultation, assessment, and hearing or trial testimony during the anticipated time period of the legal process. Many experts are quite willing to review materials and examine patients but are uncomfortable with the emotional demands imposed by formal legal depositions and trial testimony. This is also the time to ask for an update on the expert's professional status and background. There should also be an exploration of potential conflict of interest. If the neuropsychologist has been previously consulted by the opposing attorney in the case, this should be stated and the discussion brought to a close. A previous incompatible private or professional relationship with the patient and/or his or her family is another reason to terminate the consultation. Finally, the attorney and the expert should also discuss financial arrangements such as the neuropsychologist's fee schedule, the parties responsible for payment, and retainers.

Once there is agreement on these issues the attorney should clearly articulate the questions and problems that form the basis of the consultation. These may include questions of diagnosis and causation, the impact of impairment on everyday life, recommendations for treatment, opinions on prognosis, and estimates of the costs of treatment.

MATERIALS HELPFUL IN INITIAL NEUROPSYCHOLOGICAL REVIEW

The initial contact is a good time to start assembling the relevant records. A comprehensive data set is helpful in any form of neuropsychological assessment, especially in documenting the basis for opinions in forensic procedures. Such documents can include detailed and contemporaneous records of events leading to the consultation, such as police records of an accident; records of on-the-scene emergency medical technicians, ambulance personnel, and flight nurses; emergency room records; and nursing notes for the first days following trauma. Also important are other relevant medical records such as reports of neurological and/or neurosurgical examinations and interventions; neuroradiologic reports including EEG, MRI, and CT scans; hospital discharge summaries and summaries of examining and treating physicians; previous neuropsychological assessment records including the recording sheets for test and interviews; detailed medical records predating the trauma in question; school records including grade transcripts, records of individual and group aptitude, achievement and intelligence tests, special education records, school medical records, and records of college entrance examinations; military records, with special emphasis on results of the Armed Forces Qualification Test (AFQT) and the Army Classification Battery (ACB), which have been used to estimate premorbid IQ (Montague, Williams, Lubin, & Gieseking, 1957; Murphy & Langston, 1956); employment records and income tax records; and records of previous contacts with the legal system.

PLANNING THE NEUROPSYCHOLOGICAL EXAMINATION

The neuropsychologist draws on three distinct data sets when formulating opinions: history and records assembled by others; clinical impressions, test behavior, and history assembled during patient contact; and performance on individual neuropsychological tests. The latter is most clearly within the domain of neuropsychology and sets this specialty apart from other health care professions such as neurology, neurosurgery, and neuropsychiatry. Qualitative impressions and history are essential in understanding a patient's performance and guard against a robotic interpretation of numbers, but the presence of quantitative data from standardization tests adds scientific rigor and allows for precise communication to and reliability checks by other neuropsychologists. It is often helpful to explain the distinctions among the various "brain damage specialists" to juries, especially when there is a difference of opinion. One simplified explanation uses the example of a malfunctioning car. The "neurosurgeon mechanic" gets inside the engine, examines the pistons, checks the valves and measures the thickness of the break pads. The "neurologist mechanic" inspects the car on the hoist in the garage for loose or missing parts, listens to the engine and records its performance on an electrical scope, analyzes the richness of air and gas mixtures, and checks for the integrity of the electrical system. The "neuropsychologist mechanic" takes the car and driver out on a prescribed course, up and down hills, at high and low speeds, through congested areas and parking maneuvers, carefully recording the performance of car and driver. This example makes clear that the various specialists' contributions are not redundant but complementary. Experts' findings may differ and yet be valid within the context of the examination.

The neuropsychological forensic examination normally involves personal contact between the psychologist and patient. There are still some holdouts from the days when a "blind," quantitative analysis of test scores and patterns, augmented by a limited history obtained by a testing technician, was seen as sufficient and a clear indicator of the scientific rigor of neuropsychological testing. However, most psychologists would now agree that valuable information and clinical impressions can be garnered through personal contact with the patient. Another reason for personal contact is that most patients expect it and want to talk to the person who is responsible for the report and potential testimony. Finally, some credibility may be lost when the opposing attorney exploits the fact (as she or he surely will) that the expert has never personally seen the patient.

Many neuropsychologists do not themselves give tests, but employ trained technicians for this purpose. Because the test administration is standardized and described in the literature, a well-trained technician can give a prescribed series of tests just as well as the neuropsychologist, and with greater economy. The technician is typically uninformed as to the legal aspects of cases and the resulting "blind" administration of tests may even serve to reduce a possible subtle bias due to expectation factors and thus enhance objectivity. The trade-off in using a technician is that the psychologist forgoes the opportunity to observe the test-taking behavior. However, this may be remedied by training the technician to take detailed behavioral notes.

There are occasions when the patient is not available for examination and the opinion of the neuropsychologist must be based on a review of records and or preexisting neuropsychological data. When the data base is comprehensive, and the tests are representative and appear to have been administered in the standard way, a psychologist can interpret the "raw" data and use them to formulate an opinion. An incomplete data base, or tests that are inappropriately selected, administered, or scored, may also become the basis for an opinion that can contribute to the case.

CONTENT OF THE CLINICAL INTERVIEW

The interview serves several functions: collection of information, clarification of the purpose and process of testing, reduction of anxiety, and a gathering of behavioral observations relating to appearance, interactive style, and mental and emotional states. There is no single standardized interview in neuropsychology, and styles of interviewing range from open to highly structured. In general, an interview should result in the following information:

1. Basic demographic data, such as name, address, telephone number, and date of birth (a patient's ability to provide this information can be diagnostic)
2. A detailed account of current symptoms and complaints (e.g., how do memory difficulties manifest themselves in daily life, how does pain rate in intensity in a 1–10 scale?)
3. Family history including age, health status or cause of death and occupation or former occupation of parents, age and health of siblings, patient's perception of family life while growing up
4. Marital status, history of previous marriages including reason for termination, common-law marriages, cohabitation or live-in arrangements, age, health and occupation of spouse or significant other, degree of satisfaction with current marriage or relationship
5. Sex, age, health, occupation, and current whereabouts of children

6. Educational history, with highest level achieved, grade point estimates, strong and weak subjects, repeated grades, special education placements
7. Work history, with dates, type of position, and reason for leaving
8. Military history, with dates, work specialty, rank at discharge, and type of discharge
9. History of significant legal problems
10. Current life stresses, including recent death and/or illness of significant others, recent job changes or job problems and financial worries
11. Work, home, and social routines, including a description of a typical working day, a typical nonworking day, recreational activities and hobbies, exercise programs and social activities including membership in clubs, churches, and so on
12. Automobile driving status, including information on possession of driver's license and technical, emotional, or legal problems with driving
13. Medical history, including information on circumstances of birth and early development; presence of major illnesses such as diabetes, high blood pressure, stroke, epilepsy, cardiovascular disease, and cancer; inpatient hospitalization; outpatient surgeries; injuries sustained in accidents including those involving motor vehicles or suffered during sports or other related activities; exposure to toxic fumes, gas and/or high voltage; assaults and/or rape; near-drowning episodes; episodes of loss of consciousness or altered states of consciousness; previous neuropsychological testing and the reasons for it; psychiatric and psychological treatment, counseling, and hospitalization; current health care providers with type of services rendered; current and recent (within the past six months) prescriptions and over-the-counter medications with dose levels, side effects, and information as to when taken last; current and past use of recreational drugs with estimates of frequency and amount; current and past use of alcohol including amount, current or past blackouts, years of use and history of alcohol-related treatment, and legal problems
14. Vegetative state including appetite, weight gain or loss, sleep patterns, recurrent dreams and nightmares, and patterns of sexual behavior and desire
15. Sensory-motor functioning including eyesight, hearing, taste, smell, tactual sensitivity, and muscle strength
16. Appearance, including dress, grooming, gait/posture, mannerisms, and physical abnormalities

17. Interactive style, including degree of cooperation, interaction, attention, and eye contact
18. Speech rate, tone, articulation, and word fluency
19. Mood and affect

SELECTION OF TESTS

It is beyond the scope of this chapter to discuss specific neuropsychological tests; the reader may consult the many excellent works on this topic, such as Lezak (1983), Filskov and Boll (1981–1986), Grant and Adams (1986), and Hartlage, Asken, and Hornsby (1987). The array of tests chosen should allow a comprehensive sampling of behaviors correlated with the state of the central nervous system. The individual test norms should be appropriate to the cultural and educational background and the age and gender of the person tested. The array of tests should be large enough for a multiple sampling of the major dimensions of brain function as a check on reliability. When the patient has been previously tested, the advantage in repeating the same tests in order to check reliability and course of change has to be balanced against the disadvantage of practice effects. There is no single test or even a standardized battery of tests that meets all these requirements. A long-running controversy in neuropsychology pits individualized, flexible arrays or tests against standardized batteries; each camp has distinguished champions. Individual test selection has the obvious advantage of optimally matching tests to the specific individual and situation; batteries typically have a larger and statistically stronger data base and allow for more precise communication and replication among researchers. The trend in neuropsychology is toward combining the best attributes of these approaches by using all or major portions of a battery or batteries as the core, which are then augmented by individual tests selected to overcome the shortcomings of the battery and to address specific questions.

Although there are many ways of classifying brain-related behaviors, there is general agreement as to the major dimensions involved. A comprehensive test battery generally contains tests that measure (a) formal IQ functioning; (b) academic skills in such areas as reading and comprehension of written materials, writing, spelling, and arithmetic; (c) attention and concentration; (d) motor strength and sensory/perceptual skills such as gross and fine motor strength, speed and dexterity, hand-eye coordination, sensory acuity of the tactual, auditory, and visual senses, tested when appropriate on both sides of the body; (e) language and verbal skills; (f) memory (immediate, delayed, and remote) and resistance of memory to interference, for verbally and visually presented material; (g) skills in problem solving, reasoning, and self-direction; and (h) emotional/psychological state. Many tests will provide information on two or more dimensions of brain function.

INITIAL CONTACT WITH THE PATIENT

Patients expect, and deserve, an explanation of the reason for undergoing the test. They are also entitled to know what to expect, which can allay fears about pain and invasive procedures. The first meeting is also the time to discuss financial arrangements. The patient should be told who gets the test report and how she or he will be informed about the findings. It is important that the patient appreciates the limitations of confidentiality in forensic procedures and knows that the psychologist most likely will be asked to reveal in deposition or in court all of the information provided by the patient.

Some special considerations apply to independent neuropsychological examination, where the patient does not attend on his or her own behalf but is "compelled" to participate by the opposing attorney. In these contacts, the psychologist must make very clear who referred the patient, and emphasize that the psychologist's testimony will be at the request of the opposing attorney with no limits imposed by the usual doctor–patient confidentiality. A normal feedback of results through subsequent contact with the patient is often not possible because of the restrictions of the legal process. To be sure, the neuropsychologist's principal client in independent examinations is the attorney, but ethical and professional obligations to the patient remain, regardless of the source of referral. These obligations to the patient extend from the quality and objectivity of the workup to the formulation of treatment and any follow-up recommendations. The latter should be clearly stated in the report or inserted in the record in deposition or other contacts with attorneys so that the patient's attorney is aware of the rec-ommendation and can pass them on to his or her client or other health care providers.

Ultimately, the only legitimate source of "expertise" of neuropsy-chologists is their training and their data base. Speculation, hunches, casual generalization, and self-serving appeals to authority make for poor opinions as they make for poor science. Matarazzo's (1990) call for scientific rigor and psychometric sophistication in forensic work is most timely. He argues cogently that the scientific literature, not the courtroom, should be the arena to test validity. As ever better trained neuropsychologists draw on ever more validated data sets, there will be greater opportunity for consensual agreement and settlement before going to court.

REFERENCES

American Psychological Association. (1989). *Directory of the American Psychological Association*. Baltimore, MD: Port City.

Council for the National Register of Health Service Providers in Psychology. (1989). *National register of health service providers in psychology*. Baltimore, MD: Port City.

Filskov, S., & Boll, T. (Eds.). (1981–1986). *Handbook of clinical neuropsychology* (Vols. 1 & 2). New York: Wiley.

Grant, I., & Adams, K. (Eds.). (1986). *Neuropsychological assessment of neuropsychiatric disorders*. New York: Oxford University Press.

Hartlage, L., Asken, M., & Hornsby, J. (Eds.). (1987). *Essentials of neuropsychological assessment*. New York: Springer.

Lezak, M. (1983). *Neuropsychological assessment* (2nd ed.). New York: Oxford University Press.

Matarazzo, J. D. (1990). Psychological assessment versus psychological testing. *American Psychologist, 45*, 999–1034.

Montague, E., Williams, H., Lubin, A., & Gieseking, C. (1957). Army test for assessment of intellectual deficit. *U.S. Armed Forces Medical Journal, 8*, 883–892.

Murphy, D., & Langston, R. (1956). A short form of the Wechsler-Bellevue and the Army Classification Battery as measures of intelligence. *Journal of Consulting Psychology, 20*, 405.

Teasdale, G., & Jennett, B. (1974). Assessment of coma and impaired consciousness: A practical scale. *Lancet, 2*, 81–83.

PART **II**

Neuropsychiatric and Neuropsychological Perspectives

chapter 4

Neuropathology and Pathophysiology of Trauma and Toxicity

JAN E. LEESTMA

Traumatic injury to the nervous system occurs in many forms, ranging from the classic blow or fall resulting in impact to the head, blast or concussive injury, missile wounds or other penetrating injuries, spinal injury, and combinations of these. Expert analysis of trauma cases can deal with the matter of complications of trauma, such as seizure disorders, psychological deficits, neurological deficits, prognosis, life-span estimates, and other matters. To develop a framework for building knowledge and experience, we must explore the most basic aspects of neurotrauma and understand key parameters of the process in the central nervous system.

THE FUNDAMENTALS OF NEUROTRAUMA

When the head is subjected to an impact, the scalp (at the immediate site of impact), the skull beneath the impact site, the coverings of the brain, and the brain itself are affected to some degree and respond to the physical insult differently. The manner in which these various components react is a function of many things, all of which combine to yield the final observable result. Grcevic and his colleagues (Grcevic, 1982, 1988; Jadro-Santel, Grcevic, Besenski, & Kalvsek, 1989; Leestma & Grcevic, 1987) have described this process as sort of a waterfall or cascade phenomenon in which there is a physical event that may produce primary injury to one or more components of the cranium. This primary event evolves, producing local injuries that may be trivial and can be repaired promptly, those that are resolved over a longer period of time, and those that cannot be repaired.

As a result of some of the primary injuries, secondary injuries occur, such as bleeding or edema, which in turn can either be resolved or not. These injuries or lesions can produce another level of injury, such as increased intracranial pressure, which may in turn compromise intracerebral circulation, which may in turn compromise respiration, which may decrease oxygenation of the brain. Thus, vicious cycles may develop that can prevent resolution or cause expansion or extension of earlier injuries, and prolong or complicate the clinical consequences of the original traumatic episode.

From a pathological point of view, medical researchers have expended a great deal of effort over the years to understand the basic processes involved in traumatic lesions of the brain or spinal cord (Becker & Povlishock, 1985). It might seem that once a traumatic event has occurred, there is nothing more to be observed. This is patently not the case. Laboratory experiments on animals have shown that impacts to the brain or spinal cord that will cause massive lesions eventually show little or no obvious pathology grossly or microscopically at the impact site shortly after occurrence (Balentine, 1985; Kirkpatrick, Higgins, Lucas, & Gross, 1985). It appears that the earliest changes in neural tissue after traumatic injury are subtle even at the ultrastructural level and involve physiological processes. The traumatized site may, however, become hemorrhagic, necrotic, and in the case of the spinal cord, evolve into a total transection (Leestma & Grcevic, 1987; Oehmichen, 1980; Oppenheimer, 1968).

Perhaps the first lesions are those involving the neural cell membranes resulting in prolonged depolarization and what is observed clinically in the brain as spreading depression (Eisenberg, 1985; Jennett & Teasdale, 1982) or in the cord as neural shock (Balentine, 1985). This lesion may include disruption or breakage of the neural membrane. In the most minimal injury the ionic channels of the membrane are probably disrupted and made dysfunctional. Perhaps at the same instant, the traumatic force has damaged the cytoskeleton of the axon or dendrite (neurofilaments and neurotubules) or perhaps other cellular organelles. The consequence of this latter injury becomes important later as intracellular transport of neurotransmitters and nutrients as well as vital trophic substances are interfered with, and neurons may die as a result (Leestma & Grcevic, 1987).

Other early events involve movement of calcium ions into cells that may activate lipolysis and proteolytic enzymes that lyse cells and further damage neighboring structures (Balentine, 1985; Siesjö, Agardh, & Bengtsson, 1990; Siesjö, Bengtsson, Grampp, & Theander, 1989; Siesjö & Wieloch, 1985). At the same time, the vascular bed that nourished the affected traumatized region is also responding to the injury. This response may involve increased or reduced blood flow and/or rupture of vessels, which results in breakdown of the blood–brain barrier with attendant leakage of edema fluid into the extracellular compartment (Adams, Graham,

& Gennarelli, 1985; Kobrine, Timmons, Rajjoub, Rizzoli, & Davis, 1977; Muiselaar & Obrist, 1985). Inflammatory mediators and other substances released as the lesion evolves affect otherwise undamaged vessels and may cause them to be obstructed, or to dilate and leak blood (Siesjö & Wieloch, 1985). Here the "cascade" phenomenon becomes more obvious. As vessels are injured they produce edema and interstitial bleeding that can damage other vessels and neural tissue. A relatively recent concept is useful to illustrate and understand what is happening at the tissue level in the traumatic lesion. Initially there is a focal lesion, the "traumatic epicenter" that expands but gradually fades out as the various processes diminish and normal tissue is reached. This border zone is the "penumbra" of the lesion; a sort of transitional gray zone one might observe during an eclipse (Leestma & Grcevic, 1987).

Once the vascular component of the injury is well established, the lesion becomes obvious to the naked eye and to various diagnostic imaging methods such as the computerized axial tomography (CT) and magnetic resonance imaging (MRI) scans (Langfitt & Zimmerman, 1985). The CT scan at first can detect lowered density due to edema, and later higher density as hemorrhage appears. The MRI can detect the increased water in the injured region. The hemorrhagic phase of injury may last a few seconds in the case of penetrating injuries, but when when blunt force injury has occurred as in a fall or blow or concussive episode, 30 minutes or more may elapse before a significant vascular component develops. This process, of course, begins to be evident only at this point in time and continues to evolve for many hours or days. The practical consequence of this phenomenon is that the victim of trauma may show clinical deterioration as the lesions expand and the "cascade" operates. The CT or MRI scan, early in the course, may show little or nothing, but hours later shows an entirely different picture. One must bear in mind that any imaging study is a "snapshot" in time, nothing more or less. In order to fully appreciate the status of a lesion at another time, another picture must be taken.

Once a traumatic lesion is established, repair reactions begin (Baggenstoss, Kernohan, & Drapiewski, 1943; Lindenberg, 1973; Lindenberg & Freytag, 1957, 1960, 1968; Oehmichen, 1980; Unterharnscheidt, 1983). In the brain there is very little primary inflammation that would be expected in other organs. The earliest cellular reaction is swelling of glial cells in an attempt to absorb the water of edema and restore the intercellular environment. This is not always successful. As capillaries bleed, blood dissects into the interstitium. Blood eventually begins to deteriorate and release blood pigments into the tissue (Eisenmenger, Gilig, Diem, & Neuhann, 1978; Strassmann, 1949). Within a few days of injury there are attempts to mobilize macrophages in the brain to begin the process of resolution. Most macrophages (80% or more) will evolve from blood-borne monocytes, some exist in the walls of capillaries, and still others are present in a "resting" state in the brain (microglial cells) (Oehmichen, 1978, 1980). By about 10 days after injury the macrophage response is well developed and will remain as long as there is necrotic material in the lesion, perhaps for months. During this phase of repair the affected tissue becomes spongelike as the necrotic cells are removed. Fibrillary astroglial cells are proliferating as well and establish the glial scar, which will ultimately make up the physical mass of the lesion. Ultimately, the traumatic lesion will appear excavated, sunken, spongelike, tan, orange, or brown, and will have an elasticity to the touch. Little or no collagen will form. Eventually the blood–brain barrier will restore itself so that the lesion may become invisible to the CT scan, although it probably never will disappear when viewed with MRI scans.

Another important conceptual framework for an understanding of neural trauma is the basic physics involved in head trauma. Reduced to the most basic level, the following factors are of the greatest importance:

1. The force involved (pulse height) as a function of the velocity of the impact event, the mass of the impacting object (head or other object), the mass of the object in relative terms to that of the head
2. The duration of the impact (pulse width)
3. The surface area of the impacting object and the surface area of the impact site
4. The angle of impact with respect to the head
5. The ability of the head to move freely

If one knows these facts one can predict the type of injury that will result (Adams et al., 1985; Leestma & Grcevic, 1987; Thibault & Gennarelli, 1985; Unterharnscheidt, 1983; Unterharnscheidt & Sellier, 1966). Conversely, one may be able to reconstruct the circumstances of a traumatic event by observing the nature and extent of the lesions produced. The forensic implications of this are obvious (Leestma, 1987; Lindenberg, 1973; Lindenberg & Freytag, 1968).

Another important factor is the physical issue of kinetic energy in the traumatic process. One object striking another implies a differential state of motion between the two objects. Newton's laws of motion have considerable application here. Perhaps the most important is his third law that states "that a body in motion tends to remain in motion and a body at rest tends to remain at rest." This implies that energy will be required to change the state of motion of an object. In the case of a moving object striking the nonmoving head, the kinetic energy of the object as it comes to rest can accelerate the head, stretch or break the scalp or skull, and/or dissipate in the brain itself (Gurdjian, 1975; Thibault & Gennarelli, 1985).

In addition, heat may be produced. Whether a moving object strikes the immobile head or the moving head an immobile object, the kinetic energies must be accounted for. The relationship between mass, velocity, and kinetic energy is expressed in the formula $K.E. = \frac{1}{2} MV^2$.

There are different spectra of injuries produced by different kinds of impact. Thus, the pathologist's accurate interpretation of head trauma is complex, as shown in the extensive literature on the subject.

CONTUSIONS

Contusions are bruises in the brain or elsewhere. They quite obviously result in injury to blood vessels and, also by mechanisms outlined above, an evolving injury to the brain substance. Contusions can be classified in various ways (Freytag, 1963; Lindenberg & Freytag, 1957). They can occur at the surface of the brain immediately under the site of impact. Such contusions are called "coup contusions" and result most commonly from blows, not falls. The site of impact on the head can be determined by surface lacerations (cuts or incisions) and by examination of the reflected scalp at autopsy for so-called subgaleal hemorrhages. An associated skull fracture can also correlate with scalp injuries to pinpoint the site of impact because most fractures radiate away from the impact site (Leestma & Grcevic, 1987). Contusions that occur in connection with falls are called "contrecoup contusions" and occur at locations 180° away from the impact site, which can also be determined by examining the scalp. Other contusions can occur as the brain moves within and against the cranium, as in falls, strong blows, and in high-velocity missile wounds. These are usually surface contusions above bony ridges at the base of the skull. These contusions, quite aptly, have been called "gliding" contusions (Lindenberg, 1973; Voigt & Löwenhielm, 1974). There is a further category of contusions that occur within the brain substance and are variously called "intermediary coup" lesions (Lindenberg, 1973), "inner cerebral" traumatic lesions (Grcevic, 1982; Leestma & Grcevic, 1987), or "diffuse" axonal injury (Adams et al., 1985; Gennarelli et al., 1982). These lesions occur as a consequence of differential movements or shear forces within the brain itself in falls, gunshot wounds, or major blows to the head. Another form of contusion occurs during skull fractures in which the brain is lacerated and bruised as it moves over a fracture line in the skull. These fracture contusions (Lindenberg, 1973) usually closely approximate observed fracture lines, commonly in basilar skull fractures. One last form of contusion is limited to infants, the so-called contusional tear (Friede, 1975; Lindenberg & Freytag, 1969). In this situation, because of the flexibility of the infant skull, impacts (which are usually the result of child abuse) deform the skull and brain to a degree not seen in adults. Because the brain is relatively unmyelinated and biomechanical relationships between gray and white matter are different and apparently more fragile so that in adults, the cerebral cortex may be torn away from the underlying white matter resulting in a small slit, into which blood usually leaks. The mechanics of this lesion might be compared to the squeezing of an orange in which the skin may "creep" away from the underlying pulp, leaving a space. Pathologists often misinterpret these lesions as birth injuries, malformations, or some other type of lesion. Such lesions can occur in the absence of typical surface coup or contrecoup contusions or even obvious blemishes in the skin (Leestma, 1987).

Coup Contusions

As mentioned above, these contusions occur beneath an impact site caused by a blow, usually with some object of mass less than that of the head, such as a club, metal pipe, billy, or sap. The mechanism of production here may be due to inbending then outbending of the skull, which produce first a positive pressure wave into the brain followed by a negative pressure wave. Positive impulses may stretch or deform the brain and cause shearing injuries, whereas negative impulses may be sufficient to produce momentary cavitation or gas formation within tissue or small vessels, which may burst them, producing the bruise (Gurdjian, 1975; Leestma & Grcevic, 1987; Lindenberg & Freytag, 1968). The lesions evolve as discussed above and end up as a tan or brown surface irregularity that does not follow an arterial distribution and is usually focal. In cross-section the lesion is often cone shaped, with the base of the cone near the cortical surface.

Contrecoup Contusions

These lesions occur in fall-type impacts in which the impacting object is infinitely large as compared with the head. The most common situation that gives rise to contrecoup contusions is the backward fall, in which the occiput strikes the floor or pavement. In the situation, the scalp may be lacerated, the skull may or may not be fractured, but the immediately underlying brain appears undamaged. The main contusion is commonly found at the frontal and temporal lobe tips. There may also be associated gliding contusions on the orbital surfaces of the frontal lobes. Fracture contusions may also occur wherever the fractures are found.

The seeming paradox of no brain injury at the impact site and often massive injury opposite has captured the interest of physicians for nearly 300 years. Various mechanisms have been advanced to explain this phenomenon (Courville, 1942; Dawson, Hirsch, Lucas, & Sebek, 1980; Duret,

1920; Goggio, 1941; A. G. Gross, 1958; Gurdjian, 1975; Holbourn, 1943, 1945; Ommaya, Grubb, & Naumann, 1971; Pudenz & Shelden, 1946; Unterharnscheidt & Sellier, 1966). Recent texts and monographs have reviewed these in detail (Leestma, 1987; Becker & Povlishock, 1985). The most easily communicable mechanistic scenario represents a combination of several hypotheses and probably captures much of the truth.

The brain is suspended in cerebrospinal fluid (CSF) inside a relatively rigid calvarium. In the case of a fall, the head accelerates slightly before the brain does; in so doing, the brain "lags" somewhat while CSF redistributes itself toward the direction of the fall. At impact the skull decelerates first and begins to inbend, creating a positive force meeting the positive force of the forward-moving brain at the site of impact. At a location opposite to the impact site, the skull is decelerating slightly behind the brain, which is moving away from the skull. This creates a negative pressure environment at the interface between brain and skull. This negative pulse, shown in animal experiments (Gurdjian, 1975) can be sufficient to increase the vapor pressure of water over the ambient pressure, causing "boiling" and vaporization of water that may be present. This cavitation, which has been visualized in experimental animals (Pudenz & Shelden, 1946), can occur in blood vessels, in brain tissue, or in CSF and may lead to physical disruption of small blood vessels and brain tissue, creating a "traumatic epicenter" that can evolve into a contusion. At the site of impact, there is no such negative pressure pulse and cavitation cannot occur, although subtle injuries may result from shearing forces.

Contusions, at first, have a bruiselike appearance but gradually evolve over several hours or days into ragged, bloody lesions likened to raw hamburger. The lesions, being superficial excavations, will follow the crests of the gyri, sparing the sulci, not conforming to arterial perfusion territories. After many weeks they appear as sunken, tan, orange, or brown serpentine lesions on the surface of the gyri. In the older literature, these lesions have been referred to as *plaques jeaune*, or *etat vermoulou* (Leestma & Grcevic, 1987). They are most commonly located over the frontal and temporal lobe tips. But if impact has occurred laterally, the opposite hemisphere, typically the lateral temporal lobes will show the lesions (Freytag, 1963). Frontal impacts, because of the impact-absorbing action of the nose, forehead, and central facial structures (not to mention the ability to raise the hands and arms to break a fall) usually prevent occipital contrecoup contusions.

Gliding Contusions

Gliding contusions (Freytag, 1963; Lindenberg & Freytag, 1968; Voigt & Löwnehielm, 1974) occur as the brain moves over bony landmarks, usually at the base of the skull in inferior frontal or inferior temporal lobe regions in the course of falls or heavy blow injuries. The mechanisms for these lesions are even less clear than for contrecoup contusions, but are probably similar. One might envision the brain surface moving over a ridge in which the leading edge of the moving brain produces a positive pressure region, while the trailing edge produces a negative pressure region that could lead to microcavitation injury. Furthermore, shear forces could develop in the trailing edge region that could damage brain tissue as well. The lesions appear virtually identical to any other type of contusion and have the same duration. They often blend imperceptibly with frontal contrecoup contusions.

Inner Cerebral Trauma ("Intermediary Coup" Lesions)

This form of brain injury is perhaps the most complex and most serious, for it includes many lesions, both seen and unseen, that have enormous clinical consequences (Adams et al., 1985; Gennarelli et al., 1982; Grcevic, 1982; Jennett & Teasdale, 1982). This collective of injuries is caused by movements of the brain against itself (rotational or shear forces) that may damage midline structures such as the corpus callosum, periventricular structures, subcortical regions, and periaqueductal regions including the reticular formation of the upper brain stem (Grcevic, 1982, 1988; Jovanovic & Grcevic, 1977; Peerless & Rewcastle, 1967; Voigt, Löwenhielm, & Ljung, 1977). Long axons of passage may be focally or diffusely damaged, and occasionally intraventricular structures such as the choroid plexus and septum pellucidum may be avulsed (Grcevic, 1983). Some degree of inner cerebral trauma occurs in virtually every significant head injury probably as a result of axonal injury. This injury, which may be demonstrable only ultrastructurally or visible only on very careful light microscopic neuropathological examination, gives rise to cerebral concussions and postconcussive syndromes. Even mild head injuries may cause aberrations of functioning that are made worse by repeated head trauma, and may take years to reverse (Alves & Jane, 1985; Caveness, 1966; Grcevic, 1982; Levin, 1985; O'Shaughnessy, Fowler, & Reid, 1984; Povlishock, Becker, Cheng, & Vaughan, 1983). This is becoming an issue in the debate over medical implications of boxing (Carson et al., 1984; Corsellis, Bruton, & Freeman-Browne, 1973; Council on Scientific Affairs, 1983; Critchley, 1957; Thomassen, Juul-Jensen, de Fine-Olivarius, Braemer, & Christensen, 1979). In more severe cases of injury, which may or may not have contusions of one sort or another, inner cerebral trauma may render the victim unconscious for prolonged periods of time. The depth of coma and its relationship to prognosis form the basis for the now widely used Glasgow Coma Scale (Jennett & Teasdale, 1982).

COMPLICATIONS OF HEAD TRAUMA

Head injury may result in a series of complications, many of which I have referred to in passing. These include the postconcussive syndrome, diminished consciousness, alterations of mentation and psychological dysfunction including amnesia, emotional lability, dementia, and psychosis. Neurological syndromes may also occur, such as parkinsonism, other forms of tremor, paralysis or paresis, cranial nerve injury, or blindness. In addition, posttraumatic seizures, hydrocephalus, delayed cerebral hemorrhage, or delayed cerebral edema can occur, as can the development of chronic subdural hematoma, cerebral spinal fluid leaks, and meningitis or brain abscess.

Brain Concussion and the Postconcussive State

In virtually every head injury there is some element of the postconcussive state that can be manifested by subtle memory disturbances, such as amnesia for the event, confusion, disorientation, headache, blackouts, and difficulty in abstract thinking (Denny-Brown, 1945). These symptoms may be mild or severe and take some time to resolve completely (Levin, 1985; O'-Shaughnessy et al., 1984). They may or may not be associated with any readily demonstrable neuropathological finding or scan image, yet are probably caused by damage to axons in the brain and possibly in the brain stem (Gennarelli et al., 1982; Povlishock, Becker, Miller, Jenkins, & Dietrich, 1979; Povlishock et al., 1983; Tomlinson, 1970) by means of shearing and rotational forces generated in the moving brain. Although virtually all individuals who suffer contusions and other obvious forms of brain trauma will show some symptoms of concussion, the reverse is not always true.

Posttraumatic Hemorrhage

The most common form of traumatic hemorrhage is subarachnoid hemorrhage due to capillary leakage from surface contusions, rupture of intracerebral traumatic hematomas, or traumatic intraventricular hemorrhage caused by avulsion of the choroid plexus. The consequences of subarachnoid hemorrhage may be immediate and fatal if the hemorrhage is acute and massive, or more subtle if limited and small. In the latter, an important lingering complication is acquired communicating hydrocephalus, discussed below. When subarachnoid hemorrhage is fatal, death occurs probably from the mass and pressure effects of the blood, irritative and chemical effects of the hemorrhage on brain stem and periventricular structures, or intraventricular hemorrhage mass effect (Leestma, 1987).

Probably the next most common hemorrhagic complication of trauma is some form of meningeal hemorrhage such as subdural or epidural hematoma. Epidural hematomas generally occur acutely as the result of a laceration of a branch of the middle meningeal arteries by a skull fracture (Gallagher & Browder, 1968). These vessels course along the side of the head within the skull and are thus vulnerable to the shearing forces of a fracture. These rapidly accumulating hematomas are fatal in about half the cases. Subdural hematomas may be acute or chronic and result from venous bleeding. Bridging veins that drain the cortical surface traverse the subarachnoid space usually along the superior midline to enter the superior sagittal sinus. These vessels are easily sheared and bleed into the dural-arachnoid interface, creating a hematoma (Cameron, 1978; Löwenhielm, 1974; Stone et al., 1983). The biomechanics of subdural hematoma formation have been extensively modeled in experimental animal studies (Gennarelli & Thibault, 1982). Sometimes a small arteriole is also lacerated, contributing to a more rapid accumulation of blood than might otherwise be the case (McDermott, Fleming, Vanderlinden, & Tucker, 1984; O'Brien, Norris, & Tator, 1974). Acute subdural hematomas, resulting in a mortality rate approaching 50% because of their rapid evolution, are of great clinical importance. In young individuals, subdural hematomas are usually traumatically caused, but in the elderly at least 50% of them have no obvious traumatic connection. Cerebral atrophy may stretch and lengthen these vessels, making them more vulnerable to breakage. In any case, the rupture of a bridging vein results in the development of a subdural hematoma. When the bleeding is slow or intermittent, symptoms of the hematoma may be minimal for some time but may gradually increase. This propensity for subdural hematomas to become chronic and gradually increase in size has considerable medical and forensic importance (Leestma, 1987).

Complications of Brain Swelling

Cerebral edema is a common accompaniment to any form of cerebral injury (Evans & Scheinker, 1945; Povlishock, Becker, Sullivan, & Miller, 1978). It comes about because (a) the vascular bed in the brain is damaged ("vasogenic" edema), allowing water to exit the vessels into the interstitium and (b) there has been a toxic insult such as hypoxia ("cytotoxic" edema), causing intracellular water to increase. Edema is either compensated or uncompensated. Mechanisms of compensation involve the glia, which try to absorb water leaking into the intercellular spaces. When the absorptive capacity is exceeded, uncompensated edema results, and the cut brain surface appears wet (Leestma, 1987).

Any rapidly evolving mass in the brain, such as edema or hematoma, takes space. As the cranium cannot expand or contract, the space occupied by the mass must be accommodated by driving out intravascular blood into the general circulation, by causing reabsorption of the CSF, or by somehow compressing neural tissues. As long as blood and CSF can accommodate the mass effect, major problems are avoided, but once this is no longer the case, herniation and shifts of the brain may give rise to a series of major complications. These include tonsillar, uncal, and other herniations, compression of cranial nerves (usually the third-cranial nerves) (oculomotor nerves), compression of arteries with infarction (usually the posterior cerebral vessels as they cross the tentorial edge), or distortion and obstruction of the cerebral aqueduct or foramina of Monro. Herniations of the brain stem may occur rapidly (and unilaterally or unevenly) and produce Duret hemorrhages of the pons and midbrain. These are midline hemorrhages that destroy the reticular formation and the vestibulo-ocular connections, and doom the victim to a comatose state. Intracranial pressure may rise to such an extent that first venous drainage and lateral arterial perfusion cease. At this point, cerebral function may cease, leaving the brain electrically silent (Leestma, Hughes, & Diamond, 1984; Leestma, Kalelkar, Teas, & Hughes, 1984). If cerebral perfusion ceases, the brain will be irreversibly damaged, giving rise to the "respirator brain" phenomenon, one of major forensic and medical significance (Walker, 1981)

Hydrocephalus

There are many causes for hydrocephalus, which may be congenital or acquired (Hakim, Venegas, & Burton, 1976; Leestma, 1987). In head injury, the most common form of hydrocephalus as a complication is so-called communicating hydrocephalus. Here, as mentioned above, a subarachnoid hemorrhage may have damaged the ability of the arachnoidal granulations to absorb CSF, leading to increased CSF pressure and rather uniform dilatation of the ventricles (Kennady, 1967). Scarring and damage may also occur to the subarachnoid space, introducing impedance to the flow of CSF. At times, CSF production may exceed reabsorption, and at other times may equal it. This situation may give rise to the syndrome of "low-pressure" hydrocephalus. The same situation may occur following bacterial meningitis, which may complicate cerebral trauma. The development of either form of secondary hydrocephalus may have forensic and medical legal significance. Both may produce subtle behavioral changes, including dementia, which can be corrected with the installation of a shunt.

Posttraumatic Epilepsy

Epileptic seizures may occur in connection with head trauma, either early in the course or later. Early seizures occur within hours or days of injury, are usually related to intracerebral hematoma, and tend to be more common in young children (9% of cases) than in adults (2%–5% of cases) (Annegers et al., 1980; Caveness, 1966; Jamieson & Yelland, 1972; Jennett & Teasdale, 1982). Early seizures are usually indicative of very severe head injury; those who experience traumatic seizures are about four times more likely to die of their injuries than those not showing seizure activity.

Late onset trauma-related epilepsy usually does not begin to appear before 3 or 4 months posttrauma but can occur even 5 and 10 years later. Most cases will occur within 2 years of the injury. The incidence of traumatic epilepsy is highly variable and is related generally to the severity of the head injury. Penetrating brain injuries produce the highest incidence, approaching 100% in some series (Leestma, 1987). The incidence for those individuals with depressed skull fractures and/or intracerebral hematomas varies between about 35% and 60% of cases. Those who suffer early seizures are four times more likely to suffer late ones than those who did not. The likelihood of permanent epilepsy, once a traumatic seizure has occurred, approaches 80%, with about 40% showing focal and/or generalized seizure disorders and about 20% showing temporal lobe-type seizures. Recent studies have suggested that posttraumatic epilepsy, when coupled with alcohol abuse and unwillingness to take medication for seizures, may result in sudden unexpected death (Lathers & Schraeder, 1990; Leestma, Kalelkar, Teas, & Hughes, 1984).

NEUROTOXICITY

Toxic injury to the nervous system can occur as a willful criminal act (although this is uncommon), through willful consumption of substances that have toxic consequences for the brain (abuse of alcohol or drugs), or by accidental or incidental exposure to the environment, food or drink, medication, or in the workplace. These latter modes of intoxication have become increasingly important in the field of medicine and litigation. The mechanisms of neurotoxicity have become the subject of a great deal of investigation in recent years (Jacobs & LeQuesne, 1984; Leestma, 1987; Roizin, Shiraki, & Grcevic, 1977; Spencer & Schaumburg, 1980).

The actions of neurotoxins can be categorized in a number of ways: agents affecting a particular cell or groups of cells in the nervous system; those affecting particular structures such as peripheral or central myelin, vessels, blood–brain barrier, the synapses; those affecting certain cellular organelles such as the neural membrane, mitochondria, cytoskeleton; and those having global or complex actions such as developmental anomalies, neoplasms, psychosis, amnesia, seizures, unconsciousness, blindness or paralysis (Kalter, 1968; Narahashi, 1980; Roizin et al., 1977; Selikoff & Hammond, 1982; Spencer & Schaumburg, 1980). Neurotoxins might also be categorized by their physical or chemical characteristics: heavy metals, alcohols, cyclic compounds, natural products, plant or animal toxins, gases, and so on.

For purposes of this discussion, I will describe only the most important or common neurotoxins. These will include ethanol and related alcohols, the most prominent environmental neurotoxins and toxic substances important in the workplace, those drugs (both ethical and illegal) that have prominent neurological effects, and carbon monoxide and hypoxia–anoxia.

The Alcohols

Ethanol is probably the most commonly ingested toxin in the civilized world and is responsible for a host of systemic and neurological diseases (Harper, 1982a, 1982b; Torvik, Lindboe, & Rogde, 1982). Intoxication, although usually intentional, may be accidental (e.g., an industrial worker inhales alcohol vapors while on the job, or a child unwittingly ingests a medication or food that contains alcohol). Acute alcohol intoxication shows its primary manifestation in the central nervous system by virtue of the fact that it is able to pass rapidly across the blood–brain barrier into the brain from the blood.

The psychological and behavioral effects of alcohol are known to everyone. Of forensic import is the interpretation of the degree of impact any given level of blood alcohol has on judgment and motor function. Levels of blood alcohol that determine legal intoxication have been made statutory in most countries (especially in relation to the operation of motor vehicles) and range from detectable levels only to 100 mg%. Needless to say, the correlation with behavior is loose at best. By the same token, blood levels of alcohol that are considered potentially fatal also vary considerably from as little as 150 mg% in an infant or child to 600 mg% or more in an adult (Camps, 1976; Gonzales, Vance, Helpern, & Umberger, 1954). Comparatively few deaths occur due to acute alcohol intoxication, and most are considered accidental. Such incidents may occur when an infant or child ingests high-concentration alcoholic beverages or sweet liqueurs, or when inexperienced drinkers in the course of a chugalug or other form of drinking contest may ingest a large quantity of high-proof alcohol in a very short period of time. In these situations, the major cause of the fatality is either respiratory depression on the basis of the alcohol alone, or secondary to an acute alcohol-induced cerebral edema with brain stem herniation. Not infrequently, aspiration of vomitus in a semicomatose state and accidental injury while intoxicated may result in death (Leestma, 1987).

Chronic alcohol intoxication does not produce a predictable outcome in any given individual. Some persons may consume vast quantities of alcohol for a lifetime with no apparent physical ill effects. Others will develop one or more neurological conditions that may be due to some primary effect of alcohol in the nervous system with or without a secondary nutritional component (Gross & Bell, 1982; Harper, 1982; Harper & Blumbergs, 1982; Torvik et al., 1982; Victor & Adams, 1961). The neurological and neuropathological conditions associated with alcohol abuse include alcoholic cerebellar degeneration; Wernicke-Korsakoff syndrome; alcoholic myopathy and neuropathy; cerebral trauma; alcoholic cerebral atrophy; seizure disorders; central pontine myelinolysis; Marchiafava-Bignami disease; accidental intoxication with heavy metals, ethylene glycol, methanol, or other alcohols; carbon monoxide intoxication; hypoxia, and hepatic encephalopathy.

Cyclic and Other Organic Compounds

There are a number of derivatives of benzene that can produce pathologically demonstrable neurotoxicity, but toluene (methyl benzene) appears to be more frequently studied, largely in connection with neurological symptoms associated with willful sniffing of this compound (Altenkirsch, Mager, Stortenburg, & Helbrecht, 1977). There seems to be a group of devotees of toluene (Benignus, 1981; Cohr & Stokholm, 1979; Sasa et al., 1978). Repeated exposure to this compound produces hallucinations, a feeling of elation, and mental confusion in the short term, but may lead to permanent symptoms that can include ataxia, tremors, seizures, diplopia, psychosis, and other behavioral symptoms (King, Day, Oliver, Lush, & Watson, 1981; Korobkin, Asbury, Sumner, & Nielsen, 1975). Neuropathological studies are scant; nevertheless, continued use of toluene may result in cerebral and/or cerebellar atrophy.

A number of polycyclic compounds of the halogenated biphenyl group have been described as producing an encephalopathy, cranial neuropathy or peripheral neuropathy, and/or behavioral abnormalities (Chia & Chu, 1984; Martinez, Taylor, Houff, & Isaacs, 1977; Seegal, Bush, & Brosch, 1985). These observations have come mostly from environmental disasters with these compounds, which have widespread use as fire retardants and insulating oils and have inevitably contaminated groundwater and virtually all the large bodies of water of the earth. In addition to producing a group of rather ill defined and nonspecific neurological conditions, these compounds are known to be neuroteratogens.

Acrylamide monomer, a very common laboratory compound and industrial starting compound in the plastics industry, is a well-known neurotoxin. When the skin of humans or animals is exposed to this substance, enough of the compound may be absorbed to produce an encephalopathy or more commonly a peripheral neuropathy, although repeated or extensive exposure is usually required. The lesion produced is a so-called dying back neuropathy (Bradley & Williams, 1977; Cavanagh, 1982; Prineas, 1969; Spencer & Schaumburg, 1980). Acrylamide neurotoxicity has been extensively studied experimentally and is thought to interfere with orthograde neuroplasmic (axonal) transport in nerves, which can lead to a distal progressing neuropathy that may affect motor or sensory fibers. The neuropathy is reversible if exposure is halted, but prolonged or severe exposure may result in permanent damage to nerves

The hexacarbons (n-hexane, 2.5 hexanedione, methyl ethyl ketone, n-butyl ketone, and similar compounds) are widely encountered industrial solvents occurring in glues, lacquers and lacquer thinners, paints, plastics, and paint-stripping compounds. They are sometimes solvents sniffed by addicts. They all produce, after repeated exposure of many days or weeks, a distal motor and sensory neuropathy that can be reversible if exposure is halted or has been mild. Affected nerves will show demyelination and axonal balloons, presumably because of focal interference with axonal transport (Spencer & Schaumburg, 1975, 1976, 1980).

Metallic Toxins

Many metals possess variable degrees of neurotoxicity and often occur in the environment, although industrial exposures may occur. The metals may attack the neural membrane or enzyme systems of cellular organelles (Feldman, 1982; Narahashi, 1980) and produce peripheral neuropathies, encephalopathies, central nervous system malformations, and behavioral abnormalities (Hammond & Beliles, 1980). They have also been implicated in the pathogenesis of motor neuron disease (Kurlander & Patten, 1979).

Drugs and Chemotherapeutic Agents

Many drugs possess the ability to produce neurotoxicity. Classical examples are streptomycin and some other antibiotics, which may show toxicity to the eighth cranial nerve, isonicotinic hydrazide (INH) (Ochoa, 1970), which can produce a peripheral neuropathy, and the mitotic spindle inhibitors (colchicine, vinblastine, vincristine), which produce peripheral neuropathies and can be highly neurotoxic if extravasated or administered intrathecally (Schochet, Lampert, & Earle, 1968; Shelanski & Wisniewski, 1969; Stanley, Taurog, & Snover, 1984). A number of other antineoplastic agents (Shapiro & Young, 1984) such as adriamycin (Sahenk and Mendell, 1979), methotrexate (Allen, Rosen, Mehta, & Horton, 1980), and cis-platinum (Neuwelt, Barnett, Glasberg, & Frenkel, 1983) may have profound effects on the central and peripheral nervous system (Spencer & Schaumburg, 1980). Other drugs such as clioquinol (enterovioform, an over-the-counter drug sometimes employed in the treatment of traveler's diarrhea) may produce a grave neurological condition known as subacute myelo-optico-neuropathy (SMON) (Egashira & Matsuyama, 1982). Consumption of an organic tin compound (Stallinon) (Rouzaud & Lutier, 1954) some years ago in France resulted in the more than 100 deaths from massive cerebral edema caused by the drug, which has since been removed from the market.

Carbon Monoxide Poisoning

Carbon monoxide intoxication, when not immediately fatal, can produce a number of neurological lesions (LaPresle & Fardeau, 1967; Olson, 1984). Carbon monoxide is toxic by virtue of its ability to strongly and rapidly bind hemoglobin in preference to oxygen. Because it binds tenaciously to hemoglobin, significant levels of carboxyhemoglobin can accumulate very rapidly. In an environment in which CO concentration is as little as 1:10,000, one can develop a 10% level of CO-Hb very easily, in minutes. This level is not considered dangerous; many cigarette smokers and traffic officers carry this level chronically. When environmental levels climb to 1:5,000, Co-Hb levels may reach 30%. This situation will certainly produce symptoms of headache, lethargy, confusion, and nausea, and may result in some loss of neurons in the brain. When environmental levels are higher and CO-Hb levels exceed 40%, delirium and coma may result. At 50%–60% CO-Hb levels death may occur. At 80% or greater levels, most individuals will die in minutes (Camps, 1976).

One of the more commonly encountered situations involving CO occurs when an individual is rescued and promptly treated for intoxication (at the 50% CO-Hb level or higher). The victim may suffer from some degree of generalized cortical neuronal loss as well as necrosis of the inner portions of the globus pallidus and/or the striatum. Such individuals are usually never neurologically intact and may remain in coma for protracted periods of time after being poisoned. A much rarer situation occurs when exposure has been sufficient to produce coma with continued inhalation of contaminated air. Such an individual may eventually regain consciousness and even recover sufficiently to leave the hospital, only to again sink into a comatose state. Neuropathological examination of this individual's brain will show diffuse destruction, perhaps with focal white matter, and capillary and venous hemorrhages of the white matter myelin (Preziosi, Lindenberg, Levy, & Christenson, 1970). This delayed reaction to CO is sometimes known as Grinker's myelinopathy (Okeda, Song, Funta, & Higashino, 1983; Schwedenberg, 1959).

Anoxia and Hypoxia

The two most important short-term nutrients of the central nervous system are oxygen and glucose. If the brain is deprived of either, within seconds to minutes neurons may be damaged or irreversibly injured. Not all neurons are equally vulnerable to this deprivation. Although there are probably some important differences in the distribution of lesions caused by pure hypoglycemia and by pure hypoxia, we may consider them as identical for treatment purposes. The unequal vulnerability of neurons to hypoxia and other insults forms the basis for a still-contested concept known as "selective vulnerability" (Schade & McMenemey, 1963). An example of such selectivity is in connection with CO poisoning in which the globus pallidus is necrotic while the rest of the brain is relatively spared.

As a general rule, when the whole brain is made hypoxic, as in respiratory arrest or asphyxia (strangulation, ligatures, aspiration of food or objects), and when circulation is not restricted some neurons will be irreversibly damaged sooner than others. Among the most vulnerable neurons are the larger neurons in the Ammon's horn of the mesial hippocampal formation of the temporal lobe, cerebellar Purkinje cells, larger neurons of the globus pallidus and striatum, neurons of the Dentate nuclei of the cerebellum, and some of the middle and larger neurons of the cerebral cortex. More resistant are the smaller neurons of the cerebral cortex, the brain stem reticular formation, cerebellar granule cells, and neurons of the thalamus. Some of the more resistant neurons are those in the spinal cord and motor areas of the brain stem (Leestma, 1987; Schade & McMenemey, 1963).

If hypoxic neuronal damage is widespread and massive, a sufficient number of neurons may die so as to produce "laminar" or "pseudolaminar" necrosis. In this circumstance, usually after several days, the cortex may peel off from the underlying tissues. In such cases it is not uncommon to also observe cavitation bilaterally in the globus pallidus and/or striatum. Once areas damaged by hypoxia have had many weeks to react, the end result is microcavitation, and eventually gliosis.

The forensic implications of anoxia and hypoxia center mostly upon the effect of these conditions upon brain development when they are said to occur in connection with birth and are often believed to be the etiology of "cerebral" palsy. This appears to be the case in some instances, but in the vast majority of "cerebral" palsy cases, no etiology can ever be determined. It has been suggested that difficulty at birth (low Apgar scores) is more a reflection of an earlier process, and thus an epiphenomenon, which may add damage to that already present (Stevenson & Sunshine, 1989; Wigglesworth, 1984). It is unfortunate that more is not known concerning the vulnerability of the developing brain to hypoxia/anoxia and the causes of "cerebral" palsy.

REFERENCES

Adams, J. H., Graham, D. I., & Gennarelli, T. A. (1985). Contemporary neuropathological considerations regarding brain damage in head injury. In D. P. Becker & J. T. Povlishock (Eds.), *Central nervous system trauma, status report, 1985* (pp. 65–87). Washington, DC: National Institute of Neurological and Communicative Disorders and Stroke, National Institutes of Health.

Allen, J. C., Rosen, G., Mehta, B. M., & Horten, B. (1980). Leukoencephalopathy following high-dose IV methotrexate chemotherapy with leucovorin rescue. *Cancer Treatment Reports, 64,* 1261–1273.

Altenkirsch, H., Mager, J., Stortenburg, G., & Helbrecht, J. (1977). Toxic polyneuropathies after sniffing glue thinner. *Journal of Neurology, 214,* 154–172.

Alves, W. M., & Jane, J. A. (1985). Mild brain injury: Damage and outcome. In D. P. Becker & J. T. Povlishock (Eds.), *Central nervous system trauma, status report, 1985* (pp. 255–270). Washington, DC: National Institute of Neurological and Communicative Disorders and Stroke, National Institutes of Health.

Annegers, J. F., Grabow, J. D., Groover, R. V., Laws, E. R., Jr., Elveback, L. R., & Kurland, L. T. (1980). Seizures after head trauma: A population study. *Neurology, 30,* 683–689.

Baggenstoss, A. H., Kernohan, J. W., & Drapiewski, J. F. (1943). The healing process in wounds of the brain. *American Journal of Clinical Pathology, 13,* 333–348.

Balentine, J. D. (1985). Hypotheses in spinal cord trauma research. In D. P. Becker & J. T. Povlishock (Eds.), *Central nervous system trauma, status report, 1985* (pp. 455–461). Washington, DC: National Institute of Neurological and Communicative Disorders and Stroke, National Institutes of Health.

Becker, D. P., & Povlishock, J. T. (Eds.). (1985). *Central nervous system trauma, status report, 1985.* Washington, DC: National Institute of Neurological and Communicative Disorders and Stroke, National Institutes of Health.

Benignus, V. A. (1981). Health effects of toluene: A review. *Neurotoxicology, 2,* 567–588.

Bradley, W. G., & Williams, M. H. (1977). Axoplasmic flow in axonal neuropathies: I. Axoplasmic flow in cats with toxic neuropathies. *Brain, 96,* 235–246.

Cameron, M. (1978). Subacute and chronic subdural hematoma. *Journal of Neurology, Neurosurgery & Psychiatry, 41,* 834–839.

Camps, F. E. (Ed.). (1976). *Gradwohl's legal medicine* (3rd ed.). Chicago: Year Book Publishing.

Carson, I. R., Siegel, D., Shaw, R., Campbell, E. A., Tarlau, M., & DiDomenico, A. (1984). Brain damage in modern boxers. *Journal of the American Medical Association, 251,* 2663–2667.

Cavanagh, J. B. (1982). Mechanism of axon degeneration in three toxic "neuropathies": Organophosphorus, acrylamide and hexacarbon compared. In W. T. Smith & J. B. Cavanagh (Eds.), *Recent advances in neuropathology* (pp. 213–242). London: Churchill-Livingstone.

Caveness, W. F. (1966). Posttraumatic sequelae. In W. F. Caveness & A. E. Walker (Eds.), *Head injury: Conference proceedings* (pp. 209–219). Philadelphia: Lippincott.

Chia, L. G., & Chu, F. L. (1984). Neurological studies on polychlorinated biphenyl (PCB)–poisoned patients. *Progress in Clinical Biological Research, 137*, 117–126.

Cohr, K. H., & Stokholm, J. (1979). Toluene: A toxicological review. *Scandinavian Journal of Work, Environment & Health, 5*, 71–90.

Corsellis, J., Bruton, C., & Freeman-Browne, D. (1973). The aftermath of boxing. *Psychological Medicine, 3*, 270–303.

Council on Scientific Affairs. (1983). Brain injury in boxing. *Journal of the American Medical Association, 249*, 254–257.

Courville, C. B. (1942). Coup-contrecoup mechanism of craniocerebral injuries: Some observations. *Archives of Surgery, 45*, 19–43.

Critchley, Mc D. (1957). Medical aspects of boxing particularly from a neurological standpoint. *British Medical Journal, 1*, 357–362.

Dawson, S. L., Hirsch, C. S., Lucas, F. V., & Sebek, B. A. (1980). The contrecoup phenomenon: Reappraisal of a classic problem. *Human Pathology, 11*, 155–166.

Denny-Brown, D. (1945). Cerebral concussion. *Physiological Reviews, 25*, 296–325.

Duret, H. (1920). Commotions graves, mortelles, sans lesions (commotions pures) et lesions cerebrales etendues sans commotion dans les traumatismes cranio-cerebraux [Severe fatal concussions without lesions (pure concussions) and extended cerebral lesions without concussions in cranio-cerebral traumas]. *Revue Neurologique, 36*, 888–900.

Egashira, Y., & Matsuyama, H. (1982). Subacute myelo-optico-neuropathy (SMON) in Japan: With special reference to the autopsy cases. *Acta Pathologica Japonica, 32* (Suppl. 1), 101–116.

Eisenberg, H. M. (1985). Outcome after head injury: General considerations and neurobiological recovery: Part I. General considerations. In D. P. Becker & J. T. Povlishock (Eds.), *Central nervous system trauma, status report, 1985* (pp. 271–280). Washington, DC: National Institute of Neurological and Communicative Disorders and Stroke, National Institutes of Health.

Eisenmenger, W., Gilg, P., Diem, G., & Neuhann, T. (1978). Zur histologischen und histochemischen Altersbestimmung gedecker Hirnrindenverletzungen [Histological and histochemical age determination of closed cerebral cortex injuries]. *Beitrage zur gerichtlichen Medizin, 26*, 281–289.

Evans, J. P., & Scheinker, I. M. (1945). Histologic studies of the brain following head trauma: I. Post-traumatic cerebral swelling and edema. *Journal of Neurosurgery, 2*, 306–314.

Feldman, R. G. (1982). Central and peripheral nervous system effects of metals: A survey. *Acta Neurological Scandinavica, 92*(Suppl.), 143–166.

Freytag, E. (1963). Autopsy findings in head injuries from blunt forces. *Archives of Pathology & Laboratory Medicine, 75*, 402–413.

Friede, R. L. (1975). Cerebral lesions from physical trauma. In R. L. Friede (Ed.), *Developmental neuropathology* (pp. 37–45). New York: Springer-Verlag.

Gallagher, J. P., & Browder, J. (1968). Extradural hematoma: Experience with 167 patients. *Journal of Neurosurgery, 29*, 1–12.

Gennarelli, T. A., & Thibault, L. E. (1982). Biomechanics of acute subdural hematoma. *Journal of Trauma, 22*, 680–686.

Gennarelli, T. A., Thibault, L. E., Adams, J. H., Graham, D. I., Thompson, C. J., & Marcincin, R. P. (1982). Diffuse axonal injury and traumatic coma in the primate. *Annals of Neurology, 12*, 564–574.

Goggio, A. I. (1941). The mechanism of contre-coup injury. *Journal of Neurology and Psychiatry, 4*, 11–22.

Gonzales, T. A., Vance, M., Helpern, M., & Umberger, C. J. (1954). *Legal medicine and toxicology*. New York: Appleton-Century-Crofts.

Grčević, N. (1982). Topography and pathogenic mechanisms of lesion in "inner cerebral trauma." *Journal of the Yugoslavian Academy of Sciences, 402*, 265–331.

Grčević, N. (1983). Traumatic tears of the tela chorioidea: A hitherto unrecognized cause of post-traumatic hydrocephalus. *Acta Neurochirurgica, 32*(Suppl.), 79–85.

Grcevic, N. (1988). I. Head injury: The concept of inner cerebral trauma. *Scandinavian Journal of Rehabilitation Medicine, 17*(Suppl.), 25–31.

Gross, A. G. (1958). A new theory on the dynamics of brain concussion and brain injury. *Journal of Neurosurgery, 15*, 548–561.

Gross, S. G., & Bell, R. D. (1982). Central pontine myelinolysis and rapid correction of hyponatremia. *Texas Medicine, 78*, 59–60.

Gurdjian, E. S. (1975). *Impact head injury: Mechanistic, clinical and preventive correlations*. Springfield, IL: Chas. C. Thomas.

Hakim, S., Venegas, J. G., & Burton, J. D. (1976). The physics of the cranial cavity, hydrocephalus and normal pressure hydrocephalus: Mechanical interpretation and mathematical model. *Surgical Neurology, 5*, 187–210.

Hammond, P. B., & Beliles, R. P. (1980). Metals. In J. Doull, C. D. Klaassen, & M. O. Amdur (Eds.), *Casarett and Doull's toxicology: The basic science of poisons* (2nd ed., pp. 409–467). New York: Macmillan.

Harper, C. G., & Blumbergs, P. C. (1982). Brain weights in alcoholics. *Journal of Neurology, Neurosurgery and Psychiatry, 45*, 838–840.

Harper, C. (1982). Neuropathology of brain damage caused by alcohol. *Medical Journal of Australia, 2*, 276–282.

Holbourn, A. H. S. (1943). Mechanics of head injuries. *Lancet, 2*, 438–441.

Holbourn, A. H. S. (1945). The mechanics of brain injuries. *British Medical Bulletin, 3*, 147–149.

Jacobs, J. M., & LeQuesne, P. M. (1984). Toxic disorders of the nervous system. In J. Hume Adams, J. A. N. Corsellis, & L. W. Duchen (Eds.), *Greenfield's neuropathology* (4th ed., pp. 627–698). New York: Wiley.

Jadro-Santel, D., Grcevic, N., Besenski, N., & Kalusek, M. (1989). The inner cerebral trauma: The correlative pathology with CT scans. In F. Aichner, F. Gerstenbrand, & N. Grcevic (Eds.), *Neuroimaging II* (pp. 263–273). Stuttgart & New York: Gustav Fischer.

Jamieseon, K. G., & Yelland, J. D. N. (1972). Traumatic intracerebral hematoma: Report of 63 surgically treated cases. *Journal of Neurosurgery, 37*, 528–532.

Jennett, B., & Teasdale, G. (1982). *Management of head injuries*. Philadelphia: Davis.

Jovanovic, N., & Grcevic, N. (1977). Topography of the acute lesions of the brain stem in closed brain trauma of the acceleration type. *Neurologia, 25*, 3–22.

Kalter, J. (1968). *Teratology of the central nervous system*. Chicago: University of Chicago Press.

Kennady, J. C. (1967). Investigations of the early fate and removal of subarachnoid blood. *Pacific Medicine and Surgery, 75*, 163–168.

King, M. D., Day, R. E., Oliver, J. S., Lush, M., & Watson, J. M. (1981). Solvent encephalopathy. *British Medical Journal, 283*, 663–665.

Kirkpatrick, J. B., Higgins, M. L., Lucas, J. H., & Gross, G. W. (1985). In vitro simulation of neural trauma by laser. *Journal of Neuropathology & Experimental Neurology, 44*, 268–284.

Kobrine, A. I., Timmins, E., Rajjoub, R. K., Rizzoli, H. V., & Davis, D. O. (1977). Demonstration of massive traumatic brain swelling within 20 minutes after head injury: Case report. *Journal of Neurosurgery, 46*, 256–258.

Korobkin, R., Asbury, A. K., Sumner, A. J., & Nielsen, S. L. (1975). Glue-sniffed neuropathy. *Archives of Neurology, 32*, 158–162.

Kurlander, H. M., & Patten, B. M. (1979). Metal in spinal cord tissue of patients dying of motor neuron disease. *Annals of Neurology, 6*, 21–24.

Langfitt, T. W., & Zimmerman, R. A. (1985). Imaging and in vivo biochemistry of the brain in head injury. In D. P. Becker & J. T. Povlishock (Eds.), *Central nervous system trauma, status report, 1985* (pp. 53–63). Washington, DC: National Institute of Neurological and Communicative Disorders and Stroke, National Institutes of Health.

LaPresle, J., & Fardeau, M. (1967). The central nervous system and carbon monoxide poisoning: II. Anatomical study of brain lesions following intoxication with carbon monoxide (22 cases). *Progress in Brain Research, 24*, 31–74.

Lathers, C. M., & Schraeder, P. L. (Eds.). (1990). *Epilepsy and sudden death*. New York: Marcel Dekker.

Leestma, J. E. (Ed.). (1987). *Forensic neuropathology*. New York: Raven Press.

Leestma, J. E., & Grcevic, N. (1987). Impact injuries to the brain and head. In J. E. Leestma (Ed.), *Forensic neuropathology* (pp. 184–253). New York: Raven Press.

Leestma, J. E., Hughes, J. R., & Diamond, E. R. (1984). Temporal correlates in brain death: EEG and clinical relationships to the respirator brain. *Archives of Neurology, 41*, 147–152.

Leestma, J. E., Kalekar, M. B., Teas, S. S., & Hughes, J. R. (1984). Sudden unexpected death associated with seizures: Analysis of 66 cases. *Epilepsia, 25*, 84–88.

Levin, H. S. (1985). Outcome after head injury: General considerations and neurobehavioral recovery: Part II. Neurobehavioral recovery. In D. P. Becker & J. T. Povlishock (Eds.), *Central nervous system trauma, status report, 1985* (pp. 281–299). Washington, DC: National Institute of Neurological and Communicative Disorders and Stroke, National Institutes of Health.

Lindenberg, R. (1973). Mechanical injuries of brain and meninges. In W. U. Spitz & R. S. Fisher (Eds.), *Medicolegal investigation of death: Guidelines for the application of pathology to crime investigation* (pp. 420–469). Springfield, IL: Chas. C. Thomas.

Lindenberg, R., & Freytag, E. (1957). Morphology of cortical contusions. *Archives of Pathology, 63*, 23–42.

Lindenberg, R., & Freytag, E. (1960). The mechanism of cerebral contusions, a pathologic–anatomic study. *Archives of Pathology, 69*, 440–469.

Lindenberg, R., & Freytag, E. (1968). Trauma of the meninges and brain. In J. Minckler (Ed.), *Pathology of the nervous system* (vol. 2, pp. 1705–1765). New York: McGraw-Hill.

Lindenberg, R., & Freytag, E. (1969). Morphology of brain lesions from blunt trauma in early infancy. *Archives of Pathology, 87*, 298–305.

Löwenhielm, P. (1974). Dynamic properties of the parasgittal bridging veins. *Zeitschrift fur Rechsmedizin, 74*, 55–62.

Martinez, A. J., Taylor, J. R., Houff, S. A., & Isaacs, E. R. (1977). Ketone poisoning: Cliniconeuropathological study. In L. Roizin, H. Shiraki, & N. Grcevic (Eds.), *Neurotoxicology* (pp. 443–456). New York: Raven Press.

McDermott, M., Fleming, J. F. R., Vanderlinden, R. G., & Tucker, W. S. (1984). Spontaneous arterial subdural hematoma. *Neurosurgery, 14*, 13–18.

Muiselaar, J. P., & Obrist, W. D. (1985). Cerebral blood flow and brain metabolism with brain injury. In D. P. Becker & J. T. Povlishock (Eds.), *Central nervous system trauma, status report, 1985* (pp. 123–137). Washington, DC: National Institute of Neurological and Communicative Disorders and Stroke, National Institutes of Health.

Narahashi, T. (1980). Nerve membrane as a target of environmental toxicants. In P. S. Spencer & H. H. Schaumburg (Eds.), *Experimental and clinical neurotoxicology* (pp. 225–238). Baltimore: Williams & Wilkins.

Neuwelt, E. A., Barnett, P. A., Glasberg, M., & Frenkel, E. P. (1983). Pharmacology and neurotoxicity of cis-diamminedichloroplatinum, bleomycin, 5-fluorouracil, and cyclophosphamide administration following osmotic blood–brain barrier modification. *Cancer Research, 43*, 5278–5285.

O'Brien, P. K., Norris, J. W., & Tator, C. H. (1974). Acute subdural hematoma of arterial origin. *Journal of Neurosurgery, 41*, 435–439.

Ochoa, J. (1970). Isoniazid neuropathy in man: Quantitative electron microscopic study. *Brain, 93*, 831–850.

Oehmichen, M. (1978). Mononuclear phagocytes in the central nervous system. Philadelphia: Saunders.

Oehmichen, M. (1980). Timing of cortical contusion: Correlation between histomorphologic alterations and post-traumatic interval. *Zeitschrift fur Rechtsmedizin, 84*, 79–94.

Okeda, R., Song, S. Y., Funta, N., & Higashino, F. (1983). An experimental study of the pathogenesis of Grinker's myelinopathy in carbon monoxide intoxication. *Acta Neuropathologica, 59*, 200–206.

Olson, K. R. (1984). Carbon monoxide poisoning: Mechanisms, presentation, and controversies in management. *Journal of Emergency Medicine, 1*, 233–243.

Ommaya, A. K., Grubb, R. L., Jr., & Naumann, R. A. (1971). Coup and contrecoup injury: Observations on the mechanics of visible brain injuries in the rhesus monkey. *Journal of Neurosurgery, 35*, 503–516.

Oppenheimer, D. R. (1968). Microscopic lesions in the brain following head injury. *Journal of Neurology, Neurosurgery & Psychiatry, 31,* 299–306.

O'Shaughnessy, E. J., Fowler, R. S., Jr., & Reid, V. (1984). Sequelae of mild closed head injuries. *Journal of Family Practice, 18,* 391–394.

Peerless, S. J., & Rewcastle, N. B. (1967). Shear injuries of the brain. *Canadian Medical Association Journal, 96,* 577–582.

Povlishock, J. T., Becker, D. P., Cheng, C. L. Y., & Vaughan, G. W. (1983). Axonal change in minor head injury. *Journal of Neuropathology & Experimental Neurology, 42,* 225–242.

Povlishock, J. T., Becker, D. P., Miller, J. D., Jenkins, L. W., & Dietrich, W. D. (1978). The morphopathologic substrates of concussion. *Acta Neuropathologica, 47,* 1–11.

Povlishock, J. T., Becker, D. P., Sullivan, H. G., & Miller, J. D. (1978). Vascular permeability alterations to horseradish peroxidase in experimental brain injury. *Brain Research, 153,* 223–239.

Preziosi, T. J., Lindenberg, R., Levy, D., & Christenson, M. (1970). An experimental investigation in animals of the functional and morphologic effects of single and repeated exposures to high and low concentrations of carbon monoxide. *Annals of the New York Academy of Sciences, 174,* 369–384.

Prineas, J. (1969). The pathogenesis of dying-back polyneuropathies: II. An ultrastructural study of experimental acrylamide intoxication in the cat. *Journal of Neuropathology & Experimental Neurology, 28,* 598–621.

Pudenz, R. H., & Sheldon, C. H. (1946). The Lucite calvarium—a method for direct observation of the brain. *Journal of Neurosurgery, 3,* 487–505.

Roizin, L. Shiraki, H., & Grcevic, N. (Eds.). (1977). *Neurotoxicology.* New York: Raven Press.

Rouzaud, M., & Lutier, J. (1954). Oedeme subaigue cerebromeninge due a une intoxication d'actualite [Subacute cerebromeningeal edema due to an interesting form of intoxication]. *La Presse Medicale, 62,* 1075.

Sahenk, Z., & Mendell, J. R. (1979). Analysis of fast axoplasmic transport in nerve ligation and adriamycin-induced neuronal perikaryon lesions. *Brain Research, 171,* 414–453.

Sasa, M., Igarashi, S. Miyazaki, T., Miyazaki, K., Nauno, S., & Matsuda, I. (1978). Equilibrium disorders with diffuse brain atrophy in long-term toluene sniffing. *Archives of Otolaryngology, 221,* 103–169.

Schade, J. P., & McMenemey, W. H. (Eds.). (1963). *Selective vulnerability of the brain in hypoxemia.* Philadelphia: Davis.

Schochet, S. S., Lampert, P. W., & Earle, K. M. (1968). Neuronal changes induced by intrathecal vincristine sulfate. *Journal of Neuropathology and Experimental Neurology, 27,* 645–657.

Schwendenberg, T. H. (1959). Leukoencephalopathy following carbon monoxide asphyxia. *Journal of Neuropathology and Experimental Neurology, 18,* 597–608.

Seegal, R. F., Bush, B., and Brosch, K. O. (1985). Polychlorinated biphenyls induce regional changes in brain norepinephrine concentrations in adult rats. *Neurotoxicology, 6,* 13–24.

Selikoff, I. J., & Hammond, E. C. (Eds.). (1982). Brain tumors in the chemical industry. *Annals of the New York Academy of Sciences, 381,* 1–364.

Shapiro, M. R., & Young, D. F. (1984). Neurological complications of antineoplastic therapy. *Acta Neurologica Scandinavica, 100*(Suppl.), 125–132.

Shelanski, M. L., & Wisniewski, H. (1969). Neurofibrillary degeneration induced by vincristine therapy. *Archives of Neurology, 20,* 199–206.

Siesjo, B. K., & Wieloch, T. (1985). Brain injury: Neurochemical aspects. In D. P. Becker & J. T. Povlishock (Eds.), *Central nervous system trauma, status report, 1985* (pp. 513–532). Washington, DC: National Institute of Neurological and Communicative Disorders and Stroke, National Institutes of Health.

Siesjö, B. K., Agardh, C. D., & Bengtsson, F. (1990). Free radicals and brain damage. *Cerebrovascular and Brain Metabolism Reviews, 1,* 165–211.

Siesjö, Bengtsson, F., Grampp, W., & Theander, S. (1989). Calcium, excitotoxins, and neuronal death in the brain. *Annals of the New York Academy of Sciences, 568,* 234–251.

Spencer, P. S., & Schaumburg, H. H. (1975). Experimental neuropathy produced by 2, 5-hexanedione—a major metabolite of the neurotoxic industrial solvent methyl n-butyl ketone. *Journal of Neurology, Neurosurgery & Psychiatry, 38,* 771–775.

Spencer, P. S., & Schaumburg, H. H. (1976). Feline nervous system response to chronic intoxication with commercial grade of methyl n-butyl ketone, methyl isobutyl ketone and methyl ethyl ketone. *Toxicology and Applied Pharmacology, 37,* 301–311.

Spencer, P. S., & Schaumburg, H. H. (Eds.). (1980). *Experimental and clinical neurotoxicology.* Baltimore: Williams & Wilkins.

Stanley, M. W., Taurog, J. D., & Snover, D. D. (1984). Fatal colchicine toxicity: Report of a case. *Clinical and Experimental Rheumatology, 2,* 167–171.

Stevenson, D. K., & Sunshine, P. (Eds.). (1989). *Fetal and neonatal brain injury: Mechanisms, management and the risks of practice.* Philadelphia: Decker.

Stone, J. L., Rifai, M. H. S., Sugar, O., Lang, R. G. R., Oldershaw, J. B., & Moody, R. A. (1983). Subdural hematomas: I. Acute subdural hematoma: Progress in definition, clinical pathology, and therapy. *Surgical Neurology, 19,* 216–231.

Strassmann, G. (1949). Formation of hemosiderin and hematoidin after traumatic and spontaneous cerebral hemorrhages. *Archives of Pathology, 47,* 205–210.

Thibault, O. E., & Gennarelli, T. A. (1985). Biomechanics and craniocerebral trauma. In D. P. Becker & J. T. Povlishock (Eds.), *Central nervous system trauma, status report, 1985* (pp. 379–389). Washington, DC: National Institute of Neurological and Communicative Disorders and Stroke, National Institutes of Health.

Thomassen, A., Juul-Jensen, P., deFine-Olivarius, B., Braemer, J., & Christensen, A. L. (1979). Neurological, electroencephalographic and neuropsychological examination of 53 former amateur boxers. *Acta Neurologica Scandinavica, 60,* 352–362.

Tomlinson, B. E. (1970). Brain stem lesions after head injury. *Journal of Clinical Pathology, 23*(Suppl.), 154–165.

Torvik, A., Lindboe, C. F., & Rogde, S. (1982). Brain lesions in alcoholics: A neuropathological study with clinical correlations. *Journal of Neurological Sciences, 56,* 233–248.

Unterharnscheidt, F. (1983). Neuropathology of rhesus monkeys undergoing -G impact acceleration. In C. L. Ewing, D. J. Thomas, A. Sances, Jr., & S. J. Larson (Eds.), *Impact injury of the head and spine* (pp. 94–176). Springfield, IL: Chas. C. Thomas.

Unterharnscheidt, F., & Sellier, K. (1966). Mechanics and pathomorphology of closed brain injuries. In W. F. Caveness & A. E. Walker (Eds.), *Head injury: Conference proceedings* (pp. 321–341). Philadelphia: Lippincott.

Victor, M., & Adams, R. D. (1961). On the etiology of the alcoholic neurologic diseases with special reference to the role of nutrition. *American Journal of Clinical Nutrition, 9,* 379–397.

Voigt, E., & Löwenhielm, P. (1974). "Gliding contusions" des Grosshirns ["Gliding contusions" of the cerebrum]. *Hefte Unfallheilkunde, 117,* 329–335.

Voigt, G. E., Löwenhielm, C. G., & Ljung, C. B. (1977). Rotational cerebral injuries near the superior margin of the brain. *Acta Neuropathologica, 39,* 201–209.

Walker, A. E. (1981). *Cerebral death.* Baltimore: Urban & Schwarzenberg.

Wigglesworth, J. S. (1984). Perinatal pathology. In J. L. Bennington (Ed.), *Major problems in pathology* (vol. 15, pp. 1–447). Philadelphia: Saunders.

chapter 5

Neurological and Neuropsychiatric Assessment of Brain Injury

GARY J. TUCKER
and VERNON M. NEPPE

The most important part of the assessment of any patient is the history, which in large part influences the selection of the laboratory examinations as well as illuminates how particular symptoms are minimized or maximized by a patient. This history comes from many different sources: the patient, records, family, schools, and so on. However, for communication purposes it must be organized into a coherent framework, best accomplished by the traditional medical format: chief complaint, history of present illness, developmental history, family history, past medical history, social history (which includes substance abuse as well as social relationships), sleep patterns, and eventually mental status and neurological examination results.

The evaluation of the patient with brain damage must take into account the presence of preexisting psychopathology as well as psychopathology that is related to recent brain injury.

HISTORICAL COMPONENTS OF PSYCHIATRIC ILLNESS

As the psychiatric nomenclature and classification of diseases have become more objective, we can more clearly determine which historical components of psychiatric illness are critical to the diagnostic process. In particular, do the specific signs and symptoms fit an established psychiatric diagnosis? Were these signs and symptoms present prior to the brain injury? Is there a family history of psychiatric illness or behavior patterns that is similar to the patient's symptomatology? Has the patient or a family member responded to a specific pharmacological intervention? Illnesses usually have distinct courses and patterns, whereas, personality traits and characteristics are usually persistent ways of behaving that do not show a specific onset or cessation of behavior. It is too easy to take a cross-sectional approach to the patient rather than attempting to determine a longitudinal picture of the patient's symptomatology. This is essential to determine the contributing factors of brain damage to the patient's current status. A major purpose of the evaluation is to determine the degree to which a patient's symptoms and patterns of behavior existed prior to injury, or are either related to or facilitated by that injury.

DIFFERENTIATING NEUROLOGICAL FROM PSYCHIATRIC CONDITIONS

The first and most important clue to neurological illness is the fact that the patient's symptoms and signs do not clearly fit into any known psychiatric diagnostic category. Although this assumption may seem simplistic, nevertheless the symptoms most patients manifest should fit into the major psychiatric categories without too much procrustean maneuvering. When the symptomatology is not clearly that of any known psychiatric condition, one should withhold judgment to the fact that perhaps the condition is not a psychiatric one.

Second, if there is no prior history of psychiatric illness, then one should strongly suspect that this is not a psychiatric condition. In most cases, one can see the seeds of the current symptomatology in the patient's previous behavior. When psychiatric conditions become symptomatic enough to require care or evaluation, they usually manifest an increase in already preexisting personality traits.

Third, abrupt changes in personality or behavior are not characteristic of psychiatric syndromes. In most cases, we can see consistencies in behavior and personality from the premorbid to the morbid condition. One sees marked personality and behavioral changes primarily as symptoms of organic conditions. However, one must also evaluate the role of secondary gain and manipulative behavior in abrupt changes.

Fourth, psychiatric symptoms do not usually fluctuate rapidly. The resolution of psychiatric symptoms is most often gradual. The resolution of a psychotic process in schizophrenia and affective disorder is usually over a period of weeks or months. Patients with psychiatric illnesses are not hallucinated and delusional in the morning and then lucid in the afternoon. Such rapid fluctuations are frequently symptomatic of organic conditions; these fluctuations can manifest themselves as either behavioral or psychological symptomatology. Rapid fluctuations in motor activity are also much more characteristic of neurological conditions as opposed to purely psychiatric conditions.

Finally, in most cases psychiatric conditions respond to the usual psychiatric intervention (either pharmacological or psychological) in a fairly consistent manner. When a patient with "schizophrenia" does not respond in a timely fashion to the usual neuroleptic doses, then perhaps the diagnosis should be evaluated in light of the fact that the wrong medication may be being used to treat the condition. One should also reconsider the diagnosis when a patient who is usually reassured by a comment becomes more agitated and upset. Most psychiatric conditions respond in a consistent manner to customary interventions; when a person's condition does not change, the clinician should reevaluate the diagnosis.

CLINICAL EXAMINATION

The clinical examination should provide guidelines to further laboratory and diagnostic investigations. The clinical evaluation should lead to hypotheses about the anatomic aspects of the patient's disorder (Plum, 1988). We should attempt to decide whether we are dealing with a diffuse or a focal process, whether there is peripheral nervous system and/or central nervous system involvement, and whether the process is changing—either getting worse or getting better—or not changing at all.

Two forms of reasoning aid the clinician in making these decisions. One is pattern recognition. This is an *empirical* process whereby an experienced clinician, who often is highly specialized, recognizes the classic symptoms and signs that the patient presents and can categorize them into a known syndrome. This pattern recognition is probably the traditional medical approach to patients but has pitfalls in that it is often easy to force various observations and symptoms into a syndrome that may not be correct. This way of thinking weakens the critical observation powers of the clinician and allows him or her to throw out symptoms that do not quite fit the clinical picture, rather than looking at each patient with fresh eyes.

The second major form of reasoning relies on an understanding of physiology and anatomy. This is more of a *deductive* process whereby the clinician analyzes the clinical symptomatology and attempts to understand it through various anatomic and physiological principles. If the symptoms fit no known anatomical or physiological pathway, then one should be cautious in the interpretation of the data. Both of these types of clinical evaluation are critical to making hypotheses about the patient's problem and guiding further investigations to verify these hypotheses.

NEUROLOGICAL EXAMINATION

The traditional neurological exam (Table 5.1) allows preliminary thoughts about localization or neurological dysfunction as manifested by the patient. The examination should lead to further specific laboratory testing, both neuropsychological and otherwise. However, there are some aspects of the neurological examination that can confound psychiatric conditions, and these are the areas that have been termed "soft signs" or nonlocalizing neurological findings and regressive (primitive) reflexes.

Soft Signs

"Soft signs" have diffuse, nonlocalizing significance (Table 5.2). These contrast with "hard signs," which can be anatomically localized, for example, the paralysis of an arm.

TABLE 5.1. Traditional Neurological Exam

Cranial nerves
  Smell
  Visual acuity and visual fields
  Pupils size and reaction, range of eye motion
  Corneal reflexes and facial sensation
  Upper and lower facial muscles and taste
  Hearing
  Articulation, palate movement, gag reflex
  Tongue
Motor system
  Limb strength and coordination, gait
  Spasticity, flaccidity, or fasciculation
  Abnormal movements (tremor, chorea, etc.)
  Reflexes
    Deep tendon
    Other
Sensory system
  Position
  Vibration
  Stereognosis
  Graphesthesia
  2-point discrimination
  Extinction (visual, tactile)
Cerebellar system
  Finger to nose, heel-shin, rapid alternating movements
Autonomic system
  Sweating, pulse, pupils, continence

TABLE 5.2. Typical Soft Signs

Stereognosis
Graphesthesia
Bilateral simultaneous stimulation
Coordination, balance, gait
Sensory (light, touch, position, vibration, pain, slow extinction, or poor
  lateralization)
Synkinesis
Choreoathetosis
Dystonia
Tremor, tics
Speech disturbances
Adventitious motor overflow
Motor impersistence
Auditory visual integration
Vestibular dysfunctions (decreased or increased responses)
Cranial nerve disorders that are nonlocalizing
Diffuse EEG abnormalities
Decreased or increased reflexes
Hoffman's sign
Clonus
Mental retardation
Memory disturbances
Nonlocalizing indicators of cerebral dysfunction on various psychological tests

In the interpretation of clinical neurological examination findings, soft neurological signs have been clearly described for many psychiatric conditions. Although this is particularly true for schizophrenic patients, these findings have also been described in patients with affective disorders, borderline personality disorders, and attention deficit disorders (Pincus & Tucker, 1985). Soft signs have been noted for 36% to 50% of schizophrenic patients. Consequently, to use soft signs as sole indicators of brain damage would be difficult in a psychiatric population. Many of these soft signs also disappear in the nonacute, less florid psychotic state. In addition, psychotic responses, negativism, or impairments in concentration may at times be misinterpreted as "soft signs." Such features are variable and inconsistent. However, they may confound the evaluation of a patient with brain injury and an affective disorder.

There is great variability in what are called soft signs (Table 5.2). However, there are over 30 studies of increased neurological findings in schizophrenic patients alone (Heinrichs & Buchanan, 1988). Many of these signs in schizophrenic patients indicate difficulties in the sensory integrative functions, such as graphesthesia, stereognosis, and audiovisual integration. The major dysfunctions that can be categorized in terms of soft signs in all psychiatric conditions relate also to sensory integrative functions as well as motor coordination, sequencing, and patterning of movement. All of these soft signs can also be precipitated or mimicked as a result of various medications, particularly neuroleptics. Certainly the role of tardive dyskinesia in patients who have been treated with neuroleptics is also a cause for concern in that it may indicate neurological impairment that is unrelated to the specific injury being investigated. Similarly, other neuroleptic-induced extrapyramidal features—bradykinesia, 5–6 per second moderately coarse static tremor, cogwheel rigidity, and akathesia—may confound evaluations.

Neurological Signs of Diffuse Cerebral Dysfunction

A variation of soft signs are the neurological changes that correlate with diffuse cerebral dysfunction, such as delirium or dementia (Jenkyn et al., 1985). Some people have called them "regressive reflexes," as they are usually present in younger patients or are related to development in that they become inhibited as the individual matures. One may see such signs when there is a disturbance of higher cortical function. Certain clinical signs are correlated with diffuse cerebral dysfunction (Table 5.3). Many of these signs have a high false negative yield. They are similar to soft signs in that some of them can be present in severely depressed and schizophrenic patients; when the condition is in remission, these signs will often abate. Consequently, it is difficult to interpret the implication of these signs in the presence of psychiatric conditions.

TABLE 5.3. Neurological Findings Associated with Diffuse Neurological Disease

Release phenomena
  Nuchocephalic
  Glabellar tap/blink
  Snout and pout reflex
  Palmar mental reflex
Paratonia
Visual pursuit tracking
Reverse spelling/reversal of numbers
Memory-recall
Gait disturbance
Brisk deep tendon reflexes
Plantar extensor responses

LOCALIZATION

There has been considerable debate in neurological circles about whether the symptoms of organic brain dysfunction relate equally to localization or to the amount of tissue lost (Pincus & Tucker, 1985). In most cases, it is probably not either/or but a combination of both localization and amount of tissue lost that will indicate the functional deficits. However, both the neurological exam (Table 5.4) and the type of behavioral symptoms that the patient exhibits (Table 5.5) will provide rough guidelines as to neuroanatomical localization of functions or behaviors. The importance of localization or hypotheses about localization should serve as a guide to further investigation, either through neuropsychological testing, more detailed mental status testing, or various imaging and electrophysiological techniques. One further useful dichotomy is that suggested by Goldstein (1952). He perceived the development of pathological deficits in the organic patient as a "pathogenetic" process. He described the patient's attempts

---

TABLE 5.4. Probable Anatomical Localization of Various Neurological Examination Findings: Central Nervous System Lesions

Cerebral hemispheres[a]
  Hemiparesis with increased deep tendon reflexes and Babinski
  Hemisensory lost
  Homonymous hemianopsia
  Aphasias, dementia, hemi-inattention, apraxias, agnosias, aprosodias,
    nystagmus, reading, spelling, calculation, change of cognition
  Pseudobulbar palsy
Basal ganglia[a]
  Movement disorder—Parkinson's, athetosis, chorea, hemiballismus,
    dystonias, dyskinesias
Brain stem
  Cranial nerve palsy with contralateral hemiparesis, hemisensory loss—ipsi or
    contralateral ataxia
  Ophthalmoplegia
  Nystagmus
  Bulbar palsy
Cerebellum
  Tremor or intention
  Impaired rapid attending movements
  Ataxia
  Scanning speech
Spinal cord
  Para or quadraparesis
  Sensory loss (at specific levels)
  Bladder, bowel, sexual dysfunction

---

[a]Contralateral to lesion.

TABLE 5.5. Frequently Associated Simple Behavioral Dysfunctions and Anatomic Localizations

---

Frontal lobe lesions

Motor abnormalities
    May vary from total paralysis to problems with coordination and integration of movement
    Apraxias
Expressive language dysfunction
    Aphasia—nonfluent[a]
    [Broca's] (Comprehension often intact especially with left-sided lesions)
Behavioral dysfunction
    Decreased spontaneity and initiative
    Perseveration and difficulty in shifting behavior and attention
    Decreased judgment in social situation
    Loss of abstracting ability
    Amotivation and apathy
    Release phenomena (e.g., primitive reflexes)

Parietal–temporal–occipital lobe lesions, left[a] and right[b]

Sensory-integrative abnormalities
    Agnosias
    Defects in stereognosis and graphesthesia
Behavioral dysfunctions
    Visual agnosias
    Temporal lobe symptomatology
    Bilateral temporal lobe lesions—impaired new learning

Parietal-temporal-occipital lobe lesions—Left[1]

Sensory-integrative abnormalities
    Dyslexia
    Dyscalculia[a,c]
    Dysgraphia[a]
    Finger agnosia[a]
    Ideomotor apraxia[d]
    Ideational apraxia[d]
    Right–left agnosia[c]
Language dysfunctions
    Fluent aphasias (Wernicke's)
Behavior dysfunctions
    Verbal memory

Parietal-temporal-occipital lobe lesions—right[b]

Sensory integrative abnormalities
    Anosogonosia[e] and pain asymbolia
    Spatial neglect and autotopagnosia[e]
    Constructional apraxia (visuo-spatial agnosia)
    Dressing "apraxia"
    Spatial acalculia
Behavioral dysfunction
    Defective recognition and recall of complex auditory and visual stimuli (music, etc.)

---

[a] Function usually localized to dominant lobe.
[b] Function usually localized to nondominant lobe.
[c] Gerstmann's syndrome.
[d] Many of the so-called parietal lobe "apraxias" may actually be at the perceptual–organizational integrative levels constituting "agnosias."
[e] Babinski's syndrome.

at compensation as "pathoplastic." Pathoplastic compensation may at times aggravate coping—for example, an accentuation of preexisting obsessionality to the level of functional impairment in order to compensate for memory and organizational difficulties.

MENTAL STATUS EXAMINATION

The mental status examination traditionally practiced by psychiatrists is little more than a way of organizing information. The traditional format (divided into appearance and behavior, mood and affect, language and thought, cognition, volition, suicide and homicide tendencies, and judgment) is little more than the way an experienced psychiatrist will organize his or her observations of the patient's mental functions. However, it often leaves one without a knowledge of whether certain functions were tested or not, or whether they were omitted because the patient could not perform them, or whether they were tested at all. The other major drawback of this type of presentation is the lack of sufficient quantifiable data for comparing one patient to another, as well as in the same patient's mental functions over time. For example, is there a difference between the patient who can remember three objects in 5 minutes, or two objects, or only one object? Consequently, there have been attempts to standardize the mental status examination. Perhaps the most widely used has been Folstein's (Folstein, Folstein, & McHugh, 1975) Mini Mental Status Examination (MMSE). Several short batteries have also been developed to standardize the mental status examination (Rovner & Folstein, 1987).

Gurland, Cote, Cross, and Toner (1987) compared five standardized short examinations that attempt to quantify the following areas: recall of personal information, orientation to time, place and person, memory, new learning, attention, concentration, and calculation. A few of these have various paper-and-pencil components as well.

The MMSE has been recommended as a preliminary screen for medical and psychiatric patients. It covers the major areas of orientation and calculation (loaded areas covering half the items), registration, recall, language, and praxis. It is short and requires no training to use. However, like all of these brief standardized batteries, as Gurland et al. note, it shows little predictive power for classifying organic syndromes, diagnosis, prognosis, or mortality, and has a low sensitivity for identifying the mildly impaired organic patient.

One examination that is more detailed clinically, reproducible, and widely used in the evaluation of Alzheimer's patients, is the Dementia Rating Scale (Vitaliano et al., 1984). Other short instruments of interest are those developed by Kahn, Goldfarb, Pollack, and Peck (1960), Stonier

(1974), Pfeiffer (1975), and Rosen, Mohs, and Davis (1984), none of which is widely used. The recently developed neurobehavioral cognitive status examination (Schwamm, VanDyke, Kiernan, Merrin, & Mueller, 1987) uses several headings that permit quantitative assessment. However, it does not have pencil-and-paper components, so reevaluation is more difficult. It also does not adequately evaluate sensory motor reflex phenomena, gnosis, and praxis, but certainly appears to be a substantial improvement over other instruments. Recently, Trzepacz, Baker, and Greenhouse (1987) have developed a much-needed symptom rating scale for delirium, which assesses many of the fluctuating behaviors noted in delirium. From Great Britain is yet another promising dementia instrument, the Cambridge Mental Disorders of the Elderly Examination (CAMDEX), developed by Roth et al. (1986). The CAMDEX has a standardized structured interview as well as a cognitive exam (CAMCOG) of 67 items, including the 19 from Folstein's MMSE. Neppe has developed a promising, somewhat longer clinical evaluation called the BROCAS Scan—the Screening Cerebral Assessment (Neppe & Geist, 1988).

BROCAS Scan

We have been working for some time on an instrument to more adequately evaluate the interface area of neurology and psychiatry (e.g., pathology in the cerebral cortex) at the bedside clinical level. We wanted to develop an instrument that is short (taking 20 to 30 minutes), sensitive (impaired individuals will produce impaired results), and specific (normal individuals and nonorganic psychiatric patients will not show impaired results). The test therefore should be a quick-and-ready, nonintensive screen of cerebral cortical functioning, which identifies possible areas of abnormality to be followed over time; it should also screen patients for more detailed neuropsychological testing. The BROCAS Scan seems to meet all these requirements, although results are still preliminary.

The Scan provides clinical personnel with a quick assessment of a patient's mental status. We have grouped various facets of cerebral functioning and some noncerebral features into categories, spelling out the acronym BROCAS. B is for behavior rating, which is an independent score. The remaining ten items make up ROCAS: R is for recall and recognition, O for orientation and organization, C for concentration and calculation, A for apraxia and agnosia, and S for speech and "sensory-motor-reflex." These items are combined into a two-dimensional score sheet. Behavior is measured using a modified version of the Brief Psychiatric Rating Scale (Overall & Gorham, 1962). Patients are also scored in each of the remaining ten categories (ROCAS) on the basis of their performance on a series of test items. The results form a "BROCAS profile" that can be associated with clinical and neuropsychiatric features. Consequently, an interviewer unfamiliar with the patient will be able to use the BROCAS profile to assess the nature of the illness. Scores for each of the ten ROCAS categories can range from a maximum of ten, reflecting gross impairment, to a minimum of zero, which is normal. Thus, a profile can be obtained for each patient and compared with others with specific diagnoses. There is a total of 41 items. Twenty-two of them are CORE series of items given to everyone. Those patients who are not grossly impaired (who have not scored greater than 50 on the CORE) are tested on the remaining FINE items. Each item is divided into one or two subtests. Each subtest has a maximum score of 5 for gross errors of performance. This ensures that no particular item is overloaded on the scoring system level and that a grid system can be developed. Minor errors are scored as 1, generally indicating required retesting on a particular item.

We are still testing. However, at this point, it appears that the Scan has good construct validity according to overall clinical assessments by neuropsychiatrists and evaluations involving the results of magnetic resonance imaging (MRI) scan of the head and of neuropsychological testing. In addition, the instrument's interrater reliability is excellent. It appears significantly better than the Folstein's MMSE. The BROCAS Scan permits modification and can be administered without any apparatus. However, it can be used in a more rigid fashion with the exact questionnaire and answer sheets that are available. It has been used by both undergraduate psychology students and psychiatrists, and is simple enough to be learned in only a few demonstrations. Because of the short testing time, patients can easily be retested after a particular pharmacological or other intervention, or to monitor the progress of their illness, a potentially important clinical and research application.

IMAGING

With the data now available from the computerization of radiologic procedures and MRI, we are able to correlate observed behavior and performance on neuropsychological testing with the actual visualization of lesions in the central nervous system. The computerized axial tomography (CT) scan is an X-ray examination that produces an excellent transverse image of the brain and is particularly useful for detecting meningeal abnormalities associated with metastic neoplasia or inflammatory conditions. It is also very useful for finding calcified lesions, acute subarachnoid bleeding, and other hemorrhagic cortical lesions. Although a major advance over simple skull X-rays, it is not as effective as MRI, which reveals not only transverse cuts but also sagittal, coronal, and oblique sections of the brain and in addition visualizes the anatomy of the brain in exquisite detail. MRI is not sensitive to bony artifacts but is particularly useful in detecting lesions in the temporal lobes and subcortical structures (the cerebellum, brain stem, and spinal cord), all of which are not as well visualized by CT. MRI is also much better in detecting white matter lesions, such as those associated with Alzheimer's disease, multiple sclerosis, and microvascular disease (Conlon & Trimble, 1987; Garber, Weilburg, Buononno, Manschreck, & New, 1988).

Another great advantage of MRI scans is the ability to obtain not only structural data, as does the CT scan, but functional data as well. During the MRI, a pulse of energy (a particular radio frequency) applied to the nuclei in the brain (usually the hydrogen ion) generates a deflection pulse. From these pulses one can measure proton density, which in turn reflects the density of the hydrogen nuclei. Two measures give further information. The first, which is known as "time constant one" (T-1), is a measure of the relaxation of the hydrogen nuclei in a longitudinal plane. The second is spin relaxation (T-2), which is a measure in the transverse plane. These reflect in part the relationship of free water and lipids in the tissue, thereby giving us some idea of local physiological activity. MRI series weighted between T-1 and T-2 can also be performed—and also reconstructed via computers retrospectively. Thus, we not only have a good measure of the anatomical boundaries of white and gray matter but also the potential for functional studies in terms of physicochemical differences in regional brain areas. MRI has been excellent for evaluating tumors, infarctions, demyelinating disease, and seizure disorders.

There has been some controversy about the use of these technologies in regard to psychiatric patients; some have proposed that only when localizing neurological findings are present should a CT scan be ordered. However, others such as Weinberger (1984) have recommended CT scans for patients with the following clinical indications: unexpected confusion, dementia, movement disorder, psychosis, anorexia, catatonia, late onset affective or personality disturbances, and atypical symptoms of course of chronic psychiatric illness. Beresford, Blow, Hall, Nichols, and Langstrom (1986) also found high correlations, with positive findings on CT scans if formal mental status testing was abnormal. CT scans are far cheaper than MRI; however, MRI generally reveals abnormalities at least as well and sometimes better in all the above instances. Often, patients with normal CT scans end up with an MRI of the head as the index of suspicion warrants further confirmation of the absence of structural pathology.

In forensic practice, neuroradiological techniques are of increasing value. One could make a case for routine MRI of the head in all instances. However, medically such investigations are only necessary when structural intracranial pathologies—most commonly tumor, vascular, degenerative, or gliotic—are suspected. Except for the special indications noted above, MRI (when available) has eclipsed CT.

Other more dynamic measures—such as positron emission tomography (PET), single photon emission computerized tomography (SPECT), and nuclear magnetic resonance (NMR) SPECT—are more valuable for defining the functional areas of either hyper- or hypoactivity as well as measuring regional cerebral blood flow. PET has the potential for localizing various receptors. These techniques are presently in the research stage and are not yet in routine clinical use.

BLOOD TESTS

Of great importance is a second major subgroup of organic brain syndromes—namely, extracranial pathology, for example, endocrine, metabolic, and toxic disorders. These disorders require investigation generally by routine blood tests such as complete blood count, sedimentation rate, urea, electrolytes, glucose, syphilis, serology (and now AIDS testing [HIV]), and thyroid functions. B12, folate, calcium, phosphorus, magnesium, cortisols, porphyrin screens, antinuclear antibodies, and other tests may be required as clinically indicated. Urine toxicology and psychiatric drug testing are, of course, invaluable.

ELECTROENCEPHALOGRAPHY

The electroencephalogram (EEG) has been used a great deal in both psychiatry and neurology. In the presence of paroxysmal episodes of spikes or spikes and waves, the electoencephalogram is an excellent discriminator of patients having epileptic seizures as opposed to patients exhibiting hysterical or pseudoseizures. However, the rare occurence of paroxysmal episodes of spikes in psychiatric patients has limited the application of electroencephalography. It has also been used for detecting focal abnormalities. Focality, particularly associated with temporal lobe lesions, is a common phenomenon in patients with psychopathology (Neppe & Tucker, 1988a, 1988b). The meaning of this finding is hard to interpret, particularly as these abnormalities are most often dysrhythmic, slowed, nonparoxysmal patterns.

Over the past few years, the use of EEG telemetry has increased. This technique involves a prolonged monitoring of the patient, who is generally confined to one room over periods of time varying from 12 hours to 2 weeks. Most common is cable telemetry, where a lengthy cable is connected to an EEG montage on the patient's head. EEG telemetry has the advantage of providing lengthy EEG records over periods of days or weeks as opposed to record for a period of an hour (the results of routine EEGs). EEG telemetry is not easily available and is commonly a superspecialized technique in extremely difficult cases; thus, there is little forensic application at this point.

Normal EEG results do not exclude the existence of a brain disorder. Scalp electrodes may make it difficult to localize symptoms because symptoms originating from deep structures such as the mesial temporal areas may not be picked up with surface electrodes. Even depth electrode placement has its difficulties because the placements have to be in exactly the areas associated with firing. Sleep EEG records significantly increase the incidence of finding EEG abnormalities, particularly focal lesions such as temporal lobe lesions. Special electrode placements, such as sphenoidal and naso-pharyngeal electrodes, have been useful to a limited degree.

Recent advances in EEG technology may ultimately change the whole perspective of its use. This is particularly so in the context of computerized EEG monitoring, which allows a breakdown of wave forms as well as correlation of the EEG with evoked potentials, including cognitive evoked potentials. This technique is still in the experimental stage.

CONCLUSIONS

The patient with possible brain damage should be evaluated in detail using the conventional medical approach. There is no substitute for an adequate history. Evaluation should include not only a full physical and conventional neurological and psychiatric examination, but a neuropsychiatric mental status evaluation of higher cerebral functions. The history and exam will allow preliminary diagnosis and evaluation. These can be consolidated by appropriate blood and urine tests, waking and sleep EEGs, neuroradiological investigations, and neuropsychological assessment.

REFERENCES

Beresford, T. P., Blow, F. C., Hall, R. C. W., Nichols, L. O., & Langstrom, J. W. (1986). CT scanning in psychiatric inpatients: Clinical yield. *Psychosomatics, 27*, 105–112.

Conlon, P., & Trimble, M. R. (1987). Magnetic resonance imaging in psychiatry. *Canadian Journal of Psychiatry, 32*, 702–712.

Folstein, M. F., Folstein, S. E., & McHugh, P. R. (1975). "Mini-mental state": A practical method for grading the cognitive state of patients for the clinician. *Journal of Psychiatric Research, 12*, 189–198.

Garber, H. J., Weilburg, J. B., Buononno, F. S., Manschreck, T. C., & New, P. F. J. (1988). Use of magnetic resonance imaging in psychiatry. *American Journal of Psychiatry, 145*, 164–171.

Goldstein, K. (1952). The effect of brain damage on the personality. *Psychiatry, 15*, 245–260.

Gurland, B. J., Cote, L. J., Cross, P. S., & Toner, J. A. (1987). The assessment of cognitive function in the elderly. *Clinics in Geriatric Medicine, 3*, 53–63.

Heinrichs, D. W., & Buchanan, R. W. (1988). Significance and meaning of neurological signs in schizophrenia. *American Journal of Psychiatry, 145*, 11–18.

Jenkyn, L. R., Reeves, A. G., Warren, T., Whiting, R. K., Clayton, R. J., Moore, W. W., Rizzo, A., Tuzun, I. M., Bonnett, J. C., & Culpepper, B. W. (1985). Neurologic signs in senescence. *Archives of Neurology, 42*, 1154–1157.

Kahn, R. L., Goldfarb, A. L., Pollack, M., & Peck, A. (1960). Brief objective measures for the determination of mental status in the aged. *American Journal of Psychiatry, 117*, 326–328.

Neppe, V. M., & Geist, M. (1988). A new screening cerebral assessment. In Society for Biological Psychiatry (43rd Convention) Program, No. 262, p. 322.

Neppe, V. M., & Tucker, G. J. (1988a). Modern perspectives on epilepsy in relation to psychiatry: Behavioral disturbances of epilepsy. *Hospital & Community Psychiatry, 39*, 389–395.

Neppe, V. M., & Tucker, G. J. (1988b). Modern perspectives on epilepsy in relation to psychiatry: Classification and evaluation. *Hospital & Community Psychiatry, 39*, 263–271.

Overall, J. C., & Gorham, D. P. (1962). The brief psychiatric rating scale. *Psychological Reports, 10*, 799–802.

Pincus, J., & Tucker, G. J. (1985). *Behavioral neurology* (3rd ed.). New York: Oxford University Press.

Plum, F. (1988). Approach to the patient. In J. Wyngaarden & L. Smith (Eds.), *Cecil textbook of medicine*. Philadelphia: Saunders.

Pfeiffer, E. (1975). A short portable mental status questionnaire for the assessment of organic brain deficits in elderly patients. *Journal of the American Geriatric Society, 23*, 433–441.

Rosen, W. G., Mohs, R. C., & Davis, K. L. (1984). A new rating scale for Alzheimer's disease. *American Journal of Psychiatry, 141*, 1356–1364.

Roth, M., Tym, E., Montjoy, C. Q., Huppert, F. A., Hendrie, H., Verma, S., & Goddard, R. (1986). CAMDEX: A standardized instrument for the diagnosis of mental disorders in the elderly with special reference to the early detection of dementia. *British Journal of Psychiatry, 149*, 698–709.

Rovner, B. W., & Folstein, M. F. (1987). Mini-mental state exam in clinical practice. *Hospital Practice, 22*, 99–110.

Schwamm, L. H., VanDyke, C., Kiernan, R. J., Merrin, E. L., & Mueller, J. (1987). The neurobehavioral cognitive status examination: Comparison with the cognitive capacity screening examination and the mini-mental state examination in a neurosurgical population. *Annals of Internal Medicine, 107*, 486–491.

Stonier, P. D. (1974). Score changes following repeated administration of mental status questionnaire. *Age and Aging*, *3*, 91–96.

Trzepacz, P. T., Baker, R. W., & Greenhouse, J. (1987). A symptom rating scale for delirium. *Psychiatry Research*, *23*, 89–97.

Vitaliano, P., Breen, A., Russo, J., Albert, M., Prinz, P., & Vitiello, M. (1984). Clinical utility of the dementia rating scale for assessing SDAT patients. *Journal of Chronic Diseases*, *37*, 743–754.

Weinberger, D. R. (1984). Brain disease and psychiatric illness: When should a psychiatrist order a CAT scan? *American Journal of Psychiatry*, *141*, 1521–1527.

PART III

Interpreting the Findings

chapter 6

Estimating Premorbid Ability and Preexisting Neuropsychological Deficits

ROBERT S. WILSON
and GLENN T. STEBBINS

In forensic assessment, neuropsychologists are typically asked to render opinions on two questions: (a) Are there abnormalities of performance? and (b) Are these abnormalities attributable to the injury or illness in question? In this chapter, we discuss factors to be considered in making these determinations. The first question involves comparison of test performance to a normative reference group and to the individual's estimated premorbid ability level. The second question concerns causation and touches upon topics reviewed in more detail in other chapters. In this chapter, we look at preexisting neuropsychological deficits as a possible explanation for abnormalities of current performance.

Two standards are available for the evaluation of neuropsychological test performance. One is the normative data base for a given test. Although such norms are an essential part of test interpretation, their quality varies widely from test to test. Some norms may be representative of the general population (e.g., Wechsler Adult Intelligence Scale–Revised [WAIS-R]; Wechsler, 1981); others are based on local samples of convenience. Norms permit transformation of raw test scores into a form (e.g., standard scores, percentiles) that conveys information about an individual's standing relative to an appropriate reference group. Although such information is vital, it may be of little help in determining if abilities have declined since the onset of the injury or illness in question.

A second standard for evaluating test performance is an individual's level of ability prior to the injury or illness in question. Knowledge or estimation of the individual's premorbid ability level is often vital in neuropsychological assessment. Individuals with superior ability prior to, for example, a head injury may experience a significant decline in function following the injury. Yet test performance may still be in the normal range relative to the general population. Alternatively, individuals of borderline intelligence may score in the impaired range on selected neuropsychological measures without evidence of damage to the central nervous system. Knowledge of the examinee's premorbid ability, therefore, is of utmost importance in the interpretation of neuropsychological test results.

Ideally, test results obtained prior to the injury or illness would provide documented evidence of premorbid ability. Understandably, this ideal is rarely encountered in practice. When test data are available, the tests are often those used in educational or military settings. Their relation to tests used in clinical neuropsychological practice is often uncertain. Even when directly relevant tests have been administered, one should examine the test forms themselves to ensure that no gross scoring or administrative errors have been made.

In the absence of premorbid test data, clinicians are forced to estimate premorbid ability. These estimates are typically based on one or both of the following sources of information: (a) measures of present ability that are relatively insensitive to brain dysfunction and/or (b) qualitative and quantitative historical information regarding the premorbid period.

PRESENT ABILITY APPROACH

The present ability, or pattern-analytic, approach to estimation of premorbid ability is based on the assumption that some measures of current ability are relatively insensitive to brain dysfunction. This approach is not new. Binet suggested that alcoholics scattered passes and failures on the Binet Scale. Babcock (1930) developed a scale to measure mental deterioration that used a vocabulary test to estimate premorbid ability. Wechsler (1939) extended this notion somewhat in reference to the Wechsler-Bellevue Scale and later the WAIS. He observed in the cross-sectional normative data for these tests that some subtests showed little to no age-related decline (i.e., they hold with age), whereas others showed an age-related decline (i.e., they do not hold with age). These observations led Wechsler to suggest that clinicians might wish to calculate a deterioration index based on a comparison of "hold" and "don't hold" subtests. Wechsler's deterioration index stimulated considerable research interest. The results were almost uniformly negative (e.g., Larrabee, Largen, & Levin, 1985). In fairness to Wechsler, the quality of much of this work was suspect, and in 1958 he formally acknowledged the failure of his deterioration index. Curiously, the Wechsler approach continues to attract sporadic research interest today or to reappear in different guises. Nonetheless, the reasons for the failure of his and related indices have been clear for some time and were delineated in a penetrating review by Yates (1956) over 30 years ago. The essential problem is that although present ability measures such as vocabulary are highly related to IQ, these measures are not insensitive to brain dysfunction. In fact, neurological patients show a significant decline on all Wechsler subtests (Russell, 1972).

More recently, Nelson and colleagues (Nelson & O'Connell, 1978) developed a reading test specifically for the purpose of estimating premorbid IQ in neuropsychological assessment. They observed that scores on a standard reading test "held" better than did a vocabulary measure in a mixed sample of patients with brain damage. Guided by this finding, Nelson (1982) devised the National Adult Reading Test (NART). The 50 stimulus words are irregular in the sense that each violates common rules of pronunciation and phoneme production (e.g., debt, naive). The choice of such irregular words was meant to maximize the importance of previous familiarity with the words rather than current ability to decode the alphabetic array and organize the verbal response.

The NART was originally validated by showing that it has a high correlation with IQ but that NART performance in a sample of patients with cortical atrophy was apparently normal. These patients ranged from 20 to 70 years of age and scored approximately one standard deviation below a control group on the WAIS.

We recently concluded an investigation of the NART's validity, the results of which are relevant to the present discussion (Stebbins, Wilson, et al., 1990). The sample consisted of 199 dementia patients and 26 normal controls examined at the Rush Alzheimer's Disease Center. All patients had a standard dementia diagnostic evaluation (McKhann et al., 1984) resulting in clinical diagnoses of Alzheimer's disease, multi-infarct dementia, or a mixture of the two. Performance on the Mini Mental Status Examination (MMSE) (Folstein, Folstein, & McHugh, 1975) was used to divide the patients into very mild (24–27), mild (16–23), and moderate to severe (5–15) levels of dementia. Each subgroup was selected to be equivalent in age ($F (2, 196) < 1$) and education ($F (2, 196) < 1$). The normal control group consisted of patients' relatives. WAIS Full Scale IQs were estimated (a) using the NART error score and regression formula presented in Nelson (1982) and (b) using age, sex, race, education, and occupation in the regression formula of Wilson et al. (1978).

According to the results (Table 6.1), the demographically estimated IQs are equivalent in the four groups ($F (3, 221) < 1$). For the NART, however, there was a significant group effect ($F (3, 221) = 20.4$, $p < .001$). Post hoc analyses using Tukey's multiple range statistic indicated that the very mild patients did not differ from the controls on NART

TABLE 6.1. Sample Characteristics by Dementia Levels

Subgroup	n	Age	Education	DIQ[a]	NART
Normal controls	26	63.5	13.3	114.86	111.02
Very mild dementia	41	69.8	12.8	114.95	108.68
Mild dementia	81	72.9	12.6	114.74	104.53
Moderate/severe dementia	77	72.2	12.4	113.48	99.13

[a] Demographic IQ estimate.

performance. However, the mild and moderate to severe groups showed a significant impairment in NART performance ($p < .05$) relative to the control and very mild groups and to one another. The results of a subsequent study suggest that even among those with mild dementia, defined by MMS ≥ 16, the NART appears to underestimate IQ in patients who have accompanying linguistic deficits (Stebbins, Gilley, et al., 1990). These findings indicate that the NART, like its predecessors, is not insensitive to brain dysfunction. The standard error of estimate of the NART is relatively small (7.6), however, and, if used cautiously, it may yet prove to be a useful adjunct in the estimation of premorbid IQ in encephalopathic individuals.

In summary, all attempts to estimate premorbid ability from measures of present ability suffer from the same problem. Damage to the brain affects performance on all such measures. In patients with focal lesions in the dominant hemisphere, the effects may be dramatic. In patients with a diffuse encephalopathy, the effect appears to depend on the nature and extent of the damage, but there is little empirical justification for assuming that such measures have not been affected by the injury or illness in question. On the other hand, if the brain damage is diffuse and relatively mild, the NART in particular, and vocabulary tests in general, may help provide a lower limit, at or above which the true level of premorbid ability is expected to lie.

HISTORICAL APPROACH

The alternative to using present ability to estimate past ability is the historical approach. This approach is based on the empirical demonstration that numerous life history variables (e.g., education, occupation) are related to performance on standardized intelligence tests. The historical approach can be based on qualitative and quantitative information obtained from interview and past records. In addition, numerous quantitative methods are available that provide point estimates of premorbid IQ with confidence intervals given selected demographic information.

In any case, the historical assessment should include a review of the examinee's perinatal, developmental, educational, and occupational history. Looking first at the educational background, the most critical variable is the amount of formal schooling completed, or educational attainment. IQ tests were originally developed to predict educability. It should not be surprising, therefore, that educational attainment is the best single demographic predictor of IQ. Correlations with WAIS Full Scale IQ, for example, are typically around .70 (Matarazzo, 1972). Qualitative features of the educational background can provide important information as well. Specifically, it is important to determine if subjects have had to repeat a grade in school. Failure of first or second grade is common in children with a learning disability or pervasive attention deficit. Inquiry regarding special education should be routinely made. The examiner should also inquire about supplemental schooling (e.g., general equivalency diploma [GED] examination, technical training). Our clinical practice is to discount technical training in calculating educational attainment but to credit those who have passed the GED examination by adding 12 to the years of schooling completed and dividing the sum by two. Thus, an individual who completed the tenth grade and later passed the GED examination would be credited with 11 years of formal education.

In some instances, examination of school records can be helpful in evaluating premorbid functioning. Potentially helpful materials include academic transcripts, ratings and behavioral observations by teachers, and the results of academic achievement tests. School grades are moderately correlated with IQ, but considerable interpretive caution is required. Nonintellectual factors clearly play a major role in academic success. Further, grading policies differ within school levels, between institutions, and between eras. Specific observations by teachers are available in some academic records and may be helpful in identifying the presence or absence of specific strengths and weaknesses. Academic achievement tests, particularly those with representative national norms, can be helpful in determining the presence or absence of a specific disability at specific points in school. Finally, some individuals have had individually administered psychological testing through the school system. Such data can be extremely helpful, although it is advisable to obtain the raw data if possible to evaluate the adequacy of test administration.

An occupational history is another important step in evaluating premorbid functioning. IQ is highly related to level of occupational attainment but relatively uncorrelated to achievement within an occupation. The interview, therefore, should focus on the specific positions held, length of employment, and reasons for leaving, beginning with the current job and moving back in time. Some job titles (e.g., secretary) are self-explanatory, whereas others (e.g., systems operator) require amplification. Familiarity with some of the more standard occupational scales will facilitate collection of these data. The WAIS and WAIS-R manuals contain the scales used in the 1950 and 1980 censuses, respectively. Phillips (1968) presents more extensive occupational coding schemes. Length of employment in each position helps to evaluate how representative each job is of the examinee's employment history. The regularity of employment and reasons for shifting positions may also be helpful in evaluating premorbid psychiatric status.

In some instances, it is necessary or desirable to obtain the history from a collateral source (e.g., spouse, relative, friend). Such an approach is essential with children or patients whose cognitive functioning is severely compromised. With children, it is important to obtain information about the perinatal/developmental period. Most parents are able to accurately recall birth weight and approximate length of gestation. Both of these variables are related to subsequent IQ, although the relationship is changing with more aggressive neonatal care. Complications during the prenatal period or delivery, Apgar scores, and subsequent hospital course are all of potential interest. The parent should also be asked the age at which major developmental milestones (sitting, walking, talking, toilet training) were achieved. Parental report of such information, however, is not entirely reliable and tends to conform more to normative expectations than to the actual age at which the milestones were achieved (e.g., Yarrow, 1963). Thus, only extreme developmental aberrations are likely to be elicited by interview. In critical instances, medical records from this period may be helpful in clarifying ambiguities.

Although a wealth of potentially rich information can be obtained through interview and examination of educational, occupational, and medical records, integration of these data with current test results is a complex matter. A considerable body of research demonstrates that clinicians have difficulty integrating such diverse data sets to arrive at a judgment (Meehl, 1954). Fortunately, there are several actuarial methods available that use objective demographic data to estimate premorbid IQ.

The first of these methods was developed by Wilson and colleagues (Wilson et al., 1978; Wilson et al., 1979) for use with the WAIS (Table 6.2). The Full Scale IQs of the WAIS standardization sample were regressed on age, sex, race, education, and occupation. R^2 was .54, and the resulting regression equation yields point estimates of IQ. The standard error for these estimates is 10.2, meaning that the probability is approximately .68 that the actual premorbid IQ is within 10.2 points of the estimated IQ. Subsequent validity research has supported the clinical utility of this equation (Goldstein, Gary, & Levin, 1986; Karzmark, Heaton, Grant, & Matthews, 1985; Klesges, Fisher, Vasey, & Pheley, 1984; Klesges, Sanchez, & Stanton,

TABLE 6.2. Demographic Formulas for Estimation of Premorbid WAIS and WAIS-R Full Scale IQ

WAIS formula (Wilson et al.)
   IQ = (.17) age − (1.53) sex − (11.33) race + (2.97) education + (1.01) occupation + 74.05

WAIS-R formula (Barona et al.)
   IQ = (.47) age + (1.76) sex + (4.71) race + (5.02) education + (1.89) occupation + (.59) region + 54.96

Note. See original articles for coding of selected variables.

1981; Wilson, Rosenbaum, & Brown, 1979). Barona, Reynolds, and Chastain (1984) have provided a similar formula for the WAIS-R (Table 6.2). Reynolds and Gutkin (1979) developed a formula to predict Wechsler Intelligence Scale for Children–Revised (WISC-R) IQs, but the standard error of estimate is large (13.5) and the percentage of variance accounted for is relatively small. The demographic method of estimating premorbid IQ has some distinct advantages. Specifically, these formulas provide objective estimates of premorbid ability, thereby overcoming the inherent limitations of clinicians in data integration as well as perceptions of bias that may be present in forensic situations. Further, these estimates, unlike those based on present ability, are unaffected by the neurological injury or illness. These methods are far from perfect, however. The standard errors of estimate are substantial, indicating that the formulas should be viewed as providing a range within which premorbid functioning is likely to fall rather than a point estimation. Clinical experience suggests that the formulas tend to overestimate IQ for retarded individuals. The formulas may not be not applicable to children or to situations in which the onset of the injury or illness in question occurred prior to adulthood.

In a recent and promising development, Crawford, Stewart, Parker, Besson, and Cochrane (1989) used a combination of present ability and demographic information to estimate premorbid IQ. In the standardization sample, the resulting formula was superior to formulas based on either present ability information or demographic data alone. Further, the formula fared well in subsequent use with a cross-validation sample (Crawford, Cochrane, Besson, Parker, & Stewart, 1990). Although more work will be required before such formulas can be applied in clinical practice, the approach of using both age-resistant present ability measures and demographic variables to estimate IQ holds considerable promise.

In summary, although knowledge of premorbid ability is vital, clinicians are forced to estimate in nearly all situations. These estimates may be based on measures of present ability that are relatively insensitive to brain dysfunction (e.g., NART, vocabulary tests), on qualitative findings gleaned from a history of life accomplishments during the premorbid period, and/ or on formulas that estimate IQ given specific demographic data. The latter approach is the most justified empirically, but experienced clinicians also typically take qualitative historical data and various "hold" tests into account in making determinations of premorbid ability.

ESTIMATE OF PREEXISTING DEFICITS

Preexisting and/or concurrent neurological or systemic disorders may offer competing explanations for the abnormalities seen on examination. Unfortunately, many neurobehavioral abnormalities are relatively nonspecific indicators that may be seen in a variety of medical disorders. In some instances, therefore, it is simply not possible to conclude whether abnormalities are due to one condition, another, or both. In evaluating the preexisting or concurrent condition, the considerations of biological plausibility, temporal sequence of events, and specificity of outcome are germane to the differential diagnosis. In some instances, a careful history may clarify the situation. A patient with a childhood head injury and well-documented neuropsychological disability may show evidence of an abrupt or gradual behavioral decline following a second head injury or exposure to a neurotoxin, respectively.

A related issue is the possible additive effects of serial injury. For example, following a head injury an individual may recover to the extent that overall functioning 1 year later is at the estimated premorbid level. Yet mild head injury may be associated with permanent neuronal damage (Oppenheimer, 1968), and the long-term effect of the injury may be the individual's increased vulnerability to subsequent insults to the central nervous system (Gronwall & Wrightson, 1975). For example, retrospective studies of patients with Alzheimer's disease suggest that prior head injury may be a risk factor (Mortimer, French, Hutton, & Schuman, 1985). Patients with an encephalopathy, therefore, may show a more pronounced symptomatic response to subsequent events affecting the brain (e.g., neurotoxic exposure, head injury, neuronal loss with normal aging).

SUMMARY

Neuropsychological abnormalities can be inferred on the basis of deviation from (a) an appropriate normative reference group and/or (b) the premorbid level of function. Premorbid ability can be estimated from measures of present ability or from historical information. The former approach is flawed and may only be appropriate for providing a lower limit to the estimate of premorbid IQ or in situations in which there is no reason to suspect general intellectual deterioration. The latter approach may draw on a range of qualitative and quantitative information but rests on formulas that convert demographic variables into IQ estimates. These demographically estimated IQs have fared well in validation research but are associated with sizable errors of estimate suggesting caution in their application. The potential impact of preexisting or concurrent conditions should be considered in evaluating the diagnostic significance of neuropsychological abnormalities.

REFERENCES

Babcock, H. (1930). An experiment in the measurement of mental deterioration. *Archives of Psychology*, *28*, Serial #117, 1–105.

Barona, A., Reynolds, C. R., & Chastain, R. (1984). A demographically based index of premorbid intelligence for the WAIS-R. *Journal of Consulting & Clinical Psychology*, *52*, 885–887.

Crawford, J. R., Stewart, L. E., Parker, D. M., Besson, J. A. O., & Cochrane, R. N. B. (1989). Estimation of premorbid intelligence: Combining psychometric and demographic approaches improves predictive accuracy. *Personality & Individual Differences*, *10*, 793–796.

Crawford, J. R., Cochrane, R. H. B., Besson, J. A. O., Parker, D. M., & Stewart, L. E. (1990). Premorbid IQ estimates obtained by combining the NART and demographic variables: Construct validity. *Personality & Individual Differences*, *11*, 209–210.

Folstein, M. F., Folstein, S. E., & McHugh, P. R. (1975). "Mini-Mental State": A practical method for grading the cognitive state of outpatients for the clinician. *Journal of Psychiatry Research*, *12*, 189–198.

Goldstein, F. C., Gary, H. E., & Levin, H. S. (1986). Assessment of the accuracy of regression equations proposed for estimating premorbid intellectual functioning on the Wechsler Adult Intelligence Scale. *Journal of Clinical & Experimental Neuropsychology*, *8*, 405–412.

Gronwall, D., & Wrightson, P. (1975). Cumulative effects of concussion. *Lancet*, *2*, 995–997.

Karzmark, P., Heaton, R. K., Grant, I., & Matthews, C. G. (1985). Use of demographic variables to predict full-scale IQ: A replication and extension. *Journal of Clinical & Experimental Neuropsychology*, *7*, 412–420.

Klesges, R. C., Fisher, L., Vasey, M., & Pheley, A. (1984). Predicting adult premorbid functioning levels: Another look. *International Journal of Clinical Neuropsychology*, *7*, 1–3.

Klesges, R. C., Sanchez, V. C., & Stanton, A. L. (1981). Cross-validation of an adult premorbid functioning index. *Clinical Neuropsychology*, *1*, 13–15.

Larrabee, G. J., Largen, J. W., & Levin, H. S. (1985). Sensitivity of age-decline resistant ("hold") WAIS subtests to Alzheimer's disease. *Journal of Clinical & Experimental Neuropsychology*, *7*, 497–504.

Matarazzo, J. D. (1972). *Wechsler's measurement and appraisal of adult intelligence* (5th ed.). Baltimore: Williams & Wilkins.

McKhann, G., Drachman, D., Folstein, M., Katzman, R., Price, D., & Stadlan, E. M. (1984). Clinical diagnosis of Alzheimer's disease: Report of the NINCDS-ADRDA work group under the auspices of the Department of Health and Human Services task force on Alzheimer's disease. *Neurology, 34,* 939–944.

Meehl, P. E. (1954). *Clinical vs. statistical prediction.* Minneapolis: University of Minnesota Press.

Mortimer, J. A., French, L. M., Hutton, J. T., & Schuman, L. M. (1985). Head trauma as a risk factor for Alzheimer's disease. *Neurology, 35,* 264–267.

Nelson, H. E. (1982). *National Adult Reading Test (NART) test manual.* Windsor: NFER-Nelson Publishing Co.

Nelson, H. E., & O'Connell, A. (1978). Dementia: The estimation of premorbid intelligence levels using the New Adult Reading Test. *Cortex, 14,* 234–244.

Oppenheimer, D. R. (1968). Microscopic lesions in the brain following head injury. *Journal of Neurology, Neurosurgery & Psychiatry, 31,* 299–306.

Phillips, L. (1968). *Human adaptation and its failures.* New York: Academic Press.

Reynolds, C. R., & Gutkin, T. B. (1979). Predicting the premorbid intellectual status of children using demographic data. *Clinical Neuropsychology, 1,* 36–38.

Russell, E. (1972). WAIS factors analysis with brain-damaged subjects using criterion measures. *Journal of Consulting & Clinical Psychology, 39,* 133–139.

Stebbins, G. T., Gilley, D. W., Wilson, R. S., Bernard, B. A., & Fox, J. H. (1990). Effects of language disturbances on premorbid estimates of IQ in mild dementia. *Clinical Neuropsychologist, 4,* 64–68.

Stebbins, G. T., Wilson, R. S., Gilley, D. W., Bernard, B. A., & Fox, J. H. (1990). Use of the National Adult Reading Test to estimate premorbid IQ in dementia. *Clinical Neuropsychologist, 4,* 18–24.

Wechsler, D. (1939). *The measurement of adult intelligence.* Baltimore: Williams & Wilkins.

Wechsler, D. (1981). *Manual for the Wechsler Adult Intelligence Scale revised.* New York: Psychology Corporation.

Wilson, R. S., Rosenbaum, G., & Brown, G. (1979). The problem of premorbid intelligence in neuropsychological assessment. *Journal of Clinical Neuropsychology, 1,* 49–53.

Wilson, R. S., Rosenbaum, G., Brown, G., Rourke, D., Whitman, D., & Grisell, J. (1978). An index of premorbid intelligence. *Journal of Consulting & Clinical Psychology, 46,* 1554–1555.

Yarrow, M. R. (1963). Problems of methods in parent–child research. *Child Development, 34,* 215–226.

Yates, A. (1956). The use of vocabulary in the measurement of intellectual deterioration—a review. *Journal of Mental Science, 102,* 409–440.

chapter 7

Consequences of Prescription and Nonprescription Drug Use

A L B E R T   S.   C A R L I N

Although the importance of the neuropsychological consequences of drug and alcohol use is obvious for the public health sector, for those doing research on pharmacology and on brain function, and for those engaged in the treatment of substance abuse, their relevance for forensic issues seems less clear. This is particularly so because the exposure to alcohol and psychoactive drugs is voluntary, whether in the context of recreational or medical use. However, awareness of the effects of psychoactive drugs and the permanence or transience of these effects are relevant to forensic issues. Knowledge of the impact of these substances is necessary when considering the etiology of any observed neuropsychological impairment. Previous or ongoing use of psychoactive substances may have an impact on neuropsychological integrity or may affect the results of subsequent or previous head injury.

Making an Attribution

When assessing a patient in order to determine if a pattern of drug use has caused neuropsychological deficit, the task begins with the determination of whether or not a deficit exists. Assuming that the neuropsychological measures were appropriately selected and adequately administered and scored, the neuropsychologist then must construct hypotheses about the cause of any observed deficit. The greatest validity and the greatest inter-clinician reliability of judgment occur when the question is the presence of neuropsychological impairment. It is more difficult to ascribe hemispheric laterality reliably and most difficult to infer the specific sites and the nature of the lesion. The assessment task becomes more difficult if an effort is made to attribute the observed impairment to a specific cause, especially if multiple possible sources of impairment may be present. In order to attribute any impairment to psychoactive drugs, or to rule out such an attribution, the clinician must be aware of the research literature extant for neuropsychological consequences of the substances in question, as well as the history of the patient. The history of the patient may reveal not only potential alternative sources of impairment, but also factors that may interact with substances consumed to increase the likelihood of impairment.

Consequences and Effects

It is useful to differentiate between acute neuropsychological effects of drugs and the relatively enduring neuropsychological consequences of their use. Almost all psychoactive drugs have neuropsychological effects. In addition to such immediate autonomic effects as change in heart rate and blood pressure, there may be long-term central effects on concentration, memory, and motor activity. Behavioral disinhibition and euphoria may also be observed. Effects of specific psychoactive drugs vary as a function of the dose as well as route of administration. Impaired judgment and reasoning ability as well as impaired motor coordination are effects of alcohol intoxication, whereas cirrhosis and Wernicke-Korsakoff syndrome are possible consequences of chronic alcohol use. In the same manner apparent hunger, impaired short-term memory, and increased risibility are acute effects of marijuana, but amotivational syndrome is alleged to be a more enduring consequence. Many recreational drug users may be thought of as seeking out an elective transient neuropsychological impairment. Although in some forensic situations the nature of the temporary impairment may be of importance, the intermediate and long-term consequences of drug and alcohol use are more typically of greater interest. This chapter focuses primarily on intermediate and long-term consequences of alcohol and other psychoactive drugs.

CONSEQUENCES OF SPECIFIC DRUGS

Alcohol

This discussion begins by focusing on the consequences of long-term use of a well-known and notorious neurotoxic substance—alcohol. In 1881 Wernicke described a neurological syndrome that he attributed to alcohol, and in 1887 Korsakoff first reported the syndrome pattern of amnesia and confabulation that bears his name (Victor, Adams, & Collins, 1971). Both were describing different aspects of an alcohol-related neurotoxic state that is well known. The Wernicke-Korsakoff syndrome is now easily diagnosed and treated with large doses of thiamine. Although the treatment may be lifesaving through prevention of midbrain hemorrhages, and ameliorates the associated ataxia, confusional state, and peripheral neuropathy, most patients are left with neuropsychological deficit (Victor et al., 1971). The most marked residual deficit is an anterograde amnesia of striking proportions.

The association of excessive alcohol use with more subtle deficits is less straightforward. In part this may be due to the sheer volume of publications dealing with the neuropsychological effects of alcohol. For the period from January 1983 to June 1990 (American Psychological Association, 1990), the PsycLIT computerized literature search lists 157 publications that include both alcohol and neuropsychology as key words.

A number of studies have demonstrated impaired abstracting and perceptual motor skills in alcoholics (Fitzhugh, Fitzhugh, & Reitan, 1960; Fitzhugh, Fitzhugh, & Reitan, 1965; Goldman, Klisz, & Williams, 1985; Goldman, Williams, & Klisz, 1983; Grant & Reed, 1985; Jones & Parsons 1971, 1972). Deficits have also been found for complex perceptual skills (Brandt, Butters, Ryan, & Bayog, 1983; Donovan, Quiesser, & O'Leary, 1976) as well as for both verbal and nonverbal memory (Brandt et al., 1983; Butters, Cermak, Montgomery, & Adinolfi, 1977; Ron, Acker, & Lishman, 1980; Ryan & Butters, 1980). In view of the number of investigations that have found deficits, it is surprising that controversy still exists. However, a major problem in interpreting the findings of impairment among alcoholics is the difficulty of establishing a dose–response relationship. No one has yet reliably determined that greater consumption is related to more profound deficits. Melgaard, Danielsen, Sorensen, and Ahlgren (1986) failed to find any correlation between severity of alcoholism and measures of neuropsychological impairment. Tarter and Alterman (1984), in a review of the literature of etiology of neuropsychological deficits among alcoholics, concluded that lifetime alcohol consumption has less effect than frequency of consumption and amount consumed per occasion. That is, lifetime pint-weeks seems to be a less useful predictor of neuropsychological impairment than a peak-pint-week measure. Portnoff (1982) found impairment was associated with age of initiating drinking, but not years of consumption. Shaeffer and Parsons (1986) found that among alcoholics the maximum quantity frequency (a peak-week measure) in the 6 months prior to testing was associated with impairment, whereas anxiety and depression were associated with impairment with poorer performance by social drinkers. Perhaps as a correlate of the peak consumption measure, bout drinkers were found more likely to be impaired than daily drinkers (Tarbox, Conners, & McLaughlin, 1986). Tarter, Goldstein, Alterman, Petrarulo, and Elmore (1983) failed to confirm their hypothesis that frequency of withdrawal seizures may be an indicator of the severity of involvement in alcohol and hence a correlate of impairment. Although one would suspect that "more is worse," part of the problem seems to be a definition of what is "more." Should the measure of immersion be based on lifetime consumption, peak-week use, or years of drinking? Efforts to elucidate this have been confounded by some confusion of effects and consequences.

Most of the investigations cited above were examinations of patients who recently underwent withdrawal as part of their treatment. Initial work by Carlen, Wortzman, Holgate, Wilkenson, and Rankin (1978) revealed that cerebral atrophy in alcoholics is reversible over time. Decrease in cortical and central atrophy and improved neuropsychological functioning were observed in alcoholics who stopped drinking or improved their drinking patterns over a 5-year period in contrast to those who continued drinking (Muuronen, Bergman, Hindmarsh, & Telakivi, 1989). Macciocchi, Ranseen, and Schmitt (1989) found that extent of deficit immediately on entry into treatment did not predict outcome of treatment. These data also suggest that the recovery described by Muuronen et al. (1989) is not an artifact of the impact of initial level of impairment on treatment outcome or later abstinence. Long-term abstinence from alcohol has frequently been shown to be associated with a reduction in neuropsychological deficit (Adams, Grant, & Reed, 1980; Grant, Adams, & Reed, 1984), suggesting the existence of an intermediate duration period of neuropsychological deficit that slowly resolves. Adams and Grant (1984) report that drinking history does not explain cognitive findings among sober alcoholics, and they suggest that the duration of abstinence may be more important than the amount of alcohol consumed. It will be difficult to establish any sort of dose–response relationship unless both exposure to alcohol (in terms of amount, chronicity, and frequency) and interval of sobriety are examined. The slowly resolving deficit suggests that the differences between consequences and effects may be less straightforward and require a broadened time consideration.

There is also evidence that suggests that the observed neuropsychological deficit in alcoholics may not be caused by consumption of alcohol alone. Tarter, Hegedys, Goldstein, Shelly, & Alterman (1984) found that young sons of alcoholics demonstrated greater deficits than did sons of nonalcoholic fathers. This finding has given extra weight in light of the nature of the comparison group, delinquent youngsters whose fathers were not alcoholic. The delinquent comparison group had more difficulties with impulse control and had more developmental and family problems but were less neurotic. This relationship of neuropsychological dysfunction and paternal alcoholism was affirmed by Whipple, Parker, and Noble (1988), who found differences both for cognitive testing and evoked potentials. However, Shuckett, Butters, Lyn, and Irwin (1987) failed to find differences in neuropsychological functioning between sons of alcoholics and normal controls. When age of onset of paternal drinking is considered, other investigators have replicated the positive findings. For example, Tarter, Jacob, and Bremer (1989) have found that young sons of early onset alcoholics did more poorly on a battery of neuropsychological tests than did sons of later onset alcoholics and sons of normal social drinkers. The discrepancy in results suggests that age of onset of alcoholism may be an important issue not only for the alcoholic himself, but possibly for his sons. Age of onset of drinking may be a correlate of some genetic marker rather than merely of cumulative amount consumed. There is no evidence yet that having an alcoholic parent places an adult alcoholic at greater risk for experiencing neuropsychological deficit even when quite elaborate classifications of familial history are used (Alterman, Gerstley, Goldstein, & Tarter, 1987; Reed, Grant, & Adams, 1987).

In addition, as will be seen later with other drugs, a number of developmental and life-style risk factors have been found that may interact with alcohol to increase the risk of neuropsychological deficit. A premorbid history of head injury, childhood hyperkinetic syndrome, minimal brain damage, or birth problems increase the likelihood of revealing neuropsychological deficit when an individual is tested as an alcoholic adult (DeObaldia & Parson, 1984). However, Adams and Grant (1986) determined that such risk factors seem to operate in recently detoxified alcoholics, but not in alcoholics who have been sober for a longer period of time. This finding suggests that the premorbid risk factors are not merely artifacts that contribute to observed impairment, but events that either interact with alcohol or somehow reset the neurotoxic threshold.

A fuzzy but coherent picture emerges from the studies reviewed above. The severe chronic deficits from alcohol that result in Wernicke-Korsakoff syndrome are well documented. The more subtle neuropsychological deficits that seem to emerge with less terminal but nonetheless severe alcoholism are more complex. There does seem to be a pattern of deficit associated with excessive alcohol consumption. However, a clear relationship between amount consumed and extent of deficit has not been established. Several studies suggest that intensity of use rather than mere amount may be more directly related to observed deficit. The relationship is further clouded by the observation that neuropsychological deficit slowly resolves in many alcoholics over the course of months. Many studies that report impairment were done shortly after withdrawal was completed and may be describing a toxic state of intermediate duration. There are additional data that suggest that the dose–response curve will remain elusive because nondrinking risk factors may lower the threshold for the emergence of neuropsychological deficit. These risk factors include developmental markers such as childhood history of hyperkinetic syndrome, learning disorder, head injury, and being the son of an early onset alcoholic father. The neuropsychologist dealing with a client who has suffered a recent head injury, but who also has an extensive history of alcoholism, faces a difficult task. Does the previous drinking pattern contribute to impairment either in its own right or by seeming to worsen the more recent injury? A careful and detailed inquiry into drinking history should be included when obtaining the history of a client.

The neuropsychological effects of alcohol have been extensively studied for the past decade. Other psychoactive substances that are widely consumed have received less attention, but nonetheless have been investigated. Illicit drugs continue to receive greater attention than drugs that have a recognized place in the pharmacopoeia. It is as if having no legitimate purpose predisposes a substance to be suspected as more neurotoxic than one that is alleged to be therapeutic. As will be seen below, this stance of pharmacological Calvinism is not supported by the data.

Marijuana

Beginning with the LaGuardia commission report in the late 1940s, there have been efforts to determine whether marijuana use is associated with chronic impaired functioning. As the psychedelic 1960s and 1970s witnessed a marked increase in the use of marijuana, pubic concern grew and many more studies reflecting an increased sophistication in the assessment of neuropsychological functioning were carried out. Most of these studies failed to find an association between marijuana use and neuropsychological impairment (Carlin & Trupin 1977; Culver & King, 1974; Grant, Rochford, Fleming, & Stunkard 1973; Rochford, Grant, & LaVigne 1977). Reports based on clinical observations rather than empirical investigations (e.g., Kolansky & Moore 1971, 1972) have suggested that chronic marijuana use is associated with temporary impairment and a temporary personality disorder. They may have been examining individuals who were acutely intoxicated.

It is possible that the North American experience has not been extensive enough nor long enough to reveal a relationship between marijuana use and "brain damage." In an effort to examine this hypothesis, a number of studies occurred in countries with more extensive cannabis involvement. Rubin and Comitas (1975) found no relationship between marijuana use and impairment in Jamaica. However, cross-cultural considerations raise questions regarding the appropriateness of their measures, as does their use of the child version of the categories test. Satz, Fletcher, and Sutker (1976), in more carefully designed studies in Costa Rica using a battery that was relatively free of cultural bias, also found no impairment associated with marijuana use. Less sophisticated studies in India have found similar

results (Ray, Prabho, Mohan, Nath, & Neki, 1979). Although the neuropsychological consequences of the new more potent strains of cannabis
have not been investigated, a study in Greece, where hashish is typically
used, has also failed to demonstrate significant impairment (Boulougouris,
Liakos, & Stefanos, 1976; Stefanos, Liakos, & Boulougouris, 1976). The
only report that has determined a relationship between marijuana use and
impairment is by Soueif (1976) in Egypt. This was a study among prisoners,
with an odd selection of tests including tool usage. As part of a study of
multiple drug abusers, Grant et al. (1978) found a modest *negative* correlation
between lifetime marijuana use and brain damage. This may suggest that
those subjects who had neuropsychological impairment found marijuana
intoxication a negative experience and so used less marijuana than those
who were intact.

Although each of the marijuana studies described above may have
methodological weakness, the high frequency of replication of the findings
strongly suggests that marijuana, as was typically used before the late
1970s, offered little risk of chronic neurotoxicity. The past decade, however,
has seen the development of far more potent strains of marijuana, so that
the dose of tetrahydrocannabinol per unit smoked has increased markedly.
The impact of this change in dosage has not been investigated in humans
using standard neuropsychological techniques.

LSD and PCP

Lysergic acid diethylamide (LSD) is also among the more examined illicit
substances. One can only speculate about the reasons for this interest, as
there was little obvious evidence of deleterious neuropsychological consequences. In part it may be that the profound acute drug effects suggest
that equally profound consequences would be present. A study of non-
drug-abusing middle-aged persons who received LSD initially within a
psychotherapy treatment context was undertaken by McGlothlin, Arnold,
and Freedman (1969). Using the complete Halstead-Reitan battery along
with many additional tests, they found a mild impairment of spatial abilities
and improved rhythm scores associated with greater use of LSD. They
chose not to endorse a causal relationship, but raised caveats about the
use of LSD. Cohen and Edwards (1969) also found a mild spatial dysfunction
associated with LSD use. Map reading was the one test in both studies
in which poor performance was associated with increased exposure to
LSD. Acord (1972) also found impairment among neuropsychiatric patients
who used the substance at least once. In what appears to be a replication,
but in fact is a later publication based on the same sample of LSD users
with the addition of a control group, Acord and Barker (1973) found
that their patients who had used LSD were more neuropsychologically

impaired than hospital staff members. Wright and Hogan (1972), who differentiated amount of use, failed to replicate the finding of significantly greater levels of impairment among younger LSD users. When Grant et al. (1978) studied multiple drug users they found no relationship between psychedelic use and impairment. However, their drug-using sample used relatively little LSD. The findings do suggest the possibility of mild neuropsychological deficit associated with LSD use. However, those studies that did find a relationship between LSD use and neuropsychological impairment did not attend to differences in either dosage exposure or number of experiences. It is interesting to note that Acord (1972) and Acord and Barker's (1973) quixotic definition of LSD abuse is problematic for their positive findings. Arbitrary definitions of drug use or abuse must be avoided and a great deal of attention paid to the composition of both the study group and the comparison group if findings are to be meaningfully interpreted. Comparing patients with normal subjects opens the concern about the effect of psychopathology or other sources of impaired functioning on test results.

Although there is a great deal of concern about the deleterious effects of the abusive use of phencyclidine (PCP), only one neuropsychological investigation of chronic PCP users has been published. Carlin, Grant, Adams, and Reed (1979) compared a group of young male PCP abusers with a group of gender and age-matched (but otherwise nonselected) polydrug abusers who used no PCP, and a control group of normal young men who used no drugs and little or no alcohol. The PCP users consumed more LSD and fewer sedative hypnotic drugs than the polydrug users and equivalent amounts of other drugs including alcohol. Both drug-using groups contained more neuropsychologically impaired persons than did the control group. Although their results suggest that chronic PCP use may be involved in neuropsychological impairment, the pattern of multiple drug use clouds the issue.

Solvents

Glue, aerosols, and other inhalants, more clearly than any other abused substances, seem to be associated with neurological difficulties such as peripheral neuropathies and cerebellar dysfunction (Grabski, 1961; Kelly, 1975; Knox & Nelson, 1966; Lewis, Moritz, & Mellis, 1981; Malm & Lying-Tunell, 1980) as well as neuropsychological impairment (Berry, Heaton, & Kirby, 1977; Tsushima & Towne, 1977). The study by Berry et al. (1977) is of particular interest because of their care in selecting the comparison group. This investigation compared the performances of solvent sniffers with siblings who did not use drugs; thus, age, education, and socioeconomic class were matched. Solvents must be considered as a complex group of substances. There is evidence that toluene may have greater cerebellar and lesser peripheral effects as opposed to aldehydes and ketones. Also, the relative youthfulness of most solvent sniffers may exacerbate findings through the interference with growth and developmental processes. The implications of these findings in regard to voluntary exposure (with its associated high frequency and higher levels of exposure) for studies of inadvertent exposure in industrial settings (which tends to be more chronic but less intense) are not clear. It is likely that chronic low-level exposure will eventuate in some impairment as well.

Opiates

In light of the extensive history of opiates in the pharmacopoeia, the paucity of research on the neuropsychological consequences of this family of drugs is surprising. The earlier neuropsychological studies by Brown and Parrington (1942) and Pfeffer and Ruble (1946) are of greater historic than substantive interest due to methodological issues. Korin (1974) relied on the Bender Gestalt in a study of Vietnam era veterans that found heroin abusers to be impaired compared to nonopiate drug abusers. The author, however, suggested that his findings could be attributed to personality factors and psychopathology.

In a more elaborate study, Fields and Fullerton (1974) compared abstinent heroin abusers, a mixed brain-damaged population, and a group of non-drug-abusing, non-brain-damaged patients. They found that the heroin abusers did somewhat *better* than the non-brain-damaged group and that both did significantly better than the brain-damaged group. These authors concluded that opiate use is not associated with neuropsychological deficit. They relied only on statistical measures of central tendency. A series of publications by Rounsaville, Novelly, and Kleber demonstrates the potential problem of relying upon differences in measures of central tendency. They initially compared heroin abusers and epileptics and found both groups were similar. They concluded that both groups reflected significant impairment (Rounsaville, Novelly, & Kleber, 1981). However, when they later compared the same group of heroin abusers to a group of CETA workers and again found equal levels of impairment, they concluded that heroin abusers were not impaired (Rounsaville, Jones, Novelly, & Kleber, 1982). Studies that merely compare test scores of groups of patients may be difficult to interpret. Clear differences are relatively easy to interpret, but a lack of differences may reflect the poor power of an approach that does not allow for the multiple levels of inference described by Reitan and Davison (1974). A time-consuming, but more powerful approach is one in which a neuropsychologist characterizes protocols with regard to extent of impairment and compares the proportion of impairment among groups.

Grant et al. (1978) utilized this approach and then used impairment as the independent variable and drug use as the dependent variable. They found that heroin use was associated with neuropsychological deficit.

Hill, Reyes, Mikhael, and Ayre (1979) compared alcoholics, heroin abusers, and normals and found that the alcoholics performed worse than the heroin abusers and the normals. Computerized axial tomography (CT) scan results in this study are of interest both in terms of relationship between errors on the categories test and ventricle to brain size ratio. These investigators also found that heroin abusers had smaller ventricles and sulci than did normals, whereas the alcoholics had larger. The swelling they observed may suggest that the impairment among heroin abusers is a result of an allergic reaction and that a different mechanism of impairment is operating than among alcoholics. It should also be recalled that heroin abusers are subjecting themselves to greater risk than the consumption of opiates alone. The adulteration of heroin and the consequences of injecting oneself with substances of unknown purity under less than sterile conditions are potential contributors to any observed impairment. A more recent study by Strang and Guyrling (1989) addresses the issue of drug purity, at least in a more acute sense, by examining drug users who were maintained on pharmaceutical heroin in Great Britain. They found evidence of cortical atrophy and neuropsychological deficit among a small group of older, high-dose users of pharmaceutical pure heroin. Some of their subjects were still using the drug at the time of testing. Although the majority of their small sample of seven subjects had a history of multiple substance use including alcohol, concurrent use at the time of testing was minimal. It is of interest that, unlike Hill et al. (1979), they found cortical atrophy rather than swelling among heroin users. What is not clear is the extent to which their findings can be attributed to the other drugs previously abused by their subjects in the past. Once again, when multiple drug use is present, attributing any observed impairment to one drug is difficult. Nonetheless, it would be difficult to give opiates a clean bill of health, particularly if adulterated and administered intravenously with less than sterile techniques. Studies of the acute effects of opiates and sedative hypnotic drugs suggest that chronic pain patients are less impaired if they are maintained on opiates than on sedative hypnotic drugs (Hendler, Cimini, Tra, & Lanz, 1980).

Sedative Hypnotics and Antianxiety Drugs

In spite of the widespread extensive or abuse of sedative hypnotic drugs and related antianxiety agents, there is a paucity of studies on the possible deleterious neuropsychological consequences. Earlier studies by Kornetsky (1951) focused on acute drug effects and found, not surprisingly, that barbiturate drugs impaired neuropsychological functioning as an acute effect. A Swedish study by Bergman, Borg, and Holm (1980) found impairment among persons who exclusively abused sedative hypnotic drugs. They did not provide data on extent of immersion among their subjects and so could not determine a dose—response relationship. On a 5-year follow-up of the same subjects, Bergman, Borg, Engelbrektsen, and Vikander (1989) found that their subjects were somewhat improved, but a number still showed significant neuropsychological impairment. Grant et al. (1978) found that among polydrug abusers neuropsychological deficit was associated with greater sedative hypnotics use as well as with greater use of alcohol and opiates.

Stimulants

Despite reports of arteritis and deleterious vascular effects of stimulant abuse reported in the literature, there has been no neuropsychological study on humans reporting deleterious effects of stimulants (either amphetamines or cocaine). Animal studies by Ellinwood and Cohen (1971) may be of interest here. They found on autopsy that cats given large doses of methamphetamine suffered massive cortical damage. However, their group also reported that little or no damage was observed when doses were slowly escalated, thereby allowing some tolerance to develop. These authors speculate that the massive damage they observed may have been the result of the pyrexic effects of large doses rather than to any specific neurotoxic event. Grant et al. (1978) failed to implicate stimulants in the neuropsychological impairment found among their polydrug sample. This may be an artifact of a kind of "all or none" quality to the neuropsychological consequences of stimulant abuse. That is, the negative effects may be so devastating (e.g., stroke) that their victims are not likely to be included in neuropsychological investigations, but are described as case histories.

General Considerations

For many of the drugs discussed above it is difficult to determine whether their chronic use "causes" irreversible neuropsychological impairment. A greater proportion of neuropsychologically compromised persons is frequently found among abusers of many drugs. As with alcohol, it has been difficult to establish a dose—response relationship because of the interactive effects of extraneous variables. For example, Carlin, Stauss, Grant, and Adams (1978) reported that life-style and neurological risk factors not related to drug use, such as prematurity at birth, history of learning problems, or history of head injury, were significant contributors to the impairment found among polydrug abusers and precluded the elucidation of a simple dose–effect relationship between any drug and neuropsychological impairment. This state of affairs, similar to that described for alcohol by Grant (1987), suggests that for opiates and sedatives as well as alcohol the threshold for toxicity may be altered by life-style and neurological risk factors.

A further complication to completing this research is the limited "brand loyalty" among drug abusers. Patterns of multiple drug use are now more typical than not among drug abusers. Carlin and Post (1971), Culver and King (1974), and Rochford et al. (1977) found that more extensive use of marijuana was associated with greater exposure to other drugs. Grant et al. (1978) found significant moderate correlations between use of many classes of illicit drugs. The pattern of exposure to multiple drugs, either serially or contemporaneously, will make investigations of specific drugs more difficult. Characterizing groups by drug of interest alone and ignoring other drug use will confound the meaning of results.

Antidepressant Drugs

Antidepressant drugs, both tricyclic antidepressants and monoaminoxydase inhibitors, are very rarely abused. Their consumption has few immediate effects and they do not produce disinhibition euphoria—an absence of two important characteristics of most abused substances. Antidepressants have aroused little or no suspicion of implication in neuropsychological deficit. These drugs have, nonetheless, received some attention from neuropsychologists. It is likely that any effects beyond the disruption caused by initial sedation might be the positive effects associated with overall increased performance as test correlates of depression are reduced. (See Finlayson & Bird, this volume, for a more detailed discussion of the effects of depression on neuropsychological performance.) Studies of the neuropsychological correlates of tricyclic antidepressants have focused on effects. Single doses of tricyclic antidepressants administered to normals have no neuropsychological effects (Heimann, Reed, & Witt, 1968). Examination of depressed patients prior to and after 6 weeks and 12 weeks of imipramine found no differences over that period of time (Kendrick & Post, 1967), whereas other studies compared depressives who showed clinical improvement with those who did not and found improvements in memory associated with improved clinical status (Sternberg & Jarvik, 1976). Because of the typical amount of time for tricyclic antidepressants to have a clinical effect, it becomes important to separate initial negative side effects from later therapeutic effects, which may account for the worsened performance after 3 weeks reported by Legg and Stiff (1976). In any case, the tricyclic antidepressants seem to produce minimal deleterious neuropsychological effects, and there is no evidence of long-term consequences.

Lithium Carbonate

This drug has no immediate mood-altering properties nor does it cause sedation. Side effects that may acutely affect neuropsychological test performance include fine tremor, muscular weakness, twitching, and confusion. When administered to normals, lithium carbonate led to a number of unpleasant side effects and to a slight but statistically significant decrement on a number of measures of neuropsychological functioning (Judd, Hubbard, Janowsky, Huey, & Takahashi, 1977). Henry, Weingartner, and Murphy (1973) found no significant cognitive effects of lithium carbonate in patients with affective disorder. Small, Small, Milstein, and Moore (1972) administered lithium to a mixed group of psychotics including bipolars and found negative correlation between plasma lithium levels and performance on a number of measures from the Halstead-Reitan Neuropsychological Test Battery. Friedman, Culver, and Ferrel (1977) examined bipolars who were maintained on lithium and were euthymic at the time of testing; younger subjects were not impaired, but older patients were. However, because of the absence of age-relevant norms and the lack of adequate control or comparison groups, the differences are difficult to interpret. Overall, the data suggest that the chronic lithium maintenance of patients diagnosed as bipolar is not associated with deleterious effects among these patients. There are suggestions that, among patients not so diagnosed, lithium may interfere mildly with cognitive functioning. No investigations have examined the long-term consequences of lithium maintenance.

Neuroleptic Drugs

In addition to their antipsychotic action, neuroleptic drugs are capable of producing immediate and distressing neuromuscular side effects such as parkinsonism, dystonia, and akathisia. These drugs have been associated with the emergence of tardive dyskinesia and malignant neuroleptic syndrome. The former is marked by the emergence of involuntary movements that are sometimes reversible when the drug is stopped, but the disorder may become irreversible. When the disorder is more advanced, interrupting the drug may actually seem to worsen the movement disorder. Malignant neuroleptic syndrome requires acute medical intervention and support. It is marked by dyskinesia, akinesia, hyperthermia, tachycardia, dyspnea, and dysphagia, and can result in death.

Although there is an extensive literature on the acute effects of neuroleptic drugs that dates from their introduction in the late 1950s and early 1960s, the examination of more enduring effects is more recent and coincides with the recognition of tardive dyskinesia. The early studies are difficult to compare and interpret; some investigators examined psychotic patients (e.g., Legg & Stiff, 1976; Sprague, Barnes, & Werry, 1970; Weaver & Brooks, 1961), whereas others administered the drugs to normals (DiMascio, Havens, & Klerman, 1963; Safer & Allen 1971; Wenzel & Rutledge, 1962). Findings suggest that the performance of normals is more likely to be impaired by acute administration of neuroleptic drugs, whereas for schizophrenics visual–motor tasks are impaired and measures of association and memory are improved. Moses (1984) reports that schizophrenics matched for duration of illness did not differ in neuropsychological integrity if they were on medication or not. If impaired performance is observed among schizophrenics, it is difficult to differentiate the effects of the illness from those of the drugs used to treat it. (The issue of the deleterious effects of schizophrenia on neuropsychological functioning is discussed in detail by Finlayson & Bird, this volume.)

More than with other classes of drugs, it may be important to consider the specific neuroleptic drug used in the study and limit generalization because neuroleptic drugs differ in the likelihood of producing side effects, including neuropsychologically relevant effects. For example, the more sedating drugs such as thioridazine or chlorpromazine are less likely to produce parkinsonian side effects than haloperidol or fluphenazine. However, the sedation they produce is likely to interfere with neuropsychological testing if testing occurs before tolerance to side effects is developed; the parkinsonian side effects are more likely with the latter two drugs.

Studies of the effects of the chronic administration of neuroleptic drugs are less common. Klonoff, Fibiger, and Hutton (1970) found that chronic schizophrenic patients who received more medication demonstrated more obvious neuropsychological deficit on the Halstead-Reitan battery. Nearly a decade later, Grant et al. (1978) reported that greater lifetime consumption of neuroleptic drugs correlated with neuropsychological impairment among psychiatric patients. However, as greater lifetime disturbance is likely to be correlated with greater drug use, neither report can demonstrate a causal relationship.

A more recent report by Hoffman, Labs, and Casey (1987) noted that in older schizophrenics the appearance of parkinsonian symptoms was associated with poorer visual spatial performance, whereas schizophrenia symptom severity was associated with impaired verbal ability and cognitive flexibility.

The data on the effects of neuroleptic drugs suggest that if a patient who consumes neuroleptic drugs is tested for any neuropsychological deficit, it is possible that these drugs may be responsible for any visual–spatial deficit present. Unless clinically contraindicated, it may be useful to examine the patient in a drug-free state after a period of time allowing for the "washout" of drug effects.

Other more recent studies have addressed the impact of tardive dyskinesia on neuropsychological functioning. Neuroleptic drugs have been used with patients diagnosed as bipolar or manic as well as for schizophrenics. Many of the studies have focused on tardive dyskinesia in bipolar patients. Waddington et al. (1989) report that among a group of bipolar patients, those with involuntary movements associated with tardive dyskinesia performed less well on measures of cognitive flexibility than did patients without involuntary movements. Interestingly, the authors report that neither involuntary movements nor poorer test performance was related to lifetime dosage of neuroleptic drugs, but to number and severity of manic episodes. Once again, the elusiveness of the dose–response relationship becomes an issue. Struve and Willner (1983) reported that on a single measure of neuropsychological functioning, the Conceptual Level Analogy Test (CLAT), patients with tardive dyskinesia did worse than those without. However, the differences existed as well for testing carried out *prior to* the emergence of the movement disorder! These authors conclude that there may be a preexisting vulnerability for the development of tardive dyskinesia. It may also be that a unitary measure is less sensitive than multiple measures that assess visual and motor functions rather than just conceptual functioning. Mukherjee, Shukla, and Rosen (1984) found that among bipolar patients there was a strong relationship between lifelong exposure to neuroleptic drugs and agraphaesthesia. Myslobodsky (1985) suggests that when patients with preexisting brain disorder are removed from consideration, there are no differences in neuropsychological testing between patients with tardive dyskinesia and those without.

Neuroleptic drugs, similar to many of the drugs discussed above, have a suggestive but not direct relationship with neuropsychological deficits. Efforts have been made to differentiate the effects of schizophrenia from the effects of the drugs, but schizophrenia is such a protean disorder that it is difficult to separate out its effects from those of any other neuropsychological insult (see Finlayson & Bird, this volume). The studies carried out on those who received neuroleptic drugs for manic psychosis avoid this issue. But as with alcohol and many other drugs examined, other variables confuse the picture. Historical severity of the disorder seems as important as drug history. The long-term consequences of neuroleptic use and the neuropsychological correlates of tardive dyskinesia are areas that still require a great deal of research before even tentative conclusions can be reached.

GENERAL CONCLUSIONS

The relationship between many of the commonly used and abused psychoactive substances and neuropsychological consequences is not straightforward. It may be unrealistic to expect anything else. At present, the medical profession and most of the lay public generally accept the view that cigarette smoking is associated with an increased risk of heart disease and lung cancer. Yet if any 300 chronic smokers (a sample size much larger than almost any used to examine neuropsychological consequences of any drug) were selected at random and examined for the presence of those two diseases, few if any cases might emerge.

Even if some sort of association between drug use and neuropsychological impairment has been demonstrated, the elaboration of a causal relationship remains difficult. Consider alcohol, which is accepted as a neurotoxic substance. The effects of genetic background, in utero exposure to potential teratogens, and developmental and neuropsychological risk factors all enter into and confound the efforts to establish a simple causal relationship.

Events with a true but small effect size will require very large samples to be reliably established. Counting positive or negative outcomes of investigations with smaller sample sizes will accomplish little beyond generating controversy and getting more studies funded. Meta-analysis studies, in which a small effect size can be examined while controlling for adequacy of design and assessment of additional variables, may help considerably in coming to an understanding of the impact of these drugs on neuropsychological integrity.

For a particular individual, the task determining whether any observed deficit is due to consumption of any single drug or combination of drugs may be daunting but more straightforward than establishing the case within a group. A few case examples help clarify issues and problems.

A 23-year-old man who worked as a laborer had been chronically exposed to low levels of organic solvents. On one occasion a lapse in plant procedures exposed him to a heavy concentration of fumes, and he briefly lost consciousness. Upon his recovery, others noticed his impaired concentration and memory. He was fired because he began to make errors at work. As part of his grievance procedure he charged that the exposure to solvents had a deleterious impact on his mental functioning. Neuropsychological testing revealed a mild diffuse impairment. The discovery phase of the hearings revealed that he smoked marijuana three to four times a week. His employers claimed that his use of marijuana was responsible for his impaired functioning and that the exposure to solvents could not be established as the cause of his impairment. On the basis of the many replicated studies that failed to find a relationship between marijuana use and neuropsychological deficit, it is possible to conclude with some certainty that any observed deficit is not related to his marijuana use. The literature does suggest that solvents may be implicated in the observed deficit. However, familial and developmental and educational history must be considered to ascertain a level of premorbid functioning.

A factory worker was accidently exposed to sulfur dioxide gas. As his co-workers fled the site, he spent several minutes shutting down equipment before he left the scene. Once outside the building he complained of dizziness and later that night had several allergylike symptoms including difficulty in breathing, itching, and a rash. He later complained of poor concentration, low energy, insomnia, and fear-fulness. His symptoms reached such proportion that he was no longer able to work. He was evaluated by a neurologist who reported negative findings and by a psychiatrist who diagnosed the man as depressed and anxious, possibly as a response to the considerable fear and anxiety resulting from the accident at work. The patient entered treatment with another psychiatrist who started him on a regimen of antidepressants and a low potency neuroleptic for his insomnia. A neuropsychological evaluation carried out several months after the incident found evidence of mild deficit marked by impaired motor and visual motor functioning. The impairment was attributed to the sulfur dioxide exposure and described as a permanent deficit. The depression and anxiety, which are still present, were seen to be organic disorders or responses to the loss of neuropsychological integrity. Litigation began on behalf of the worker. The theory underlying the litigation was that the plaintiff had experienced significant neuropsychological impairment due to exposure to sulfur dioxide and now was no longer employable. No literature supports the contention that exposure to sulfur dioxide is associated with neu-ropsychological effects. One year after the accident, the patient was removed from neuroleptic drugs and retested several weeks later. Although still anxious and depressed, he tested well within normal limits with no evidence of neuropsychological impairment. In this case, deficit was initially attributed to exposure to a substance with no known psychoactive properties. The presence of a neuroleptic drug, a substance that has known psychoactive effects, was ignored, perhaps because it is a therapeutic agent.

A 43-year-old woman with a long history of chronic pain became concerned that her mind was not working as well as it had in the past. On the basis of her subjective complaints, she underwent a neuropsychological evaluation. The results of the evaluation were equivocal, but the plaintiff's neuropsychologist concluded that there was evidence of a mild impairment. She attributed the impairment to large doses of acetaminophen consumed while under the care of an orthopedist, but made no comment about the antianxiety agents, narcotics, or sedative hypnotic drugs she had consumed, frequently at a high rate, in the past. There is no empirical evidence that even chronic high-level use of acetaminophen is associated with neuropsychological changes of any sort, whereas there is some evidence that sedative hypnotic drugs and narcotics may impair neuropsychological functioning. In the light of the patient's multiple drug use, focusing on one substance obscures any genuine effort to make a realistic attribution of etiology.

These three cases demonstrate relatively straightforward application of the existing literature to aid the determination of whether drug use may have contributed to neuropsychological impairment. Despite the lack of clarity in the literature, neuropsychologists can make use of what knowledge is available to either help resolve the issue or prevent premature closure. More complex cases do exist, for example:

A 45-year-old woman with an extensive history of psychiatric disorder marked by suicide attempts by drug overdose and by drug and alcohol abuse underwent a course of electroconvulsive therapy (ECT). ECT was recommended after several unsuccessful courses of treatment with neuroleptic and antidepressant drugs. She had been hospitalized on a number of occasions; her admissions to the hospital were frequently associated with suicide attempts through drug and alcohol overdose. After a course of several shocks, she became concerned that her memory and cognitive abilities were impaired and attributed her impairment to the ECT. Neuropsychological evaluation revealed a mild diffuse impairment. She sued the psychiatrists who administered the ECT, claiming that the procedure caused the deficit. Later she claimed that the deficit was caused by improper induction of anesthesia.

Here multiple factors are present that preclude drawing any firm conclusion regarding the etiology of the observed deficit. Drug-based suicide attempts and a history of alcoholism and drug abuse, as well as ongoing psychopathology, may render the issue unanswerable for the neuropsychologist except for speculation.

REFERENCES

Acord, L. D. (1972). Hallucinogenic drugs and brain damage. *Military Medicine, 137,* 18–19.

Acord, L. D., & Barker, D. D. (1973). Hallucinogenic drugs and cerebral deficit. *Journal of Nervous & Mental Diseases, 156,* 281–283.

Adams, K. M., & Grant, I. (1984). Failure of non-linear models of drinking history variables to predict neuropsychological performance in alcoholics. *American Journal of Psychiatry, 141,* 663–667.

Adams, K. M., & Grant, I. (1986). The influence of premorbid risk factors on neuropsychological performance in alcoholics. *Journal of Clinical & Experimental Neuropsychology, 8,* 362–370.

Adams, K. M., Grant, I., & Reed, R. (1980). Neuropsychology in alcoholic men in their late thirties: One year follow-up. *American Journal of Psychiatry, 137,* 928–931.

Alterman, A. I., Gerstley, L. J., Goldstein, G., & Tarter, R. E. (1987). Comparisons of functioning in familial and non-familial alcoholics. *Journal of Studies on Alcohol, 48,* 425–429.

American Psychological Association. (1990). PsycLit database.

Bergman, H., Borg, S., & Holm, L. (1980). Neuropsychological impairment and exclusive abuse of sedative hypnotics. *American Journal of Psychiatry, 137,* 215–217.

Bergman, H., Borg, S., Engelbrektsen, K., & Vikander, B. (1989). Dependence on sedative hypnotics: Neuropsychological impairment, field dependence, and clinical course in a 5 year follow-up study. *British Journal of Addiction, 84*, 547–553.

Berry, G. J., Heaton, R. K., & Kirby, M. W. (1977). Neuropsychological deficits of chronic inhalant abusers. In B. Rumac & A. Temple (Eds.), *Management of the poisoned patient* (pp. 9–31). Princeton: Science Press.

Boulougouris, J., Liakos, A., & Stefanos, C. (1976). Social traits of heavy hashish users and matched controls. In R. Dornbush, A. M. Freedman, & M. Fink (Eds.), *Chronic Cannabis Use: Annals of the New York Academy of Sciences, 282*, 217–323.

Brandt, J., Butters, N., Ryan, C., & Bayog, R. (1983). Cognitive loss and recovery in long term alcohol abusers. *Archives of General Psychiatry, 40*, 435–442.

Brown, R. R., & Parrington, J. E. (1942). A comparison of narcotic addicts with hospital attendants. *Journal of General Psychology, 27*, 71–79.

Butters, N., Cermak, L. S., Montgomery, B. A., & Adinolfi, A. (1977). Comparisons of the memory and visioperceptive deficits of chronic alcoholics and patients with Korsakoff's disease. *Alcoholism: Clinical & Experimental Research, 1*, 245–257.

Carlen, P. L., Wortzman, G., Holgate, R. C., Wilkenson, D. A., & Rankin, J. G. (1978). Reversible cerebral atrophy in recently abstinent alcoholics measured by computed tomography scans. *Science, 200*, 1076–1078.

Carlin, A. S., Grant, I., Adams, K. M., & Reed, R. (1979). Is phencyclidine (PCP) abuse associated with organic brain impairment? *American Journal of Drug and Alcohol Abuse, 6*, 273–281.

Carlin, A. S., & Post, R. D. (1971). Patterns of drug use among marijuana smokers. *Journal of the American Medical Association, 218*, 867–868.

Carlin, A. S., Stauss, F. F., Grant, I., & Adams, K. M. (1978). Prediction of neuropsychological impairment among polydrug abusers. *Addictive Behavior, 5*, 5–12.

Carlin, A. S., & Trupin, E. W. (1977). The effects of long term chronic cannabis use on neuropsychological functioning. *International Journal of the Addictions, 12*, 617–624.

Cohen, S., & Edwards, A. E. (1969). LSD and organic brain impairment. *Drug Dependence, 2*, 1–4.

Culver, C. M., & King, F. W. (1974). Neuropsychological assessment of undergraduate marijuana and LSD users. *Archives of General Psychiatry, 31*, 707–711.

DeObaldia, R., & Parson, O. A. (1984). Relationship of neuropsychological performance to primary alcoholism and self reported symptoms of childhood minimal brain dysfunction. *Journal of Studies on Alcohol, 45*, 386–392.

DiMascio, A., Havens, L. L., & Klerman, G. L. (1963). The psychopharmacology of phenothiazine compounds: A comparative study of chlorpromazine, promethazine, trifluoperazine, and perphenazine in normal males. *Journal of Nervous & Mental Diseases, 136*, 1–28, 168–186.

Donovan, D., Quiesser, H., & O'Leary, M. R. (1976). Group embedded figures as a predictor of cognitive impairment among alcoholics. *International Journal of the Addictions, 11*, 125–139.

Ellinwood, E. H., & Cohen, S. (1971). Amphetamine abuse. *Science, 171*, 420–421.

Fields, F. R. J., & Fullerton, J. R. (1974). The influence of heroin addiction on neuropsychological functioning. In *Newsletter for Research in Mental Health & Behavioral Science*. Washington, D.C. Department of Medicine & Surgery, Veterans Administration.

Fitzhugh, L. C., Fitzhugh, K. B., & Reitan, R. M. (1960). Adaptive abilities and intellectual functioning in hospitalized alcoholics. *Quarterly Journal of Studies on Alcohol, 21*, 414–423.

Fitzhugh, L. C., Fitzhugh, K. B., & Reitan, R. M. (1965). Adaptive abilities and intellectual functioning in hospitalized alcoholics: Further consideration. *Quarterly Journal of Studies on Alcoholism, 26*, 402–411.

Friedman, M. J., Culver, C. M., & Ferrel, R. B. (1977). On the safety of long term treatment with lithium. *American Journal of Psychiatry, 134*, 1123–1126.

Goldman, M. S., Klisz, D. K., & Williams, D. L. (1985). Experience dependent recovery of cognitive functioning in young alcoholics. *Addictive Behaviors, 10*, 169–176.

Goldman, M. S., Williams, D. L., & Klisz, D. K. (1983). Recoverability of psychological functioning following alcohol abuse: Prolonged visual–spatial dysfunction in older alcoholics. *Journal of Consulting & Clinical Psychology, 51*, 370–378.

Grabski, D. A. (1961). Toluene sniffing producing cerebellar degeneration. *American Journal of Psychiatry, 118*, 461–462.

Grant, I. (1987). Alcohol and the brain: Neuropsychological correlates. *Journal of Consulting & Clinical Psychology, 55*, 310–324.

Grant, I., Adams, K. M., Carlin, A. S., Rennick, P. M., Judd, L. L., & Schoof, K. (1978). The collaborative neuropsychological study of polydrug abusers. *Archives of General Psychiatry, 35*, 1063–1073.

Grant, I., Adams, K. M., & Reed, R. (1984). Aging, abstinence, and medical risk factors in the prediction of neuropsychological deficit among long term alcoholics. *Archives of General Psychiatry, 41*, 710–718.

Grant, I., & Reed, R. (1985). Neuropsychology of drug and alcohol abuse. In A. I. Alterman (Ed.), *Substance use & psychopathology* (pp. 289–341). New York: Plenum Press.

Grant, I., Rochford, J., Fleming T., & Stunkard, H. (1973) A neuropsychological assessment of the effects of moderate marijuana use. *Journal of Nervous & Mental Disease, 156*, 278–280.

Heimann, H., Reed, C. F., & Witt, P. N. (1968). Some observations suggesting preservation of skilled motor acts despite drug induced stress. *Psychopharmacologia, 13*, 287–298.

Hendler, N., Cimini, C., Tra, T., & Lanz, D. (1980). A comparison of cognitive impairment due to benzodiazapines and to narcotics. *American Journal of Psychiatry, 137*, 828–830.

Henry, G. M., Weingartner, H., & Murphy, D. L. (1973) Influence of affective states and psychoactive drugs on verbal learning and memory. *American Journal of Psychiatry, 130*, 966–971.

Hill, S. Y., Reyes, R. B., & Mikhael, M., & Ayre, F. (1979). A comparison of alcoholics and heroin abusers: Computerized transaxial tomography and neuropsychological functioning. *American Journal of Psychiatry, 137*, 828–830.

Hoffman, W. H., Labs, S. M., & Casey, D. E. (1987). Neuroleptic induced parkinsonism in older schizophrenics. *Biological Psychiatry, 22*, 427–439.

Jones, B., & Parsons, O. A. (1971). Impaired abstracting ability in chronic alcoholics. *Archives of General Psychiatry, 24*, 71–75.

Jones, B., & Parsons, O. A. (1972). Specific versus generalized impaired abstracting ability in chronic alcoholics. *Archives of General Psychiatry, 26*, 380–384.

Judd, L. L., Hubbard, B., Janowsky, D. S., Huey, L. Y., & Takahashi, K. I. (1977). The effect of lithium carbonate on cognitive functions in normal adults. *Archives of General Psychiatry, 34*, 355–357.

Kelly, T. (1975). Prolonged cerebellar dysfunction associated with paint sniffing. *Pediatrics, 56*, 605–606.

Kendrick, D. C., & Post, F. (1967). Differences in cognitive status between healthy, psychiatrically ill, and diffusely brain damaged elderly subjects. *British Journal of Psychiatry, 113*, 75–81.

Klonoff, H., Fibiger, C. H., & Hutton, G. H. (1970). Neuropsychological patterns in schizophrenia. *Journal of Nervous and Mental Disease, 150*, 291–300.

Knox, J., & Nelson, J. (1966). Permanent encephalopathy from toluene inhalation. *New England Journal of Medicine, 275*, 1494–1496.

Kolansky, H., & Moore, W. T. (1971). Effects of marijuana use on adolescents and young adults. *Journal of the American Medical Association, 216*, 486–492.

Kolansky, H., & Moore, W. T. (1972). Toxic effects of chronic marijuana use. *Journal of the American Medical Association, 222*, 35–41.

Korin, H. (1974). Comparison of psychometric measures in patients using heroin and other drugs. *Journal of Abnormal Psychology, 83*, 208–212.

Kornetsky, C. H. (1951). Psychological effects of chronic barbiturate intoxication. *Archives of Neurological Psychiatry, 65*, 557–567.

Legg, J. F., & Stiff, M. P. (1976). Drug related patterns of depressed patients. *Psychopharmacology, 50*, 205–210.

Lewis, J. D., Moritz, D., & Mellis, L. (1981). Long term toluene abuse. *American Journal of Psychiatry, 138*, 368–370.

Macciocchi, S. N., Ranseen, J. D., & Schmitt, F. A. (1989). The relationship between neuropsychological impairment in alcoholics and treatment outcome at one year. *Archives of Clinical Neuropsychology, 4*, 365–370.

Malm, G., & Lying-Tunell, U. (1980). Cerebellar dysfunction related to glue sniffing. *Acta Neurologica Scandanavica, 62*, 188–190.

McGlothlin, W. H., Arnold, D. O., & Freedman, D. X. (1969). Organicity measures following repeated LSD ingestion. *Archives of General Psychiatry, 21*, 704–709.

Melgaard, B., Danielsen, U., Sorensen, H., & Ahlgren, P. (1986). The severity of alcoholism and its relation to intellectual impairment and cerebral atrophy. *British Journal of Addiction, 81*, 77–80.

Moses, J. A. (1984). The effect of presence or absence of neuroleptic medication treatment on Luria Nebraska Battery Performance in schizophrenic population. *International Journal of Clinical Neuropsychology, 6,* 249–251.

Mukherjee, S., Shukla, S., & Rosen, A. (1984). Neurological abnormalities in patients with bipolar disorders. *Biological Psychiatry, 19,* 337–345.

Muuronen, A., Bergman, H., Hindmarsh, T., & Telakivi, T. (1989). Influence of improved drinking habits on brain atrophy and cognitive performance in alcoholic patients. *Alcoholism: Clinical and Experimental Research, 13,* 137–141.

Myslobodsky, M. S. (1985). Cognitive impairment in patients with tardive dyskinesia. *Journal of Nervous and Mental Disease, 173,* 156–160.

Pfeffer, A. Z., & Ruble, D. C. (1946). Chronic psychosis and addiction to morphine. *Archives of Neurological Psychiatry, 56,* 665–672.

Portnoff, L. A. (1982). Halstead-Reitan impairment in chronic alcoholics as a function of age of onset of drinking. *Clinical Neuropsychology, 4,* 115–119.

Ray, R., Prabho, G. G., Mohan, D., Nath, L. M., & Neki, J. J. (1979). Chronic cannabis use and cognitive functioning. *Indian Journal of Medical Research, 69,* 991–1000.

Reed, R., Grant, I., & Adams, K. (1987). Family history of alcoholism does not predict neuropsychological performance in alcoholics. *Alcoholism: Clinical and Experimental Research, 11,* 340–344.

Reitan, R. M., & Davison, L. A. (1974). *Clinical neuropsychology: Current status and applications.* Washington, DC: Winston.

Rochford, J., Grant, I., & LaVigne, G. (1977). Medical students & drugs: Neuropsychological and use pattern considerations. *International Journal of the Addictions, 12,* 1057–1065.

Ron, M. A., Acker, W., & Lishman, W. A. (1980). Morphological abnormalities in the brains of chronic alcoholics: A clinical psychological and computerized tomographic study. *Acta Psychiatrica Scandanavica, 62,* 41–46.

Rounsaville, B. J., Jones, C., Novelly, R. A., & Kleber, M. D. (1982). Neuropsychological functioning in opiate addicts. *Journal of Nervous & Mental Disease, 70,* 209–216.

Rounsaville, B. J., Novelly, R. A., & Kleber, M. D. (1981). Neuropsychology and impairment in opiate addicts: Risk factors. *Annals of the New York Academy of Science, 362,* 79–90.

Rubin, J., & Comitas, L. (1975). *Ganja in Jamaica: A medical and anthropological study of chronic marijuana use.* The Hague: Mouton.

Ryan, C., & Butters, N. (1980). Learning and memory impairments in young and old alcoholics: Evidence for the premature aging hypothesis. *Alcoholism: Clinical & Experimental Research, 4,* 288–293.

Safer, D. J., & Allen, R. P. (1971). The effect of fluphenazine in psychologically normal volunteers: Some temporal, performance, and biochemical relationships. *Biological Psychiatry, 3,* 237–249.

Satz, P., Fletcher, J. M., & Sutker, L. S. (1976). Neuropsychologic, intellectual and personality correlates of chronic marijuana use in native Costa Ricans. In R. Dornbush, A. M. Freedman, & M. Fink (Eds.), *Chronic Cannabis Use: Annals of the New York Academy of Sciences, 282,* 266–306.

Shaeffer, K. W. S., & Parsons, O. A. (1986). Drinking practices and neuropsychological test performance in sober male alcoholics and social drinkers. *Alcohol, 3,* 175–179.

Shuckett, M. A., Butters, N., Lyn, L., & Irwin, M. R. (1987). Neuropsychologic deficits and the risk for alcoholism. *Neuropsychopharmacology, 1,* 45–53.

Small, I. F., Small, J. G., Milstein, V., & Moore, J. E. (1972). Neuropsychological observations with psychosis and somatic treatment. *Journal of Nervous & Mental Disease, 155,* 345–354.

Soueif, M. I. (1976). Differential association between chronic cannabis use and brain function deficits. In R. Dornbush, A. M. Freedman, & M. Fink (Eds.), *Chronic Cannabis Use: Annals of the New York Academy of Sciences, 282,* 323–343.

Sprague, R. L., Barnes, K. R., & Werry, J. S. (1970). Methylphenidate and thioridazine: Learning, reaction time, activity and classroom behavior in disturbed children. *American Journal of Orthopsychiatry, 40,* 615–628.

Stefanos, C., Liakos, A., & Boulougouris, J. (1976). Incidence of mental illness in hashish users and controls. In R. Dornbush, A. M. Freedman, & M. Fink (Eds.), *Chronic Cannabis Use: Annals of the New York Academy of Sciences, 282,* 258–263.

Sternberg, D. E., & Jarvik, M. E. (1976). Memory functions in depression: Improvement with antidepressant medications. *Archives of General Psychiatry, 33,* 219–224.

Strang, J., & Guyrling, H. (1989). Computerized tomography and neuropsychological assessment in long term high dose heroin addicts. *British Journal of Addiction, 84,* 1011–1019.

Struve, F. A., & Willner, A. E. (1983). Cognitive dysfunction and tardive dyskinesia. *British Journal of Psychiatry, 143,* 597–600.

Tarbox, A. R., Conners, G. J., & McLaughlin, E. J. (1986). Effects of drinking pattern on neuropsychological performance among alcohol misusers. *Journal of Studies on Alcoholism, 47,* 176–179.

Tarter, R. E., & Alterman, A. I. (1984). Neuropsychological deficits in alcoholics: Etiological considerations. *Journal of Studies on Alcohol, 45,* 1–9.

Tarter, R. E., Goldstein, G., Alterman, A., Petrarulo, E. W., & Elmore, S. (1983). Alcoholic seizures: Intellectual and neuropsychological sequelae. *Journal of Nervous & Mental Disease, 171,* 123–125.

Tarter, R. E., Jacob, T., & Bremer, D. L. (1989). Specific cognitive impairment in sons of early onset alcoholics. *Alcoholism: Clinical & Experimental Research, 13,* 786–789.

Tarter, R. E., Hegedys, A. M., Goldstein, G., Shelly, C., & Alterman, A. I. (1984). Adolescent sons of alcoholics. *Alcoholism: Clinical & Experimental Research, 8,* 216–222.

Tsushima, W. T., & Towne, W. S. (1977). Effects of paint sniffing on neuropsychological test performance. *Journal of Abnormal Psychology, 869,* 402–407.

Victor, M., Adams, R. D., & Collins, G. H. (1971). *The Wernicke-Korsakoff syndrome.* Philadelphia: Davis.

Waddington, J. L., Brown, K., O'Neil, J., McKeon, P., & Kinsella, A. (1989).

Cognitive impairment, clinical course, and treatment history in outpatients with bipolar affective disorder: Relationship to tardive dyskinesia. *Psychological Medicine, 19*, 897–902.

Weaver, L. A., & Brooks, G. W. (1961). The effects of drug induced parkinsonism on the psychomotor performance of chronic schizophrenics. *Journal of Nervous & Mental Disease, 133*, 148–154.

Wenzel, D. G., & Rutledge, C. O. (1962). Effects of centrally acting drugs on human motor and psychomotor performance. *Journal of Pharmaceutical Sciences, 51*, 631–644.

Whipple, S. C., Parker, E. S., & Noble, E. P. (1988). An atypical neurocognitive profile in alcoholic fathers and their sons. *Journal of the Studies on Alcohol, 49*, 240–244.

Wright, M., & Hogan, T. P. (1972). Repeated LSD ingestion and performance on neuropsychological testing. *Journal of Nervous & Mental Disease, 154*, 432–438.

chapter 8

Psychopathology and Neuropsychological Deficit

M. A L A N J. F I N L A Y S O N
and D A N I E L R. B I R D

The increasing emphasis upon the interaction of neuropsychology and psychiatry (Goldstein, 1987; Grant & Adams, 1986) and the development of the discipline of neuropsychiatry (Rogers, 1987; Rutter, 1983) now permit a closer examination of several issues of concern for practicing neuropsychologists. For example, the impact of psychopathology and its treatment on neuropsychological findings and the relative contribution of biological and psychological parameters to pathology are each relevant topics for consideration. In this chapter we examine these issues through a discussion of potential confounding elements of psychopathology in the neuropsychological examination.

AFFECTIVE DISORDERS AND NEUROPSYCHOLOGICAL PERFORMANCE

The extent to which functionally based disturbances confound neuropsychological interpretation troubles neuropsychologists practicing in psychiatric settings (Heaton & Crowley, 1981). However, in spite of this concern in the clinical lore, relatively few investigators have examined or explored the issues. Although the impact of such factors as anxiety on neuropsychological performance has been investigated occasionally, most of the reported findings relate to depression and its effects. Some researchers view such factors as irrelevant in the clinical interpretation of neuropsychological findings (Reitan & Wolfson, 1985) and train their examiners to engage the patient/client in the examination so that the behavioral effects of anxiety or depression are diminished or eliminated entirely (Heaton & Heaton, 1981).

In a recent review, Caine (1986) complained of the paucity of comprehensive investigations of the neuropsychology of depression. The studies that he reviewed had focused more on the cognitive process involved and less on the neuropsychological underpinnings. Nevertheless, Caine concluded that, although there was some evidence for deficiencies in aspects of fundamental attention and concentration, higher level or cortical functioning was not affected.

In their review, Heaton and Crowley (1981) reached a similar conclusion on the lack of relationship between neuropsychological ability scores and extent of depression. Heaton and Crowley also presented correlational data demonstrating a stronger association between degree of neuropsychological impairment and emotional distress in neurological patients than in psychiatric patients. They cited a number of studies (Heaton & Crowley, 1981) that documented emotional disturbance in neurological patients. They further reported a positive correlation between degree of neuropsychological impairment and level of emotional distress. Such data imply that emotional distress is secondary or reactive to the underlying neuropsychological dysfunction. Caution is needed when interpreting these findings because the cited reports depended upon the Minnesota Multiphasic Personality Inventory (MMPI) as the index of emotional distress. Recent evidence suggests that many of the MMPI items represent valid neurological complaints and, therefore, the MMPI must not be interpreted literally in neurological patients (Alfano, Finlayson, Stearns, & Neilson, 1990).

The evidence presented in these two reviews (Caine, 1986; Heaton & Crowley, 1981) supports the minimal impact of functional disturbance on measures of higher cortical functioning. However, data from studies of cognitive processes suggest that attention, concentration (and, therefore, memory) and visual–spatial functions may be disturbed (Richards & Ruff, 1989). Recent investigations using the Luria-Nebraska Neuropsychological Battery and related tests (Goulet Fisher, Sweet, & Pfaelzer-Smith, 1986; Heinrichs, 1987; Newman & Sweet, 1987) have also been consistent with this view. Thus, in preparing for a forensic examination the neuropsychologist should assemble a set of measures that permits other than level of performance interpretations because such procedures would be most vulnerable to the general effects of reduced attention, concentration, and psychomotor slowing. The ability to compare differential score patterns, evaluate left–right differences and document pathognomonic signs will give the neuropsychologist the data base necessary to evaluate the impact of psychopathology on neuropsychological functioning.

IMPACT OF SOMATIC THERAPIES

Of the somatic methods employed in the treatment of psychopathology (chemotherapy, electroconvulsive therapy, psychosurgery) chemotherapy's impact upon cognitive functioning has received the most attention from neuropsychologists. Although research in psychopharmacology tends to focus on specific compounds, their symptomatic effectiveness, and mechanisms of action, some researchers have argued that the impact of these drugs on cognitive and behavioral functioning requires closer scrutiny in the pharmacotoxicology literature (DeMaio, 1988). In the neuropsychological literature, however, these effects are becoming increasingly understood. The current knowledge has accumulated from several routes: (a) investigations of the behavioral toxicology of nonprescription drug use (Carlin, this volume); (b) studies of anticonvulsive medications (Dodrill, 1975, 1988; Evans & Gaultieri, 1985; Reynolds & Trimble, 1985; Trimble, 1988); (c) research on common psychiatric medications (Medelia, Gold, & Merriam, 1988; Shaw, Stokes, Mann, & Manevitz, 1987; Van Putten & Marder, 1987); and (d) explorations of the biochemistry of the central nervous system (White & Rumbold, 1988). Although a discussion of this extensive literature is beyond the scope of this chapter, we can make several comments.

Significant variability exists among studies in this field with respect to patient selection and description, choice of experimental measures, drug treatment conditions, and selection of control patients, making generalization difficult. Such variability may explain how an early review can conclude that medication effects are minimal (Heaton & Crowley, 1981), whereas a later review can report specific, differential cognitive effects (Medalia et al., 1988). Medalia et al. (1988) specifically commented upon the impact of medications on psychomotor coordination and felt that they may also have an impact upon other measures requiring motor skill for successful performance. In a "drug-on, drug-off, drug-on" paradigm, Shaw et al. (1987) demonstrated a similar detrimental motoric effect for lithium. The extent to which motor slowing or coordination difficulties are related to the toxic side effect of akinesia, as discussed by Van Putten and Marder (1987), is not yet known. Reviewers of anticonvulsive drug effects also mention psychomotor effects but cite attention, concentration, and memory difficulties as predominant (Dodrill, 1988; Trimble, 1987). However, these effects are characterized as "slight to mild" (Dodrill, 1988), and a number of potential confounding factors have been identified (Dodrill, 1988; Dodrill & Troupin, 1991; Medalia et al., 1988). As in the case of psychopathology, the impact of medications upon neuropsychological functioning appears to be limited to basic aspects of attention and related processes, although specific motor effects could occur as well. Again, for the forensic neuropsychologist, the careful selection of test instruments will circumvent this problem and permit accurate interpretation of neuropathological findings.

In considering the impact of psychopathology on neuropsychological measures the question is often raised as to whether or not the psychopathology actually reflects underlying, undiagnosed neuropathology. The role of one, or the other, cerebral hemisphere in depression is a case in point. Electrophysiological evidence (Tucker, Stenslie, Roth, & Shearer, 1981) suggests right cerebral hemisphere dysfunction may be crucial, a finding that supports the earlier position of Flor-Henry (1969). However, evidence from poststroke patients suggests that left cerebral dysfunction may play a greater role in precipitating depressed mood in this population (Robinson, Starr, Kubos, & Price, 1983). Subsequent investigators, however, failed to replicate this latter finding (Sinyor et al., 1986) and questioned whether sampling biases may have clouded their own and previous investigations.

THE NEUROPSYCHOLOGY OF SCHIZOPHRENIA

Two recent reviews of the neuropsychological and neuropathological evidence supporting brain impairment in schizophrenia (Goldstein, 1986; Seidman, 1983) reached the conclusion that the presentation of cerebral dysfunction in schizophrenia is quite varied and complex, and that the relationship between the neuropsychological (behavioral) characteristics and neurological (brain) features are not clearly understood. Goldstein (1986) did suggest that the neuropsychological exploration of subtypes of schizophrenia, particularly the positive and negative symptom syndromes proposed by Crow (1980; Crow, Cross, Johnstone, & Owen, 1982) and Andreason (1982; Andreason & Olsen, 1982) might shed further light on the matter. According to Crow (1980), one syndrome (Type I) is characterized by positive symptoms (e.g., delusions, hallucinations, and thought disorder), neuroleptic responsivity, biochemical abnormality, and minimal cognitive impairment. The other (Type II) is characterized predominantly by negative symptoms (e.g., affective flattening, poverty of speech, and social withdrawal), structural brain changes, neuroleptic unresponsivity, and cognitive impairment.

Much of the recent appeal of the positive/negative distinction lies in the fact that it unites the current understanding of phenomenology, pharmacology, pathophysiology, and neurocognitive features into a single comprehensive hypothesis (Andreasen, 1985). This distinction has now gained prominence in schizophrenia research (Bilder, Mukherjee, Rieder, & Pandurangi, 1985; Crow, Ferrier, & Johnstone, 1986; Green & Walker, 1985; Johnstone et al., 1986a, Johnstone, Owens, Frith, & Crow, 1986b; Liddle 1987; Meltzer & Locascio, 1987; Mortimer, Lund, & McKenna, 1990; Tandon & Greden, 1989; Walker, Harvey, & Perlman, 1988); although the origin of this concept in neurology can be argued (Berrios, 1985), there is little doubt about its impact on current research (Lewine, 1985).

Citing abundant evidence of structural and functional brain abnormalities in at least some subtypes of schizophrenia, Crow (1980) hypothesized that negative symptoms are associated with structural abnormalities (i.e., ventricular enlargement) as revealed through computerized axial tomography (CT), whereas positive symptoms are not. Positive symptoms, on the other hand, are purportedly related to biochemical (i.e., dopaminergic) rather than structural brain changes. The latter hypothesis is supported by data that suggest positive symptoms respond better to neuroleptics than do negative ones (Johnstone, Crow, Frith, Carnery, & Price, 1978), and that amphetamines exacerbate the condition of patients with positive but not negative symptoms (Angrist, Rotrosen, & Gershon, 1980; Dennert & Andreasen, 1983).

Another assumption of the two-syndrome hypothesis is that negative symptoms are uniquely associated with generalized cognitive impairment; however, evidence for this purported relationship is largely speculative (Crow, 1980). Furthermore, assumptions about their relative stability, neuroleptic responsivity, and neuropsychological characteristics are now being reexamined (Andreason, Flaum, Swayze, Tyrell, & Arndt, 1990; Green & Walker, 1985; Johnstone et al., 1986b; Liddle, 1987; Volkow et al., 1987).

Although negative symptoms are uniquely associated with cognitive and attentional impairment (Andreason & Olsen, 1982; Crow, 1980) recent neuropsychological studies (Bilder et al., 1985; Green & Walker, 1986a; 1986b; Walker & Harvey, 1986) suggest that each syndrome may be associated with a unique pattern of deficit.

Recently in our laboratory, Bird (1990) further examined the relationship between neuropsychological functioning and positive versus negative symptoms of schizophrenia in order to test the assumption (Crow, 1980) that negative symptoms are uniquely associated with cognitive and attentional impairment. Forty chronic schizophrenics were subtyped on the basis of symptoms that were predominantly positive, predominantly negative, both positive and negative, or neither positive nor negative according to Andreasen's (1982) criteria. These patients were then administered a comprehensive battery of neuropsychological tests.

Based on mean comparisons, test data suggested that positive-and negative-symptom schizophrenics were equally impaired according to various global indices of neuropsychological functioning, including the Halstead Impairment Index (Reitan & Wolfson, 1985), as well as on various aspects of attention and concentration (visual versus auditory; immediate versus sustained). These findings were interpreted as inconsistent with the hypothesis that cognitive and attentional deficits are unique to negative-symptom schizophrenia and suggest that differences in neuropsychological functioning may be more qualitative than quantitative.

Bird (1990) also explored the possibility that patterns of deficits among subtypes, when found, reflect lateralized or localized brain dysfunction. Green and Walker (1985) found negative symptoms to be associated with visual–motor and visual–spatial deficits and positive symptoms with deficits in short-term verbal memory; Bird (1990) also reported that positive-symptom schizophrenics showed deficits in verbal learning and memory. However, negative-symptom schizophrenics showed differential impairment on measures of verbal fluency and productivity (Bird, 1990). Although the findings of Green and Walker (1985) suggest that negative symptoms may be associated with right and positive symptoms with left-hemisphere dysfunction, the deficit pattern reported by Bird (1990) supports a negative-frontal (or left anterior) and positive-temporal (left posterior) hypothesis. However, post hoc analyses failed to support any significant relation between neuropsychological indices of right versus left or anterior versus posterior dysfunction and a patient's symptomatic status. In fact, a low correlation between psychiatric symptoms and neuropsychological performance was generally observed.

In summary, these studies support the validity of the positive–negative symptom distinction to the extent that differential patterns of neuropsychological performance deficit have been associated with the two-symptom complexes. However, there should be a reconceptualization regarding defining characteristics, particularly with respect to assumptions about cognitive and attentional correlates. Furthermore, the known interindividual variability in neuropsychological performance among schizophrenics and its apparent dissociation from the patient's symptomatic status point to the need for an independent, objective assessment of attention, memory, and cognition in each individual case.

MILD MINOR HEAD INJURY

Nowhere is the need to differentiate neuropathology and psychopathology more clearly illustrated than in the examination of mild head injury. The search for a definitive answer to the conundrum of the postconcussional syndrome (PCS) has increased of late and has been the subject of several recent reviews (Alves, Colohan, O'Leary, Rimel, & Jane, 1986; Binder, 1986; Levin, Eisenberg, & Benton, 1989). At issue is the elucidation of the persisting, apparently subjective, complaints of persons who have experienced mild head injury yet in whom clinical neurological signs are minimal or absent. Although there is no general agreement on the symptom constellation, the list of complaints usually includes headache, irritability, fatigue, dizziness, insomnia, reduced concentration, and poor memory. No such agreement exists, however, about the factors contributing to these complaints. Indeed, a recent survey of professionals dealing with individuals with PCS indicates that these differences of opinion may well reflect a declaration of faith rather than fact (McCordie, 1988). A better understanding of PCS can develop from a brief review of the existing literature with regard to definition, neuropsychological sequelae, underlying mechanisms, and other factors relevant to mild head injury.

Definition of Mild Head Injury

The adequate definition of inclusion criteria has been a major problem limiting the interpretation of findings from investigations of mild head injury. The absence of objective criteria was particularly handicapping in the earlier literature, but with the increasing use of the Glasgow Coma Scale (GCS) (Teasdale & Jennett, 1974) reliable quantification has become possible (Levin, Gary, et al., 1987). A GCS score of 13–15 at admission is considered the minimum standard; however, by limiting loss of consciousness to minutes or less, and including patients with hospitalization under 48 hours, further rigor is possible. Thus, with subtle variations, this operational definition has become the norm in recent work (Dikmen, McLean, & Temkin, 1986; Gentilini et al., 1985; Levin, Mattis, et al., 1987; Rimel, Giordani, Barth, Boll, & Jane, 1981). The strength of such a definition is that it binds the syndrome to its entry point rather than identifying it in terms of variable outcome. The definition does not require a documented loss of consciousness; by limiting hospitalization to 48 hours, major complicating medical factors can be discounted. Agreement on this definition is not unanimous; other investigators (Hugenholtz, Stuss, Stetham, & Richard, 1988) employed a graded scale of concussion developed by Ommaya and Gennarelli (1974). The differential utility of these two definitional procedures has yet to be established. However, even groups identified with established criteria could still be heterogeneous with respect to other potential biasing factors relating either to present trauma or premorbid conditions. Substance abuse, previous head injury, heterogeneity of lesion parameters, and etiology are examples of factors commonly cited (Dikmen & Temkin, 1987; Levin, Mattis, et al., 1987). We will show many of the neuropsychological sequelae are subtle, so that adequate definition of sample characteristics and careful documentation of potentially biasing factors are essential in the study of minor head injury.

Neurological Sequelae

In a review of the earlier studies of mild head injury Binder (1986) concluded that neuropsychological/cognitive deficits are invariably present in the period immediately following trauma. This position has been echoed in more recent articles (Armstrong, 1987; Davidoff, Kessler, Laibstain, & Mark, 1988). The extent to which these deficits persist, however, is less evident.

One of the most frequently cited, recent investigations of mild head injury is that by Rimel et al. (1981). In this study, 538 patients with defined mild head injury were initially examined with 424 being available for further investigation 3 months posttrauma. Researchers reported high incidence of subjective complaint in the patient group. They also noted a strikingly low employment rate. In a smaller subgroup of this sample available for neuropsychological examination, difficulties with concentration, memory, and judgment were identified. In a later paper, Barth et al. (1983) elaborated these deficits neuropsychologically and postulated a significant relationship between cognitive efficiency and successful return to the workplace. However, the absence of appropriate control groups and the lack of premorbid descriptors in these studies raise concerns about the adequacy of the findings.

In a more carefully controlled study, Gentilini et al. (1985) examined 50 patients with mild head injury 1 month posttrauma on selected cognitive tests and compared the results with those of a carefully selected control group. They reported lack of statistical difference between the patient and control groups, and concluded that substantial recovery from injury generally occurs within the first month. However, the performance of the head injury group was consistently poorer than that of the control group on a test of selective attention, although significance was documented using univariate statistical techniques.

In a similar well-controlled study, Dikmen et al. (1986) evaluated a small sample of patients 1 month and 1 year posttrauma using a more extensive set of procedures including a comprehensive battery of neuropsychological tests and measures of psychosocial adjustment. On the neuropsychological measures, impairment was present at 1 month on tests of attention, concentration, and delayed recall. No intergroup differences were apparent after 1 year, although the head injury group performed slightly poorer overall than did the control group. Psychosocial difficulties, apparent on first examination, were less prominent after 1 year. The researchers further reported that factors other than head injury (e.g., physical complications) were contributing to residual adjustment problems. Additionally, the researchers asked both control and patient subjects to complete a symptom checklist. Although the patients endorsed more items than control subjects, they also identified similar complaints. At the 1-year examination the groups no longer differed on this dimension. The researchers concluded with the comment that their findings were relevant only for groups of patients and with a plea to consider the uniqueness of each individual case.

Data from three American centers were combined in a prospective study reported by Levin, Mattis, et al. (1987), who adopted criteria and controls similar to those of Dikman et al. (1986). Fifty-seven patients (of an original 155) were followed at 1 month, and a smaller subgroup of 32 patients returned for a 3-month follow-up examination. The researchers limited their assessment and interview procedures to 1 hour, and consequently were only able to assess a limited sample of cognitive functions. Nevertheless, clear decrements in the performance of patients with head injury were apparent in all centers at initial evaluation conducted within 1 week of trauma. During reexamination at 1 month posttrauma, a more complicated picture arose, with two of the centers reporting no difference between patient and control groups, whereas one center reported persisting neurobehavioral deficits in its patient sample. Nevertheless, significant improvement from baseline was reported at the 1-month follow-up from each center. By the 3-month follow-up all patient-control comparisons were nonsignificant, with an exception that seemed to relate to a sampling bias in patients returning for follow-up. Patients had also been asked to endorse any emotional or adjustment difficulties at each examination. Virtually all patients endorsed symptoms at baseline that gradually reduced over time, although some patients were not symptom free at the 3-month follow-up. Thus, a pattern of recovery of both cognitive deficits and subjective complaints is present in these patients. However, because of the rigor of the controls established by the investigators in their selection of uncomplicated cases, the conclusions may not be generalizable to the population of minor head injury victims seen in clinics or emergency rooms.

Hugenholtz et al. (1988) were able to serially examine a small group ($n = 22$) of patients with mild head injuries on five visits up to 90 days posttrauma. Using simple and complex reaction time paradigms, the investigators were able to evaluate attention and information processing capabilities in their patients. Although the patients consistently showed a slower simple reaction time than controls, the difference did not reach significance. However, on complex reaction-time measures, the patients were significantly slower on all occasions except the last visit (90 days). Although they remained slower than controls, the difference between the two groups did not reach statistical significance.

It is important to note that these studies involve several independent centers in several countries, yet they consistently show evidence of neuropsychological deficits following mild head injury. The nature of these deficits can best be characterized as reduced cortical efficiency and are most clearly reflected in measures of attention and complex information processing. Furthermore, there appears to be a recovery of these functions over several months to the extent that performance is not different from that of carefully selected controls. The studies have not yet fully factored out the effects of previous head injury, although some researchers have postulated a cumulative effect (Gronwall & Wrightson, 1975; Reitan & Wolfson, 1988). We need further investigation and isolation of premorbid personal factors (the so-called cracked vase). Finally, the role of the caregiver or family in the maintenance of complaints is only beginning to be addressed (Peters, Stambrook, Moore, & Esses, 1990; Rosenthal & Geckler, 1986). The recent application of cluster analysis techniques to this area (Levin, Mattis, et al., 1987; Lidvall, Linderoth, & Norlin, 1970) holds promise as a way to further elucidate these variables.

Underlying Mechanisms

Evidence is mounting regarding the possibility of pathophysiological changes following mild head injury (Binder, 1986; Gennarelli, 1986; Ommaya, 1982). In summarizing the clinical literature on electroencephalogram (EEG), Binder (1986) concluded that "a mild head injury can result in the findings of an abnormal EEG" (p. 330). Changes in intercranial pressure, cerebral circulation, and evoked potentials have also been documented in animals and humans. There is microscopic evidence of brain lesions following minor head trauma in both animals (Jane, Steward, & Gennarelli, 1985) and humans (Oppenheimer, 1968). Recent investigations using magnetic resonance imaging (MRI) have documented intracerebral lesions previously undetected on conventional CT scans (Gandy, Snow, Zimmerman, & Deck, 1984; Levin, Eisenberg, Amparo, McArdle, & Williams, 1986). When these discoveries are placed in the context of the superiority of the CT scan to conventional tomography, it is clear that finer and more accurate methods of delineating pathology are evolving.

Beyond Compensation

Miller (1961) presented a review of clinical cases of head injury referred for medicolegal assessment in which approximately 25% displayed clear neurotic symptoms that were negatively correlated with severity of head injury. He further postulated that the availability of compensation was directly related to the maintenance of these symptoms. This view was later reiterated and substantiated by comparing symptom patterns among patients with mild head injury of different etiologies (Miller, 1969). Other authors have provided modest support for this contention (Bremner & Gillingham, 1974). Lishman (1978) agreed that psychogenic factors play a substantial role in the maintenance of symptomology but was less enthusiastic as to the role that compensation may play.

Miller's (1961) claim has been directly challenged on many occasions (Merskey & Woodforde, 1972; Weller, 1985). McKinlay, Brooks, and Bond (1983) specifically assessed the impact of litigation/compensation on subjective complaints, neuropsychological functioning, and relatives' reports in groups of patients with severe head injury. No differences were found between the groups, although the self-reports of those seeking compensation were slightly more symptomatic. Recent investigators have felt the role of compensation factors to be overly emphasized in the development of subjective symptomatology (Stuss, Ely, Hugenholtz, Richard, & LaRochelle, 1985). In their study, Dikmen et al. (1986) pointed out that return to work or school was less likely to occur if other system injuries were present. In his extensive review, Binder (1986) systematically explored evidence for and against Miller's (1961) contention and left little doubt that compensation was not necessarily a causal factor in the development of subjective complaints, as the evidence for a neuropathological basis was substantial. Such a view of the neuropathological evidence is echoed by Gennarelli (1986), who felt that mechanical strain to axonal membranes was the most probable underlying mechanism. However, one could argue that compensation as a source of stress might contribute to the maintenance of such symptoms following mild head injury.

Historically it would seem that the pendulum has swung from early attempts to understand subjective complaints as neurotic or psychogenic features through a period of increased attention to the neuropathological and neuropsychological factors involved. However, such a neurological view has been unable to explain the persistence of subjective complaints exceeding 1 year in some individuals (Alves et al., 1986). Although continuing neuropsychological problems cannot be totally discounted, most of the evidence from carefully controlled studies suggests that cognitive recovery typically occurs in the first 3 months following injury (Dikmen et al., 1986; Hugenholtz et al., 1988; Levin, Mattis, et al., 1987). Perhaps the pendulum could pause briefly in midswing to allow for the systematic investigation of both psychological and neuropsychological parameters and their interactions as determining factors in PCS.

Although premorbid individual difference is frequently postulated as a contributing factor, there have been no conclusive investigations of its role in minor head injury (Binder, 1986). It is important to note that those studies that excluded subjects with psychiatric disorders, alcohol abuse, and previous history of trauma generally reported a gradual dissipation of symptomatology (Dikman et al., 1986; Levin, Mattis, et al., 1987). On the other hand, those studies with less stringent controls presented a more complicated picture of subjective complaints following trauma (Alves et al., 1986).

Binder (1986) also identified several areas of selective vulnerability (or risk) and individual differences in persistent subjective complaints. In particular, lower socioeconomic status, previous history of brain trauma, and increasing age were specified as factors contributing to an increased reporting of symptomatology. Such conclusions are not surprising given the known contribution of these factors to neuropsychological performance (Reitan & Wolfson, 1988). Individuals also differ in their responses to stress (Fordyce, 1988), a factor that may also contribute to the maintenance of symptom complaints. A recent case study suggests that stress reduction therapy may have a positive impact in reducing the symptoms associated with persistent subjective complaints (Groveman, Reba, Pollack, Lehrer, & Miller, 1987).

Not only individuals but also families vary in their ability to cope. Among patients with severe head injury relatives' distress is often related to the patient's level of complaining (Livingston, Brooks, & Bond, 1985). Peters et al. (1990) reached a similar conclusion in their investigation of the marital dyad. Relatives of patients with head injury can also show different coping styles (Hinkeldy & Corrigan, 1988). A distressed spouse may contribute to the stress of the partner and consequently both individuals experience increasing levels of discomfort unless the cycle can be broken. However, the specific impact of personal coping style and family coping style on the maintenance of persistent subjective complaints has not yet been investigated. Unfortunately, although intervention/treatment, if only in the form of information sharing and reassurance, is often advocated (Levin, Gary, et al., 1987), it is rarely included in rehabilitation programs for persons with mild head injury (Gronwall, 1986). Needless to say, the impact of such efforts in reducing subjective complaints remains to be evaluated.

In summary, the differentiation of neuropsychological and psychological contributors to mild head injury is indeed complex. The issue facing the forensic expert in such cases is to quantify these subjective experiences for the court. This brief survey would suggest that in order to do so, the clinician should be collecting systematic data from a number of sources. A history of premorbid medical and psychological factors (including coping style) would be important. Documentation of neuropathological, neuro-psychological, and psychological factors is essential in the immediate injury phase as well as during appropriate follow-up investigation. The exploration of psychological aspects should include an evaluation of individual and family coping. The nature of interventions should be noted, and although such procedures have not been validated with this population, consideration should be given to their implementation. With a careful evaluation of this information, a clinician would then be able to provide reasonable probability statements for the court.

REFERENCES

Alfano, D. P., Finlayson, M. A. J., Stearns, G. M., & Neilson, P. M. (1990). The MMPI and neurologic dysfunction. *Clinical Neuropsychologist, 4,* 69–79.

Alves, W. M., Colohan, A. R. T., O'Leary, T. J., Rimel, R. W., & Jane, J. A. (1986). Understanding post-traumatic symptoms after minor head injury. *Journal of Head Trauma Rehabilitation, 1,* 1–12.

Andreasen, N. C. (1982). Negative symptoms in schizophrenia: Definition and reliability. *Archives of General Psychiatry, 39,* 784–788.

Andreasen, N. C. (1985). Positive versus negative schizophrenia: A critical evaluation. *Schizophrenia Bulletin, 11,* 380–389.

Andreasen, N. C., Flaum, M., Swayze, V. W. II, Tyrell, G., & Arndt, S. (1990). Positive and negative symptoms in schizophrenia. *Archives of General Psychiatry, 47,* 615–621.

Andreasen, N. C., & Olson, S. C. (1982). Negative versus positive schizophrenia: Definition and validation. *Archives of General Psychiatry, 39,* 789–794.

Armstrong, C. L. (1987). Psychological and cognitive longterm dynamics of mild head injuries. *Neuropsychology, 1,* 15–19.

Angrist, B., Rotrosen, J., & Gershon, S. (1980). Differential effects of neuroleptics on positive versus negative schizophrenias. *Psychopharmacology, 72,* 17–19.

Barth, J. T., Macciocchi, S. N., Giordani, B., Rimel, R., Jane, J. A., & Boll, T. J. (1983). Neuropsychological sequelae of minor head injury. *Neurosurgery, 13,* 529–533.

Berrios, G. E. (1985). Positive and negative symptoms and Jackson: A conceptual history. *Archives of General Psychiatry, 42,* 95–97.

Bilder, R. M., Mukherjee, S., Rieder, R. O., & Pandurangi, A. K. (1985). Symptomatic and neuropsychological components of defect states. *Schizophrenia Bulletin, 11,* 409–419.

Binder, L. M. (1986). Persisting symptoms after mild head injury: A review of the postconcussive syndrome. *Journal of Clinical & Experimental Neuropsychology, 8,* 323–346.

Bird, D. R. (1990). *Neuropsychological characteristics of positive and negative symptoms of schizophrenia: Implications for cognitive remediation.* Unpublished doctoral dissertation, McMaster University, Hamilton, Ontario.

Bremner, D. N., & Gillingham, F. J. (1974). Patterns in convalescence after minor head injury. *Journal of the Royal College of Surgery Edinborough, 19,* 94–97.

Caine, E. D. (1986). The neuropsychology of depression: The pseudodementia syndrome. In I. Grant & K. M. Adams (Eds.), *Neuropsychological assessment of psychiatric disorders* (pp. 221–243). New York: Oxford University Press.

Crow, T. J. (1980). Molecular pathology of schizophrenia: More than one disease process? *British Medical Journal, 280,* 66–68.

Crow, T. J., Cross, A. J., Johnstone, E. C., & Owen, F. (1982). Two syndromes in schizophrenia and their pathogenesis. In F. A. Henn & H. A. Nassrallah (Eds.), *Schizophrenia as a brain disease* (pp. 196–234). New York: Oxford University Press.

Crow, T. J., Ferrier, I. N., & Johnstone, E. C. (1986). The two-syndrome concept and neuroendocrinology of schizophrenia. *Psychiatric Clinics of North America*, *9*, 99–113.

Davidoff, D. A., Kessler, H. R., Laibstain, D. F., & Mark, V. H. (1988). Neurobehavioural sequelae of minor head injury: A consideration of post-concussive syndrome versus post-traumatic stress disorder. *Cognitive Rehabilitation*, *3*, 8–13.

DeMaio, D. (1988) Notes on human behavioural pharmacotoxicology. *Progress in Neuro-Psychopharmacology & Biological Psychiatry*, *12*, 33–40.

Dennert, J. W., & Andreasen, N. C. (1983). CT scanning and schizophrenia: A review. *Psychiatric Developments*, *1*, 105–121.

Dikmen, S., McLean, A., & Temkin, W. (1986). Neuropsychology and psychosocial consequences of minor head injury. *Journal of Neurology, Neurosurgery & Psychiatry*, *11*, 1227–1232.

Dikmen, S., & Temkin, N. (1987). Determination of the effects of head injury and recovery in behavioural research. In H. S. Levin, J. Grafman, & H. M. Eisenberg (Eds.), *Neurobehavioural recovery from head injury* (pp. 73–87). New York: Oxford University Press.

Dodrill, C. B. (1975). Diphenylhydantoin serum levels, toxicity and neuropsychological peformance in patients with epilepsy. *Epilepsia*, *16*, 593–600.

Dodrill, C. B. (1988). Effects of antiepileptic drugs on abilities. *Journal of Clinical Psychiatry*, *49*, 570–581.

Dodrill, C. B., & Troupin, A. S. (1991). Neuropsychological effects of carbamazepine and phenytoin: A reanalysis. *Neurology*, *41*, 141–143.

Evans, R. W., & Gaultieri, C. T. (1985). Carbamazepine: A neuropsychological and psychiatric profile. *Clinical Neuropharmacology*, 1985, *8*(3), 221–241.

Flor-Henry, P. (1969). Schizophrenia-like reactions and affective psychoses associated with temporal lobe epilepsy: Etiological factors. *American Journal of Psychiatry*, *126*, 148–162.

Fordyce, W. E. (1988). Pain and suffering: A reappraisal. *American Psychologist*, *43*, 276–283.

Gandy, S. E., Snow, R. B., Zimmerman, R. D., & Deck, M. D. F. (1984). Cranial nuclear magnetic resonance imaging in head trauma. *Annals of Neurology*, *16*, 254–257.

Gennarelli, T. (1986). Mechanisms and pathophysiology of cerebral concussion. *Journal of Head Trauma Rehabilitation*, *1*, 23–29.

Gentilini, M., Nichelli, P., Schoenhuber, R., Bortolotti, P., Tonelli, L., & Falasca, A. (1985). Neuropsychological evaluation of mild head injury. *Journal of Neurology, Neurosurgery & Psychiatry*, *48*, 137–140.

Goldstein, G. (1986). The neuropsychology of schizophrenia. In I. Grant & K. M. Adams (Eds.), *Neuropsychological assessment of neuropsychiatric disorders* (pp. 17–171). New York: Oxford University Press.

Goldstein, G. (1987). Neuropsychiatry: Interfaces between neuropsychology and psychopathology. *Clinical Neuropsychologist*, *1*, 365–380.

Grant, I., & Adams, K. M. (1986). *Neuropsychological assessment of psychiatric disorders*. New York: Oxford University Press.

Green, M., & Walker, E. (1985). Neuropsychological performance and positive and negative symptoms in schizophrenia. *Journal of Abnormal Psychology*, *94*, 460–469.

Green, M., & Walker, E. (1986a) Attentional performance in positive-and-negative symptoms schizophrenia. *Journal of Nervous & Mental Disease*, *174*, 208–213.

Green, M., & Walker, E. (1986b). Symptom correlates of vulnerability to backward masking in schizophrenia. *American Journal of Psychiatry*, *142*, 181–186.

Gronwall, D. (1986). Rehabilitation programs for patients with mild head injury: Components, problems, and evaluation. *Journal of Head Trauma Rehabilitation*, *1*, 53–62.

Gronwall, D., & Wrightson, P. (1975). Cumulative effect of concussion. *Lancet*, *2*, 995–997.

Groveman, A. M., Reba, P., Pollack, I. W., Lehrer, P. M., & Miller, M. H. (1987). Post-concussional syndrome and stress reduction therapy. *Neuropsychology*, *1*, 19–22.

Goulet Fisher, D., Sweet, J. J., & Pfaelzer-Smith, E. A. (1986). Influence of depression on repeated neuropsychological testing. *International Journal of Clinical Neuropsychology*, *8*, 14–18.

Heaton, R. K., & Crowley, T. J. (1981). Effects of psychiatric disorders and their somatic treatments on neuropsychological test results. In S. B. Filskov & T. J. Boll (Eds.), *Handbook of clinical neuropsychology* (pp. 481–525). Toronto: Wiley.

Heaton, S. R., & Heaton, R. K. (1981). Testing the impaired patient. In S. B. Filskov & T. J. Boll (Eds.), *Handbook of clinical neuropsychology* (pp. 526–544). Toronto: Wiley.

Heinrichs, R. W. (1987). Does depression in patients with known or suspected cerebral disease contribute to impairment on the Luria-Nebraska Neuropsychological Battery? *International Journal of Neuroscience*, *32*, 895–899.

Hinkeldy, N. S., & Corrigan, J. D. (1988). *Psychological distress and coping in relatives of closed head injury patients*. Paper presented at the 56th annual meeting of the American Psychological Association, Atlanta.

Hugenholtz, A., Stuss, D. T., Stetham, L. L., & Richard, M. T. (1988). How long does it take to recover from a mild concussion? *Neurosurgery*, *22*, 853–858.

Jane, J. A., Steward, O., & Gennarelli, T. (1985). Axonal degeneration induced by experimental noninvasive minor head injury. *Journal of Neurosurgery*, *62*, 96–100.

Johnstone, E. C., Crow, T. J., Frith, C. D., Carnery, M. W. P., & Price, L. (1978). Mechanisms of antipsychotic effect in the treatment of acute schizophrenia. *Lancet*, *1*, 848–851.

Johnstone, E. C., Crow, T. J., MacMillan, J. F., Owens, D. G. C., Bydder, G. M., & Steiner, R. E. (1986a). A magnetic resonance study of early schizophrenia. *Journal of Neurology, Neurosurgery & Psychiatry*, *49*, 136–139.

Johnstone, E. C., Owens, D. R. C., Frith, C. D., & Crow, T. J. (1986b). The relative stability of positive and negative features in chronic schizophrenia. *British Journal of Psychiatry*, *150*, 60–64.

Levin, H. S., Eisenberg, H. M., Amparo, E. G., McArdle, C. B., & Williams, D. (1986). *Magnetic resonance imaging and correlated neurobehavioural findings in patients with minor or moderate closed head injury.* Paper presented at the annual meeting of the American Association of Neurological Surgeons, Denver, CO.

Levin, H. S., Eisenberg, H. M., & Benton, A. L. (1989). *Mild head injury.* New York: Oxford University Press.

Levin, H. S., Gary, H. E. J., High, W. M., Mattis, S., Ruff, R. M., & Eisenberg, H. M. (1987). Minor head injury and the postconcussional syndrome: Methodological issues in outcome studies. In H. S. Levin, J. Frafman, & H. M. Eisenberg (Eds.), *Neurobehavioural recovery from head injury* (pp. 262–275). New York: Oxford University Press.

Levin, H. S., Mattis, S., Ruff, R. M., Eisenberg, H. M., Marshall, L. F., Tabaddor, K., High, N., & Frankowski, R. (1987). Neurobehavioural outcome of minor head injury: A three-center study. *Journal of Neurosurgery, 66,* 234–243.

Lewine, R. R. J. (1985). Negative symptoms in schizophrenia: Editor's introduction. *Schizophrenia Bulletin, 11,* 361–363.

Liddle, P. F. (1987). The symptoms of chronic schizophrenia: A re-examination of the positive–negative dichotomy. *British Journal of Psychiatry, 151,* 145–151.

Lidvall, H. F., Linderoth, B., & Norlin, B. (1970). Causes of the postconcussional syndrome. *Acta Neurologica Scandinavica, 50,* 1–144.

Lishman, W. (1978). *Organic psychiatry.* Boston: Blackwell Scientific Publications.

Livingston, M. G., Brooks, D. N., & Bond, M. R. (1985). Patient outcome in the year following severe head injury and relatives psychiatric and social functioning. *Journal of Neurology, Neurosurgery and Psychiatry, 48,* 876–881.

McKinlay, W. W., Brooks, D. N., & Bond, M. R. (1983). Postconcussional symptoms, financial compensation and outcome of severe head injury. *Journal of Neurology, Neurosurgery & Psychiatry, 46,* 1084–1091.

McCordie, W. R. (1988). Twenty-year follow up of prevailing opinion on the posttraumatic or postconcussional syndrome. *Clinical Neuropsychologist, 2,* 198–212.

Medelia, A., Gold, J., & Merriam, A. (1988). The effects of neuroleptics on neuropsychological test results of schizophrenics. *Archives of Clinical Neuropsychology, 3,* 249–271.

Meltzer, H. Y., & Locascio, J. (1987). Positive and negative subtypes in schizophrenia. *Amercan Journal of Psychiatry, 144,* 1366–1367.

Merskey, H., & Woodforde, J. M. (1972). Psychiatric sequelae of minor head injury. *Brain, 95,* 521–528.

Miller, H. (1961). Accident neurosis. *British Medical Journal, 1,* 919–925.

Miller, H. (1969). Problems of medicolegal practice. In A. E. Walker, W. F. Caveness, & M. Critchley (Eds.), *The late effects of head injury.* Springfield, IL: Cha. C. Thomas.

Mortimer, A. M., Lund, C. E., & McKenna, P. J. (1990). The positive:negative dichotomy in schizophrenia. *British Journal of Psychiatry, 157,* 41–49.

Newman, P. J., & Sweet, J. J. (1987). The effects of clinical depression on the Luria-Nebraska neuropsychological battery. *International Journal of Clinical Neuropsychology, 8*, 109–114.

Ommaya, A. K. (1982). Mechanisms of cerebral concussion, contusions, and other effects of head injury. In J. R. Youmans (Ed.), *Neurological surgery* (pp. 1877–1895). Philadelphia: Saunders.

Ommaya, A. K., & Gennarelli, T. A. (1974). Cerebral concussion and traumatic unconsciousness. *Brain, 97*, 633–654.

Oppenheimer, D. R. (1968). Microscopic lesions in the brain following head injury. *Journal of Neurology, Neurosurgery & Psychiatry, 31*, 299–306.

Peters, L. C., Stambrook, M., Moore, A. D., & Esses, L. (1990). The psychosocial sequelae of closed head injury: Effects on the marital relationship. *Brain Injury, 4*, 39–47.

Reitan, R. M., & Wolfson, D. (1985). *The Halstead-Reitan Neuropsychological Test Battery: Theory and clinical interpretation*. Tucson, AZ: Neuropsychology Press.

Reitan, R. M., & Wolfson, D. (1988). *Traumatic brain injury* (vol. 2). Tucson, AZ: Neuropsychology Press.

Reynolds, G. P., & Trimble, M. R. (1985). Adverse neuropsychiatric effects of anticonvulsent drugs. *Drugs, 29*, 570–581.

Richards, P. M., & Ruff, R. M. (1989). Motivational effects on neuropsychological functioning: Comparison of depressed versus non-depressed individuals. *Journal of Consulting & Clinical Psychology, 57*(3), 396–402.

Rimel, R. W., Giordani, B., Barth, J. T., Boll, T. J., & Jane, J. A. (1981). Disability caused by minor head injury. *Neurosurgery, 9*, 221–228.

Robinson, R. G., Starr, L. B., Kubos, K. L., & Price, T. R. (1983). A two-year longitudinal study of post-stroke mood disorders: Findings during the initial evaluation. *Stroke, 14*, 736–741.

Rogers, D. (1987). Neuropsychiatry. *British Journal of Psychiatry, 150*, 425–427.

Rosenthal, M., & Geckler, C. (1986). Family therapy issues in neuropsychology. In D. Wedding, A. M. Horton, Jr., & J. Webster (Eds.), *The neuropsychology handbook* (pp. 325–344). New York: Springer.

Rutter, M. (1983). *Developmental neuropsychiatry*. New York: Guilford Press.

Seidman, L. J. (1983). Schizophrenia and brain dysfunction: An integration of recent neurodiagnostic findings. *Psychological Bulletin, 94*, 195–238.

Shaw, E. D., Stokes, P. E., Mann, J. J., & Manevitz, A. Z. A. (1987). Effects of lithium carbonate on memory and motor speed of bipolar outpatients. *Journal of Abnormal Psychology, 96*, 64–69.

Sinyor, D., Jacques, P., Kaloupek, D. G., Becker, R., Goldenberg, M., & Coopersmith, H. (1986). Post-stroke depression and lesion location: An attempted replication. *Brain, 109*, 537–546.

Stuss, D., Ely, P., Hugenholtz, H., Richard, M., LaRochelle, S., & Poirier, C. (1985). Subtle neuropsychological deficits in patients with good recovery after closed head injury. *Neurosurgery, 17*, 41–47.

Tandon, R., & Greden, J. F. (1989). Positive and negative syndromes in schizophrenia. *American Journal of Psychiatry, 146*, 407.

Teasdale, G., & Jennett, B. (1974). Assessment of coma and impaired consciousness: A practical scale. *Lancet, 2*, 81–83.

Trimble, M. R. (1987). Anticonvulsant drugs and cognitive function: A review of the literature. *Epilepsia*, 1987, *28*(Suppl. 3), S37–S45.

Trimble, M. R. (1988). Cognitive hazards of seizure disorders. *Epilepsia, 29*(Suppl. 1), S19–S24.

Tucker, D. M., Stenslie, C. E., Roth, R. S., & Shearer, S. L. (1981). Right frontal lobe activation and right hemisphere performance: Decrement during a depressed mood. *Archives of General Psychiatry, 38*, 169–174.

Van Putten, T., & Marder, S. R. (1987). Behavioural toxicity of antipsychotic drugs. *Journal of Clinical Psychiatry, 48*, 13–19.

Volkow, N. D., Wolf, A. P., Van Gelder, P., Brodie, J. D., Overall, J. E., & Cancro, R. (1987). Positive and negative subtypes of schizophrenia. *American Journal of Psychiatry, 144*, 1367–1368.

Walker, E., & Harvey, P. (1986). Positive and negative symptoms in schizophrenia: Attentional performance correlates. *Psychopathology, 19*, 294–302.

Walker, E. F., Harvey, P. D., & Perlman, D. (1988). The positive/negative symptom distinction in psychoses: A replication and extension of previous findings. *Journal of Nervous & Mental Disease, 176*, 359–363.

Weller, M. P. (1985). Head injury-organic and psychogenic issues in compensation claims. *Medical Science & Law, 25*, 11–25.

White, J. M., & Rumbold, G. R. (1988). Behavioural effects of histamine and its antagonists: A review. *Psychopharmacology, 95*, 1–14.

chapter 9

Psychogenic Factors Influencing Neuropsychological Performance:
Somatoform Disorders, Factitious Disorders, and Malingering

C. MUNRO CULLUM,
ROBERT K. HEATON,
and IGOR GRANT

Despite the well-established sensitivity of many neuropsychological tests and test batteries to cerebral dysfunction, the validity of neuropsychological evaluations nevertheless is also very dependent upon the patients' levels of motivation and effort during the testing process. If a patient has not put forth adequate effort, his or her results may well be within the "impaired" range yet are not valid indications of the presence and degree of impaired brain functions. In the majority of cases referred for assessment, it is in the patient's best interest to perform well (as in the case of the recovering head injury patient who wishes to return to work). There nevertheless remains a significant minority of patients referred for testing who may not want to, or may not be able to, perform to the best of their abilities. Some of these individuals may be consciously faking deficits to achieve some obvious gain (e.g., monetary compensation in litigation cases), whereas others may suffer from nonorganic psychiatric disorders that result in neurological symptomatology.

The forensic neuropsychologist is all too familiar with the question "Isn't it *possible*, Doctor, that the patient may have consciously or unconsciously exaggerated or even feigned his or her deficits on your tests?" The final answer to this question, albeit following appropriate qualification by the expert witness, is 'yes.' In any neurobehavioral evaluation, the possibility of faking or exaggerating symptoms is present and should be recognized. The likelihood of a feigned or exaggerated performance in any given case must be determined by the clinical neuropsychologist as part of his or her interpretation of the results. This interpretation requires all available data pertaining to the patient, including the purpose of the testing, the referral source (and the patient's relation to it), the past psychiatric and neuromedical history of the patient, the nature of the injury and the presenting complaints, behavioral observations made during testing, the patterns of performance across and within the neuropsychological tests, personality assessment results, and results of any previous testing.

To address the question of whether the test results have been faked or exaggerated, neuropsychologists should be familiar with various factors and disorders that may affect patients' test-taking behavior, as well as with aspects of the test findings themselves that suggest invalidity.

In this chapter we review personality and other factors that may result in suboptimal test-taking effort. Although affective disorders and schizophrenia are sometimes associated with neuropsychological impairment, our focus here is on nonorganic conditions that more typically involve physical symptoms as primary presenting complaints: somatoform disorders, factitious disorders, and malingering. We refer the reader to Finlayson and Bird (this volume) for a discussion of the impact of psychopathology on neuropsychological testing. A second goal of this chapter will be to review the available research concerning the detection of exaggerated or feigned deficits on neuropsychological testing. Finally, we present case examples to illustrate methods that neuropsychologists can use to help identify invalid test results.

SOMATOFORM DISORDERS

According to the DSM-III-R (American Psychiatric Association, 1987), this is a class of psychiatric syndromes in which physical symptoms having no identifiable organic origin represent the presenting complaint. Although the precise mechanisms involved in the development and maintenance of these disturbances are not well understood, the presumed etiology of the physical symptoms lies in underlying psychological factors. By definition, the symptoms displayed represent unconscious processes that are *not* under voluntary control. We will briefly discuss two of the major types of somatoform disorders that may have particular relevance with regard to neuropsychological test performance and interpretation.

Somatization Disorder

This disorder involves multiple somatic complaints for which no physical etiology can be found. It is most frequently diagnosed in women (the reported prevalence is approximately 2%), and starts early in life (Cloninger, Reich, & Guze, 1975). Repeated visits to numerous physicians, often including many hospitalizations and even surgeries over the course of several years, are common. The complaints generally have a dramatic, attention-getting quality (histrionic personality disorder often is present) and tend to be described in vague and chronologically complicated terms. Patients with this disorder often consult general medical practitioners or specialists other than psychiatrists or psychologists because of the nature of their complaints and because they may have a history of actual physical disorders concomitant with the somatization disorder.

To qualify for a DSM-III-R diagnosis of somatization disorder, a patient must display a history of at least 13 of 35 listed physical symptoms for several years, beginning before age 30. There also cannot be any identifiable organic etiology for the symptoms. The complaints typically include pseudoneurologic or conversion symptoms, gastrointestinal complaints, psychosexual difficulties, cardiopulmonary symptoms, pain, and female reproductive symptoms. Also known as Briquet's syndrome, the patients' dramatic but vague polysymptomatic complaints are sometimes referred to as an "organ recital." Even though symptoms may wax and wane, the overall clinical picture tends to remain stable over time (Perley & Guze, 1962).

Conversion Disorder

Like somatization disorder, conversion disorder involves the presentation of a loss or alteration in physical functioning. In addition, the diagnosis requires the clinician's judgment that psychological factors are etiologically involved in the production of the symptom(s). Some of the more common symptoms are "pseudoneurological" in nature. As in the case of the more pervasive somatization disorder, by definition the symptoms are not under voluntary control, even though environmental factors may affect their manifestation. Conversion disorder differs from somatization disorder in that the symptoms are fewer and tend to be more circumscribed, even though conversion symptoms are rarely found in isolation (Pincus & Tucker, 1985). In addition, bona fide physical symptoms are not infrequently observed in patients with conversion symptoms. Beyond the fact that the presence of conversion need not exclude concurrent physical illness, Slater's (1965) 9-year follow-up of diagnosed conversion found that 28 of 85 persons so diagnosed eventually developed significant medical problems that, in retrospect, might have explained the "conversion".

A past history of psychosomatic symptoms is almost universally present, and the absence of such a history may even make the diagnosis suspect (Pincus & Tucker, 1985). Specific prevalence estimates for conversion disorder are lacking, although one survey of 500 male and female psychiatric outpatients noted that 24% of the cases experienced conversion at some time in their course (Guze, Woodruff, & Clayton, 1971).

FACTITIOUS DISORDER

This diagnostic category pertains to the presence of physical or psychological symptoms, without a detectable organic etiology, that apparently are under the conscious control of the individual. Factitious disorders do not involve obvious gain or have a readily apparent external goal, in contrast to malingering, which we discuss below. In factitious disorder, the only "goal" is to have the symptom or set of symptoms and to adopt the role of "patient."

DSM-III-R divides the factitious disorders into "chronic factitious disorder with physical symptoms" and "chronic factitious disorder with psychological symptoms." In chronic factitious disorder with physical symptoms (Munchausen syndrome), there commonly is an extensive history of medical contacts and hospitalizations, and when consistently negative medical results are obtained, new symptoms may emerge. These individuals may spend much of their lives gaining entry or attempting to gain entry into hospitals. Precise prevalence estimates for this class of disorders are unavailable, and the diagnosis itself can be difficult because of concomitant bona fide physical disorder(s).

Chronic factitious disorder with psychological symptoms (Ganser syndrome) is characterized by "approximate answers" and a strange pattern of cognitive impairment. For example, a patient might miss the current date by several days, be off as to the time of day by several hours, name the wrong month (February or April instead of March), miss simple calculations by a few digits, misidentify a close relative, or forget his or her telephone number or address while retaining an excellent memory of less overlearned material.

MALINGERING

Malingering refers to voluntary production or exaggeration of symptoms or disability. As in factitious disorder, the symptoms may be physical or psychological in nature. It is customary not to consider malingering a diagnosable psychiatric disorder, because, like lying, this activity is under conscious, voluntary control and is directed toward some objective that is readily understood (e.g., a car accident victim might feign paralysis or amnesia in order to gain a large settlement). In practice, however, malingering tends to be associated with certain psychopathological disorders and traits (e.g., antisocial personality, mixed personality disorders, and substance abuse). Furthermore, psychologically determined physical symptoms sometimes have both volitional and nonvolitional elements, as in the case of a soldier developing paralysis prior to battle.

GAIN

In the language of classical psychoanalysis, two forms of "gain" are obtained from psychologically determined physical symptoms. Primary gain is the reduction of anxiety generated by unconscious conflict. Secondary gain describes the psychosocial benefit—escape from an intolerable situation— of the symptom that is produced. Frequently, the term "secondary gain" is used (inappropriately) to describe consciously sought benefits. We propose to use the simple term "gain," irrespective of whether the benefit is conscious or unconscious. It then follows from our use of this term that all psychologically determined physical symptoms involve gain. When symptoms are part of somatoform disorders, the gain, which is some combination of anxiety reduction, symbolic communication, and psychosocial readjustment, is unconsciously determined. In malingering, the gain is consciously understood and sought.

SYMPTOM PERSISTENCE

How long symptoms persist depends partly on their etiology. Simple conversion symptoms tend to have a remission rate of up to 70% on long-term follow-up (Carter, 1949; Ljungberg, 1957). At the same time, the longer a conversion symptom persists, the less the likelihood of remission. Symptoms that are part of a somatization (Briquet's) disorder might disappear, but will tend to be replaced by others. Feigned symptoms of malingering usually diminish once the gain is achieved, but this is not always true.

In a setting of protracted litigation and repeated evaluation some individuals develop learned symptoms—that is, the symptoms gradually become woven into their self-image. This can occur no matter what the underlying etiology of the symptoms. For example, in order to build a strong case for a patient being disabled as a result of a brain injury, the attorney must clearly document the individual's acquired deficits to the court. To do so requires (typically) multiple evaluations by neurologists, psychologists, psychiatrists, and neuropsychologists, and then the deficits must be portrayed to the court in a manner that leaves little doubt as to the impaired status of the patient. Thus, the patient is frequently being confronted with data from numerous sources attesting to his or her level of impairment, and is also being asked to demonstrate and justify that impairment in the various medicolegal contexts.

Even though a patient may have no conscious awareness of a desire or tendency to exaggerate deficits, the repeated exposure to evaluations and testimony regarding level of impairment is likely to have a significant impact on the patient's self-perceptions. In many cases, therefore, the process of litigation may promote an increased focus on the patient's now-public deficits—possibly when in fact the deficits are not so severe as they are being portrayed. An analogy is the child who is constantly referred to as "stupid" by his or her parents; even though the child may not in fact be below average in intelligence, constant exposure to such a belittling environment may result in an adoption of the alleged role.

DIAGNOSIS OF PSYCHOGENIC PHYSICAL SYMPTOMS

Patients with somatoform or factitious disorders, and particularly those who are malingering, may pose significant diagnostic problems for health care professionals, including neuropsychologists. Except in the case of blatantly feigned performance, careful analysis of test behavior and results is required in order to identify those patients in whom cognitive complaints may be exaggerated or fabricated. In addition, attention should be paid to patients' past psychosocial, neuromedical, and psychiatric history.

Consideration of Patient History

Neuropsychological deficits caused by psychogenic factors can often be suspected from a careful look at a patient's history. Conversion phenomena tend to have a sudden onset in the context of an interpersonal conflict that the patient feels powerless to resolve, and often about which the patient feels incapable of comment.

In addition to deriving clues from the patient's recent life history, the clinician can also note whether there have been poorly explained psychoneurological phenomena in the past, and whether the patient tends to have an impressionable, somewhat immature cognitive style. Although histrionic personality is not necessary for conversion to develop, the presence of this personality disorder may be supportive evidence. Major mood disorders may also be associated with conversion. The person with somatization disorder may reveal a history of alcohol and drug abuse syndrome or may have a family history of psychiatric disorder, for example, Briquet's syndrome (mother) or antisocial personality or alcoholism (father). There may be a parent who was chronically medically ill.

The historical antecedents to malingering may include a personality style or attitude wherein the person believes the world owes him or her a living, and a "manipulative" stance characterized by viewing other people and institutions as tools to be used for one's own purposes. In some instances, distinct antisocial tendencies might be evident, or there may be a history of substance abuse. Malingerers often have difficulties in key interpersonal relationships, unable to modulate anger or manage authority–subordinate relationships. Thus, malingering should not be viewed as simply cheating the system, but rather the culmination of a series of maladaptations and mismatches between the person's aspirations and life circumstances. Without a history that reveals the possibility of clear gain the diagnosis of malingering is not tenable.

Facts of the Case

The correlation between the severity of an initial brain insult and the severity of ultimate neurocognitive sequelae is far from perfect. Nevertheless, exclusive reliance upon neuropsychological test findings and patient reports—without verification of the nature and circumstances of an alleged brain injury—can lead to erroneous conclusions about the etiology of any observed impairment. For example, in many cases it would be a mistake to attribute severely impaired neuropsychological test performance to brain trauma in patients for whom there is no corroborative evidence of serious initial CNS injury (e.g., extensive posttraumatic amnesia and/or evidence of structural injury on brain imaging) or subsequent neurological complications (e.g., development of a subdural hematoma). Useful information about the injury itself can be sought in available accident reports, paramedic and emergency-room notes, initial hospitalization records, as well as in reports of family members and other observers.

Mental Status Findings

On mental status examination the patient with conversion typically appears curiously unconcerned with an apparently serious disability (la belle indifference). Furthermore, these patients often seem passively content during evaluation, without betraying many of the typical anxieties that people undergoing such diagnostic procedures ordinarily display.

The polysymptomatic picture of somatization disorder may be accompanied by features of histrionic or borderline personality disorder. The patient may be irritable, moody, and interpersonally manipulative. With regard to the malingerer, the mental status examination may be entirely unremarkable. The clinician might get the impression of underlying hostility and manipulativeness, but these findings are nonspecific. The key to the diagnosis remains in understanding the history of symptom evolution in the context of current circumstances—especially the likelihood of gain.

Neurological and Ancillary Examinations

Sometimes the nonanatomic nature of the deficit is an indication of conversion symptoms, for example, hemianesthesia from head to toe or a "spiral" visual field defect. In most instances, the symptoms and signs are more equivocal. Although a clear pathological sign may *rule in* a pathophysiological causation (or contribution), the *absence* of a pathological sign (e.g., an upgoing toe, a reflex change, etc.) does not necessarily mean a neurological lesion is absent. In addition, although the presence of such a sign strongly suggests neuropathology, this does not preclude the operation of symptom exaggeration.

The same applies to ancillary tests. Normally brain imaging, electrophysiological testing, or cerebrospinal fluid studies do not guarantee absence of disease; abnormal findings indicate disease that may or may not fully explain the symptoms. Nonetheless, the disparities between symptoms and some objective measures may be able to establish psychogenic causation—for example, the presence of absolutely normal visual evoked responses (VER) in patients with major visual symptoms, or somatosensory evoked responses (SSEP) and electromyography (EMG) in those with limb weakness.

NEUROPSYCHOLOGICAL FINDINGS IN PATIENTS WITH SOMATOFORM DISORDERS

Whereas a few neuropsychological studies of patients with somatoform disorders have been published, to our knowledge none has examined groups of these patients within the context of forensic–neuropsychological issues.

Somatization Disorder

In one of the few published neuropsychological studies of somatization disorder, Flor-Henry, Fromm-Auch, Tapper, and Schopflocher (1981) compared the performance of ten patients with somatization disorder with that of ten nonpsychiatric and nonneurological controls on a comprehensive battery of neuropsychological tests. Using blind clinical ratings by two neuropsychologists (who reportedly demonstrated 100% agreement), 90% of the patient group were classified as having evidence of neuropsychological abnormalities, compared with 0% of controls.

Although this represents a rare neuropsychological study of patients with somatization disorder, a number of methodological limitations exist. In addition to the small sample size and small subject-to-variable ratio, the researchers did not provide information on sampling procedures (i.e., representativeness is uncertain), and apparently did not employ specific methods or criteria to rule out organic risk factors for neuropsychological impairment (e.g., substance abuse, previous head trauma) in the hysterics. Therefore, even though the results are interesting, their generalizability is limited.

Conversion Disorder

Because conversion disorder typically involves pseudoneurological symptoms, a number of *neurological* studies of suspected conversion disorder patients have been reported in the literature, but neuropsychological studies of patients with conversion disorder are few. Because of the heterogeneous manifestation of symptoms (hemiparesis, visual disturbance, amnesia), obtaining a relatively homogeneous and representative sample is obviously difficult.

Matthews, Shaw, and Klove (1966) conducted a well-designed study of neuropsychological functioning in "pseudoneurologic" patients. The pseudoneurologic group ($n = 32$) consisted of consecutive hospital admissions who had symptoms that were strongly suggestive of a neurological disorder (e.g., paresthesias, visual difficulties, motor weakness and/or incoordination, seizurelike spells), but for whom extensive neurological evaluations were entirely normal. A demographically matched group of 32 brain-damaged subjects also was included. The brain-damaged group scored significantly worse than the pseudoneurologic group on 17 of 26 measures from the Halstead-Reitan Battery. Also, the standard cutoff on the Halstead Impairment Index classified 72% of the brain-damaged subjects and only 6% of the pseudoneurologic subjects as having a brain disorder.

In an interesting single case study, Levy and Jankovic (1983) described a patient who demonstrated a variety of conversion symptoms, including pseudoseizures, aphasia, and even coma. Using a multiple baseline method, the authors alternately administered a placebo saline or phenytoin injection. The patient was led to believe that the saline injection was the active substance (phenytoin) to which she claimed to have had adverse reactions, and the phenytoin injection was presented as a neutral substance. Following the initial (placebo) injection, the patient began displaying a variety of dose-related symptoms (as the amount of the injection was announced, the symptoms often changed or became more severe). Brief neuropsychological assessment following injection revealed significantly diminished finger oscillation speeds bilaterally, along with the development of paraphasic errors during tests of naming, repetition, and spontaneous speech. As the announced dose increased, the patient became progressively unresponsive to oral commands, and eventually to all stimuli. Interestingly, as the patient went into a pseudocoma, not only did her pain responsivity decrease dramatically, but two involuntary reflexes, the corneal reflex and the optokinetic nystagmus reflex, disappeared. During the entire procedure, the patient's electroencephalogram (EEG) was normal. Subsequent administration of phenytoin (which the patient believed was a neutral substance) resulted in no neuropsychological or neurological abnormalities.

This case illustrates the fact that "psychological" and "neurophysiological" events occur on a continuum. Certain phenomena that are traditionally regarded as "mental" can have measurable physiological and neuropsychological correlates. Conditioning of EEG alpha rhythm is perhaps the best known example, but we recognize also that neuropsychological change can occur in severe depression, and that electrophysiological change can occur in hypnosis and other trance states. This suggests that whereas some of the variation in neuropsychological performance in hysteria (conversion and dissociative disorders) might reflect unconscious or partially voluntary motivation to appear "impaired," there may also be subtle alterations in central nervous system function that are by-products or correlates of such hysterical states.

In summary, the limited available research concerning neuropsychological performance of patients with somatoform disorders has produced inconsistent findings. According to results from the Matthews et al. (1966) study, most such patients for whom an organic basis of neurological symptoms can be adequately ruled out do not show significant impairment on comprehensive neuropsychological testing. On the other hand, the case presented by Levy and Jankovic (1983) suggests somatoform symptoms can be associated with neurophysiological changes that are susceptible to the influence of personality and environmental factors. Few published psychiatric studies have addressed factitious disorders, and to our knowledge no systematic neuropsychological study of patients with these disorders has been published.

STUDIES OF FEIGNED DEFICITS ON NEUROPSYCHOLOGICAL TESTS

It is virtually impossible to identify and study *real* malingerers because such people rarely (if ever) admit that they have fabricated test results. As a consequence, investigators in this area have had to rely upon analog studies that use normal subjects who have been instructed to simulate malingering. The comparability of such subjects' performances to those of real malingerers is unknown. In addition, actual patients who exaggerate or malinger deficits may have some "real" (organically based) deficits to build upon, and exaggerated real deficits may be easier to produce and more difficult to detect than deficits that are entirely fabricated. On the other hand, patients who have real deficits may be less clever about exaggerating these and fabricating others. Another difficulty with analog studies of malingering is that, typically, the neuropsychologists who are asked to interpret the results are deprived of much potentially useful information that is available in the actual clinical situation. Usually in the analog study one or more sets of test results are sent to multiple clinicians for diagnostic ratings. What is not provided is detailed information regarding the patient's history, behavior during testing, and consistency of responding within tests. It is possible, although as yet unproven, that failing to provide these types of information may artificially put the clinician at a disadvantage in making the required diagnostic judgments.

One of the earliest published studies of the potential for faking deficits on neuropsychologial tests was that by Benton and Spreen (1961). They obtained samples of 47 college students and 23 medical patients who had no evidence or history of cerebral damage. Following a standard administration of Form E of the Benton Visual Retention Test (Benton, 1955), all subjects were given Form C under "malingering" conditions: They were instructed to perform as if they had suffered a head injury and brain damage. The results of the second administration were compared with those of a group of 48 patients who had verified cerebral damage. The researchers found that the malingering and brain-damaged groups' performances differed both quantitatively and qualitatively. The normal subjects who feigned brain damage obtained significantly *lower* (worse) total scores than their brain-damaged counterparts and evidenced more errors of distortion. The actual brain-damaged group demonstrated more errors of omission, perseveration, and size in their recall of the test stimuli. Spreen and Benton (1963) obtained similar results in a study where subjects were instructed to simulate the performance of a mentally retarded individual on the Benton Visual Retention Test.

Several similar reports pertaining to the falsification of deficits on the Bender-Gestalt test have appeared, although the results are mixed, perhaps because of differences in methodology. Bruhn and Reed (1975), for example, applied two different Bender-Gestalt scoring procedures to the test data of college students who were instructed to perform as brain-damaged persons would. When relying upon a standardized scoring system, the test results of the "malingerers" could not be discriminated from those of a group of patients with genuine brain disorders. On the other hand, when the protocols were sorted into "malingering" and "organic" groups based on qualitative evaluation by an experienced clinician, 89% of the records were correctly classified.

The aforementioned studies used single tests in attempting to differentiate feigned from brain-damaged performances. One could argue that faking deficits on a single test might be easier than faking believable deficits on an entire battery of tests. One of the means to clinically assess the likelihood of malingering on neuropsychological measures is to evaluate the consistency of results across a variety of measures and/or over repeated administrations (we discuss the latter in detail below).

Heaton, Smith, Lehman, and Vogt (1978) were the first to examine the potential for faking deficits on a comprehensive battery of neuropsychological tests. This study compared the performances of 16 volunteer malingerers and 16 head-injury patients on an expanded Halstead-Reitan Neuropsychological Test Battery (HRB) and the Minnesota Multiphasic Personality Inventory (MMPI).

Examination of the groups' mean HRB summary scores (Average Impairment Rating and Halstead Impairment Index) and Wechsler Adult Intelligence Scale (WAIS) IQ scores indicated that both groups obtained scores that suggested similar levels of overall impairment. When the pattern of performances across measures was examined, however, it was noted that the malingering and head injury groups differed in their relative strengths and weaknesses. Specifically, the head injury group evidenced greater impairment on measures of abstract conceptual reasoning, cognitive shifting, and psychomotor problem solving. In contrast, the malingering group demonstrated greater deficits in sensory–perceptual and motor functioning, and on some measures of auditory attention and discrimination.

To assess clinicians' ability to detect probable malingerers, copies of all subjects' neuropsychological and MMPI protocols were sent to ten experienced neuropsychologists. The clinicians were asked to rate whether each protocol was most likely faked, or whether it was that of a nonfaking head-injured patient. The diagnostic accuracy of the clinicians was only modest, ranging from chance to approximately 20% above chance.

Stepwise discriminant function analyses of the neuropsychological and MMPI data explored whether group membership could be accurately predicted on statistical grounds. Although an unfavorable subject-to-variable ratio suggests that significant "shrinkage" of classification accuracy might occur on cross-validation, the discriminant analysis of the neuropsychological data alone yielded a perfect (100%) correct classification rate. A separate discriminant analysis of the MMPI scores resulted in misclassification of only one subject in each group, or a correct classification rate of 94%. These results suggest that pattern analysis of neuropsychological test results, particularly when supplemented with information from the MMPI, may provide important information in helping to identify suspected malingerers. As the authors pointed out, however, large-scale cross-validation of their findings is needed, although application of the discriminant function formulas to 84 additional head injury cases revealed that patients who were litigating and/or who gave strong clinical evidence of exaggerating deficits were much more likely to be classified as malingering (Heaton et al., 1978).

In a more recent study, Goebel (1983) attempted to extend the findings of Heaton et al. (1978). This study examined the performance of a heterogeneous group of 52 brain-damaged patients in comparison with performances of a normal control group ($n = 50$) and four additional normal groups (total $n = 152$) who were instructed to feign nonspecific, right, left, and diffuse brain damage on the HRB. The results indicated that the patient group performed at a significantly lower level than the control group and combined faking groups on the majority of tests, and that the malingering group was not distinguishable from controls overall. The subgroups that were asked to fake different types of brain damage did not produce different results. In a "blind" clinical review of the test protocols, Goebel correctly classified 94% of the subjects with respect to presence or absence of brain damage.

Although Goebel (1983) used these findings to claim that it is very difficult for neurologically normal subjects to successfully feign brain damage on neuropsychological testing, several methodological limitations preclude drawing firm conclusions from the results. For example, whereas the brain-damaged group performed more poorly than the members of the faking groups, the patients were rather severely impaired on the average, and were older and less educated than the members of the faking groups. Although subject demographic data were not included on the test protocols, the clinician was aware of the demographic differences in his subject groups; such differences could well have contributed to the discrimination process. In addition, most of the subjects did not produce test results that are in the "impaired" range. The problem here is that it is of little interest to determine whether impaired results from brain-damaged patients can be discriminated from normal protocols. The design of this study, therefore, failed to address the essential questions of whether "real" and feigned neuropsychological deficits are different, and whether neuropsychologists can discriminate one from the other.

Using the discriminant function formulae of Heaton et al. (1978), Thompson and Cullum (1991) examined two groups of clinical patients, one that was judged by the examiners to have put forth adequate effort on neuropsychological evaluation, and one judged to have not put forth adequate effort. All patients were involved in litigation or seeking disability benefits. The discriminant equations using neuropsychological test scores or MMPI scales were unable to distinguish these groups. However, several individual test results showed some promise along these lines, including measures of sensory-perceptual, learning, and memory abilities.

In a recent small-scale investigation, Faust, Hart, and Guilmette (1988) instructed children ($n = 3$) to fake deficits on a large battery of neuropsychological tests. The researchers gave no specific instructions regarding the nature of faking, although they asked the children (aged 9–12) not to be obvious, and offered an additional financial incentive for successful (undetected) faking. The results of one of the cases, along with a brief history (depicting the patient as having had a head injury with brief loss of consciousness) were sent to 240 psychologists listed in the National Register of Health Care Providers as offering neuropsychological services. Of the 77 psychologists who responded, none judged any of the three cases to be malingering. These results are obviously limited in generalizability, as the authors note, because of the small sample size. The results also may have been affected by bias produced by the low response rate of the clinical judges. Furthermore, fewer than 10% of respondents had completed postdoctoral training in neuropsychology. Nevertheless, these analog findings are consistent with previous ones (Heaton et al., 1978) in suggesting that detection of feigned neuropsychological deficits may not be easily accomplished when based on test scores and brief history alone (also see Faust, Hart, Guilmette, & Arkes, 1988; Franzen, Iverson & McCracken, 1990).

Simulated Amnesia

In a review of the literature on genuine and simulated amnesia, Schacter (1986b) commented that even though amnesia is a widely researched clinical entity, relatively little is known regarding the nature of simulated amnesia. Trankell (1972) has suggested that the nature of memory content may be useful in identifying false memories. For example, he reports that actual memories typically contain more sensory and context-related detail than fabricated ones. In another investigation Schacter (1986a) asked experienced clinicians to study subjects' verbal descriptions of their retrieval attempts and to judge whether subjects were genuinely amnesic or simulating amnesia. As has been found with other studies using neuropsychological test results, the judges' classification rates were not different from chance.

Subjects in the Schacter (1986a) study were also asked to assess their ability to remember forgotten material if they were provided with adequate cues. Not surprisingly, it was found that both the genuinely forgetful and simulating groups felt least likely to remember if simply given more time for recall, whereas they felt they would be more likely to recall information with the provision of cues, and *most* likely if given a recognition format. However, the simulators rated themselves as less confident than the genuinely forgetful subjects that they could recall a target even if given cues or a recognition trial.

Another means by which the simulation of amnesia has been studied is by comparing groups' recall and recognition abilities with the performance level that would be expected on the basis of chance alone (e.g., see Pankratz, 1983). Brandt, Rubinsky, and Lassen (1985) reported that a group of college students asked to fake amnesia demonstrated a level of performance similar to that of groups of head injury and Huntington's disease patients on a free recall word list task. On a subsequent yes–no forced recognition trial, however, the faking group demonstrated chance-level performance, whereas both patient groups obtained above-chance scores. Although the faking group in this study was small ($n = 10$) and only three of the 10 subjects performed significantly below chance on the recognition trial, the results suggest that performance at or below the chance level on recognition tasks may be suggestive of an exaggerated or feigned performance (see also Pankratz, 1983).

In a recent investigation of qualitative aspects of simulated amnesia, Wiggins and Brandt (1988) compared a group of subjects asked to simulate amnesia, a group of nonsimulating controls, and a group of genuinely amnesic patients. Using an implicit memory paradigm, they found that all three groups demonstrated clear priming effects on a stem-completion task. On an explicit memory task (word list recall), the simulators' total scores were lower than those of controls, but superior to those of the amnesic group. In addition, both the control and simulator groups displayed typical primacy and recency recall effects, whereas the genuine amnesics demonstrated only a recency effect. On a delayed forced-choice recognition task, the simulators obtained lower total scores than either the control or memory-disordered group. On the recognition task, fewer than 2% of controls and 8% of the memory-disordered subjects had scores at the chance level, in comparison to almost 21% of the simulators.

Overall, the results of the studies on simulated amnesia suggest that although below average performance on memory tests in general is not difficult for simulators to achieve, qualitative or pattern differences in memory test performance may be useful in the discrimination of simulated and nonsimulated amnesia. In particular, the data suggest that most simulators are not aware that cued recall and recognition formats after free recall improve the performance of most memory impaired persons (see Butters & Miliotis, 1985; Squire & Butters, 1984). Additional analysis of qualitative patterns of memory-test performance using data from patients with known memory disorders may also be helpful (e.g., see Brandt, 1988; Rawling & Brooks, 1991).

SPECIFIC TECHNIQUES FOR ASSESSING
FUNCTIONAL COMPLAINTS

Lezak (1983) has described several brief tests, originally developed by Andre Rey, that can be used to help assess whether patients may be faking or exaggerating neuropsychological deficits. These measures generally involve simplistic tasks administered in such a way as to suggest that they are more difficult than they appear. One popular example of this is Rey's 15-item recall task, wherein an array of easily encoded stimuli is presented, after which recall is assessed. Until recently, however, little was known about performance on this test in patients with known neurological disorders. Lee, Loring, and Martin (1991) suggest a cutoff of 7 in suggesting the possibility of a factitious memory disorder, although more studies in this area are needed. The underlying assumption is that poor performances on easy tasks may be indicative of faking or exaggeration.

The symptom validity test procedure (Binder & Pankratz, 1987; Pankratz, 1988; Pankratz, Fausti, & Peed, 1975) is a similar measure that was devised to assess the validity of patients' complaints of sensory deficits by examining patients' responses on a 100-item forced choice format. Performances much below chance reportedly suggest a functional etiology; this format may be modified to assess other complaints (Hiscock & Hiscock, 1989; Lezak, 1983).

Binder and colleagues (e.g., Binder, 1990; Binder & Willis, in press) have developed a standard symptom validity testing procedure, the Portland Digit Recognition Test. This involves digit recognition procedures using a series of 5-digit numbers, with a distractor task prior to forced-choice recognition. Initial studies have shown some promising results in detecting motivational difficulties among some minor head injury patients seeking compensation (Binder & Willis, in press). This task is somewhat lengthy, however, and, as with other similar measures, the results may not be clinically useful in the absence of grossly feigned results (i.e., a response error rate that is well below chance).

Using a battery of standard neuropsychological measures, Bernard (1990) examined groups of college students instructed to feign cognitive deficits. As has been found previously (e.g., Heaton et al., 1978), malingering subjects consistently performed worse than controls, and the majority of subjects were correctly classified using discriminant function analysis. It was noted that feigned memory deficits were not grossly exaggerated, and may be difficult to identify clinically. Consistent with the work of Brandt (1988), it was found that recognition performance was particularly affected, compared with free recall. Interestingly, in this sample, the Rey 15-item test was not found to be useful in distinguishing malingerers from controls, although it was pointed out that test order may have affected this result.

Overall, such techniques are interesting and may have potential for helping to detect exaggerated or feigned neuropsychological deficits in a limited percent of cases. However, as yet there is little available research documenting their effectiveness in this regard, and it appears that symptom validity procedures have greater specificity than sensitivity. In addition to using these techniques, clinicians must carefully evaluate patients' behaviors, histories, and neuropsychological results within and across measures. For a current review of malingering studies in clinical neuropsychological assessment, see Franzen et al. (1990).

MALINGERING AND THE MMPI

Although the MMPI is not a neuropsychological test, it is often used in neuropsychological evaluations and can be helpful in identifying faking or exaggerated responses. Extremely elevated scores on the F scale, for example, may indicate an amplification of complaints, and the F minus K index (using raw scores) is also useful in assessing invalid response styles (Hathaway & Meehl, 1951). Graham (1987) notes that the "typical" malingering profile has a saw-toothed appearance, with spikes on scales F, 2, 4, 6, and 8. Additional subscales have been derived from the MMPI to characterize further the nature of patients' complaints, including the Obvious and Subtle subscales (Wiener, 1948), the Test–retest index (Greene, 1979), and the Dissimulation scale (Gough, 1954).

Although the literature pertaining to faking on the MMPI is extensive (see Franzen et al., 1990), only a few studies have examined the profiles of individuals attempting to fake brain damage in the context of a neuropsychological evaluation. In the Heaton et al. (1978) study, the malingerers produced more globally elevated MMPI profiles, with mean scores on 7 of 13 scales being significantly higher than those of the actual head injury group. The head injury patients demonstrated significant elevations (above $T = 70$) only on scales 2 and 8, a pattern that tends to be characteristic of such groups (Cullum & Bigler, 1988). Thus, within the context of a neuropsychological evaluation, the MMPI may provide additional information that can be useful in identifying potential malingerers. On the other hand, a normal MMPI profile, and even a "defensive" pattern of results on the MMPI validity scales, does not necessarily argue against malingering on neuropsychological testing. Although some malingerers may display general tendencies to exaggerate pathology on both neuropsychological and personality measures, others may deny psychopathology but exaggerate neurological disability.

SUMMARY OF RESEARCH ON MALINGERING

In summary, it appears that the detection of feigned or exaggerated deficits can be more difficult than is typically acknowledged. Although this point is of critical importance to neuropsychological test interpretation, there has been surprisingly little systematic research devoted to the detection of invalid test results.

The research described in the previous sections provides no adequately validated (and especially *cross-validated*) guideliness that have both sensitivity and specificity for detecting exaggeration or faking on standard neuropsychological test batteries. However, it seems that sensorimotor tests may be especially vulnerable to faking, and that higher level cognitive deficits may be somewhat more difficult to feign. Assessment of performance patterns on measures of learning and memory may also be useful in detecting malingering or exaggerated deficits. Obviously, however, more research is needed in this area.

Although this specific issue has not yet been thoroughly investigated, the detection of malingering may be enhanced with the use of batteries of neuropsychological tests that contain groups of instruments known to measure common constructs. Potentially, indices of consistency of performances across related tests may help identify unreliable (and therefore invalid) performances within any single evaluation. Consistency of performances across multiple neuropsychological evaluations also can be an important indication of reliability of responding. We discuss this at some length below.

In the next section, we present three cases in which a malingered or otherwise invalid performance was suspected, and we discuss the nature of each individual's performance that led to our conclusions.

CASES OF SUSPECTED MALINGERERS

The data presented in the following cases are based on actual performances of head injury patients who were involved in litigation. However, we have made minor adjustments to the test scores and histories to ensure anonymity.

All of these patients had multiple neuropsychological evaluations, a common occurrence in litigation cases; that is, the plaintiff and the defense

attorneys (and sometimes the treating physicians) frequently obtain independent neuropsychological evaluations and opinions. Often there is
considerable (although rarely total) overlap in the tests used. For example,
many neuropsychologists use the WAIS-R and HRB as a core battery and
add various supplemental tests of memory, aphasia, and so on.

Whenever there has been previous testing, the neuropsychologist should
obtain the results and consider them in relation to those of the current
evaluation. There are three major reasons for this. First, it is important to
consider practice effects on repeated testings. In the absence of any real
change in the patient, performances on many tests will tend to be better
on the second and subsequent administrations because of the previous
exposure to the test stimuli and procedures (i.e., due to learning). When
this has occurred, in the absence of confounding factors, the earlier result
may be the more valid indication of the patient's actual ability in question
because the later one(s) may overestimate that ability.

The second reason for obtaining and considering the results of all
testings is that the pattern of differences on the testings may reflect real
(organically based) changes in the patient. The most common example of
this in litigation cases is when the initial testing was performed relatively
acutely after a head injury or other brain insult, and later testings occurred
after at least partial recovery of brain function. In this situation, results of
the later testing (adjusted for practice effects) would represent the more
valid indication of the patient's ultimate level of functioning and of any
permanent sequelae of the injury. Furthermore, a history of multiple risk
factors for neuropsychological impairment (e.g., learning disability, substance
abuse, or earlier head trauma, in addition to the injury in question) and
a clear pattern of recovery (total or partial) demonstrated on multiple
testings can help establish which abilities were affected by the injury in
question. Similarly, a decline over serial evaluations may suggest the influence
of nonneurological factors, providing no new neurological risk factors
have arisen.

The final reason for considering results of multiple testings is to help
detect possible unreliable responding by the patient. If a patient (consciously
or unconsciously) puts forth less than optimal effort on neuropsychological
testing, we think it is highly likely that this will affect the *consistency* of
results across multiple evaluations. To produce consistent (but exaggerated
or feigned) results, the patient would have to replicate the same levels of
inadequate effort across multiple tests and time periods. We propose that
this would be difficult to accomplish, especially on lengthy (6- to 8-hour)
test batteries and when long test–retest intervals are involved. Although
this hypothesis has not yet been subjected to systematic research, we believe
that a consideration of response consistency over multiple evaluations is

apt to be one of the most powerful techniques available to neuropsychologists for detecting invalid test results.

The three patients discussed below were all seeking compensation for alleged neuropsychological deficits suffered as a result of traumatic head injuries. All but one had initial testing relatively acutely after an injury, when additional spontaneous recovery could still occur. None had any evidence of complications (e.g., seizures, chronic subdural hematoma, infection, hydrocephalus) that might cause worsening of the patient's functioning over time. Thus, we expected successive neuropsychological evaluations to show improvement (due to recovery and/or practice effects) or no significant change in the patients.

To facilitate analysis of these patients' results across their multiple evaluations, we calculated the baseline minus follow-up differences scores of 126 neurologically normal individuals who had been tested twice using the same comprehensive battery of neuropsychological tests. These data are part of an ongoing study of the test–retest reliability of an expanded HRB. (The detailed results of that project will be published elsewhere.) The sample comprised 86 males and 40 females, with a mean age of 43.8 years (SD = 19.6) and a mean educational level of 12.1 years (SD = 3.25). The mean test–retest interval was 5.5 months (SD = 2.5). Using the performance of this sample, we will indicate when the changes in the patients' scores over successive evaluations fall outside 95% of the controls; that is, we will identify those scores that improve or decline beyond the level of at least 95% of our control sample. Furthermore, when 26% or more of the patients' test scores show statistically significant change in either direction these changes (when compared to the performance of the control sample on the entire battery) strongly suggest either genuine improvement or worsening of the patient, or a nonreliable performance. Finally, discrimination among the latter possibilities is based upon the nature (direction and consistency) of the changes observed.

Case 1

This patient was a 35-year-old right-handed male college graduate who was involved in litigation concerning an alleged head injury suffered in a motor vehicle accident. By the patient's report, he had no history of prior neurological insult, learning disability, major psychiatric disorder, or substance abuse. There was a question as to whether the head injury involved a loss of consciousness, although the patient claimed that he did not recall the impact. His earliest reported memory following the incident was within several minutes of the injury. The patient claimed that several hours later, he developed pains in his head, neck, and back. Subsequently, various other symptoms arose, including memory difficulties. The results of computerized axial tomography (CT) and EEG studies were normal.

The complaints of neurocognitive deficits persisted, and about 3 years after the accident the patient completed a neuropsychological evaluation. We would expect no significant additional spontaneous recovery from the injury so long afterward. The results suggested moderate to severe cerebral dysfunction. Approximately 1 month following the initial evaluation, the patient's attorney requested a repeat testing at a different center.

Consider first the initial testing (Table 9.1). Some results are worse than we would expect after a head injury that had such mild acute sequelae (Time component of Tactual Performance Test, Trail Making Test, numerous bilateral errors on Sensory Perceptual Exam). Also, considering the overall level of impairment suggested, normal results on the Category Test and Location component of the Tactual Performance Test are atypical. Nevertheless, it would be difficult to conclude with confidence that this single set of results is unreliable or invalid.

When we compare the results of the two evaluations, however, a clearer picture emerges (Table 9.1). The patient's WAIS-R performance improved dramatically, particularly on the Verbal subtests. His Verbal IQ increased from 87 to 117, a 30-point difference well beyond expected test–retest gains. To illustrate, of the 119 subjects in Matarazzo and Herman's (1984) study of normal subjects retested on the WAIS-R at 2- to 7-week intervals, the average gain in Verbal IQ was 3.3 IQ points, and none showed increases greater than 15 points. It is particularly noteworthy that the patient's Vocabulary subtest scaled score went from 9 to 17, a substantial increase on a subtest that typically shows little or no practice effect. By contrast, the patient's Performance IQ improved by only 4 points, from 82 to 86, which is more consistent with what would be expected on the basis of practice effects (Matarazzo & Herman, 1984).

On the Category Test, the patient's initial score of 35 errors is within normal limits, although his subsequent performance 1 month later was impaired (69 errors). This much deterioration in Category Test performance is significantly greater than would be expected on the basis of the test–retest findings of the 126 subjects in our study. Moreover, this change is in the opposite direction of the changes on the Wechsler subtests. Other inconsistencies occurred on the Tactual Performance Test, where the patient showed greater than expected improvement on the first trial but actually showed some deterioration in performance (compared to the previous evaluation) on the subsequent two trials. Memory studies revealed seriously impaired results, which would be inconsistent with relatively normal functioning in routine daily situations. Also, nonverbal learning performances were highly variable across trials. The patient's MMPI at Testing 2 appeared valid and reflected severe levels of psychological distress. The validity scales

TABLE 9.1. Neuropsychological Test Performance of Patient 1

Variable	Test 1	Test 2	Difference[a]
WAIS-R Verbal IQ	87	117	+30[b]
WAIS-R Performance IQ	82	86	+4
WAIS-R Full Scale IQ	84	101	+17[b]
Information	13	15	+2
Digit Span	5	13	+8[b]
Vocabulary	9	17	+8[b]
Arithmetic	6	8	+2
Comprehension	5	10	+5[b]
Similarities	7	11	+4[b]
Picture Completion	5	10	+5[b]
Picture Arrangement	5	6	+1
Block Design	7	6	−1
Object Assembly	6	7	+1
Digit Symbol	8	6	−2[b]
Category Test (errors)	35	69	−34[b]
Trail Making Test A (sec.)	70	62	+8
Trail Making Test B (sec.)	145	115	+30
TPT Dominant (min.)	15	7	+8[b]
TPT Nondominant (min.)	9	11	−2
TPT Both (min.)	5	8	−3
TPT Memory	5	6	+1
TPT Location	5	4	−1
Speech Sounds (errors)	10	9	+1
Seashore Rhythm Test (correct)	23	23	0
Aphasia Screening Test (errors)	2	1	+1
Spatial Relations (errors)	5	6	−1
Dynamometer−dom. (Kgs.)	25	17	−8
Dynamometer−nondom. (Kgs.)	38	35	−3
Finger Tapping−dom.	42	42	0
Finger Tapping−nondom.	47	53	+6
Grooved Pegboard−dom. (sec.)	150	139	+11
Grooved Pegboard−nondom. (sec.)	140	152	−12
Sensory−Right (total errors)	14	13	+1
Sensory−Left (total errors)	17	11	+6[b]
Tactile Form Recog.−dom. (sec.)	11	15	−4
Tactile Form Recog.−nondom. (sec.)	12	10	+2

[a] A positive sign indicates improved performance, whereas a negative sign indicates worse performance on the later evaluation.
[b] indicates significant change in score beyond the range seen in 95% of 126 control subjects.

were all under $T = 70$ $(F = 62)$, yet all clinical scales except 9 and 0 were significantly elevated over $T = 70$.

Overall, this patient demonstrated "significant" changes on 27% of the 33 individual test measures that were administered in both evaluations. The test–retest data from our sample of 126 subjects indicate that this much change on the HRB is statistically quite rare in a neurologically stable person (which Case 1 should be); that is, not one of the subjects in the normative study demonstrated this much change on this many measures. Also, during the second neuropsychological evaluation, it was the examiner's impression that the patient was not putting forth his best effort at all times; some tests were readministered at this point, with highly variable results. In addition, several historical discrepancies were noted between evaluations (e.g., the patient reported higher educational and occupational accomplishments than he actually had attained). Thus, considering this patient's highly variable performances within and across neuropsychological evaluations, his misrepresentations of historical information, and litigation status, the overall impression was one of malingering, although the possibility of a conversion disorder (i.e., with unconscious motives) could not be ruled out.

Case 2

Patient 2 was a 35-year-old right-handed man with 18 years of education who reportedly suffered a head injury in a motorcycle accident. It was unclear whether the patient actually lost consciousness, although a brief period of altered consciousness was suspected based on observers' reports. The patient was not hospitalized at the time, but he contacted his family physician several days later with multiple somatic complaints. With the continuation of symptoms (and the development of additional complaints, which included memory problems), he was subsequently referred for a neurological examination. The results of the clinical examination as well as EEG were within normal limits, although neuropsychological testing performed 3 weeks following the accident was interpreted as indicating severe cerebral compromise. A cranial CT scan was normal.

The results of the initial neuropsychological evaluation (Table 9.2) do indeed suggest significant neurocognitive as well as sensorimotor impairment. As with Case 1, this patient's apparent neuropsychological impairment was surprisingly severe, given his history of an apparently mild concussion and normal results on the clinical neurological exam and neurological laboratory tests (EEG and CT). Nevertheless, there is nothing striking about his pattern of results on this single testing that would indicate an unreliable or invalid exam.

TABLE 9.2. Neuropsychological Test Performance of Patient 2

Variable	Test 1	Test 2	Test 3	Test 4	1–2 Diff.[a]
WAIS-R Verbal IQ	101	91	98	91	−10[b]
WAIS-R Performance IQ	90	77	87	81	−13[b]
WAIS-R Full Scale IQ	97	84	93	85	−13[b]
Information	9	9	10	8	0
Digit Span	9	4	12	4	−5[b]
Vocabulary	9	10	9	9	+1
Arithmetic	8	5	5	3	−3[b]
Comprehension	15	14	10	16	−1
Similarities	12	7	12	9	−5[b]
Picture Completion	10	8	6	9	−3[b]
Picture Arrangement	8	5	7	6	−3[b]
Block Design	8	6	9	6	−2[b]
Object Assembly	6	3	8	4	−3[b]
Digit Symbol	7	4	6	5	−3[b]
Category Test (errors)	80	115	70	100	−35[b]
Trail Making Test A (sec.)	40	80	50	43	−40[b]
Trail Making Test B (sec.)	114	243	118	149	−129[b]
TPT Dominant (min.)	10	10	13	11	0
TPT Nondominant (min.)	5	8	11	7	−3[b]
TPT Both (min.)	7	6	8	6	+1
TPT Memory	2	5	6	10	+3[b]
TPT Location	0	5	2	2	+5[b]
Speech Sounds (errors)	16	11	8	4	+5[b]
Seashore Rhythm Test (correct)	18	15	20	18	−3[b]
Aphasia Screening Test (errors)	2	3	3	3	−1
Spatial Relations (errors)	2	2	2	2	0
Dynamometer–dom. (Kgs.)	27	35	21	30	+8[b]
Dynamometer–nondom. (Kgs.)	23	43	44	49	+20[b]
Finger Tapping–dom.	25	31	43	50	+6
Finger Tapping–nondom.	35	45	53	55	+10[b]
Grooved Pegboard–dom. (sec.)	93	87	88	93	+6
Grooved Pegboard–nondom. (sec.)	83	79	70	77	+4
Sensory–Right (total errors)	10	8	8	9	+2
Sensory–Left (total errors)	6	5	4	6	+1
Tactile Form Recog.–dom. (sec.)	22	12	10	20	+10[b]
Tactile Form Recog.– nondom. (sec.)	18	9	11	7	+9[b]

[a] A positive sign indicates improved performance, whereas a negative sign indicates worse performance on the later evaluation.
[b] indicates significant change in score beyond the range seen in 95% of 126 control subjects.

A second comprehensive neuropsychological evaluation was obtained approximately 2 years later, with two additional evaluations performed as a consequence of the patient's involvement in litigation regarding his head injury (Table 9.2). If one assumes that the patient had a significant brain injury in the accident, his worst neuropsychological performances would be expected in the initial evaluation, when some relatively acute (and potentially reversible) impairment might be present. The expected finding across subsequent testings would be initial "real" improvement (beyond what would result from practice effects) followed by considerable stability in performance from Test 2 through Test 4.

Comparing the results from Tests 1 and 2, we see that the patient obtained scores that were markedly different on 21 (64%) of the 33 individual test measures administered (excluding IQs). Moreover, these changes are inconsistent in direction and do not reflect a pattern of recovery that might occur between 1 month and 2 years following a brain injury. Excluding summary scores, 13 significant changes were in the direction of deteriorating functioning, whereas 8 were in the direction of improvement. Particularly since there was no evidence of additional neurological complications during the period between Test 1 and Test 2, both the inconsistency and the decrements in performance are highly unusual.

Other inconsistencies can be seen in this patient's performance over the various evaluations; the increase, then decrease, then increase in Category Test errors and Trail Making Test times, and the extreme variability in grip strength. In addition, the examiner during the third testing noted that the patient did not appear to exert his best effort on many tests. When the patient was retested on some of the same measures during that examination, his performance was often highly variable. For example, when initially presented with a story memory task, the patient forgot 25% of the information he originally learned, which is suggestive of a mild verbal recall deficit. In contrast, his recall on a second story memory task was above average. MMPI results obtained during the third evaluation seemed to indicate prominent, multiple somatic complaints, mild depression, and some manipulative, and acting-out tendencies.

In summary, across his four neuropsychological evaluations Patient 2 showed a grossly inconsistent pattern of performance that cannot be explained by practice effects or any likely changes in his neurological status.

Case 3

This patient was 26 years old when he sustained a closed head injury in an industrial accident. He was right-handed and had completed 12 years of formal education. He was reportedly unconscious for several minutes

TABLE 9.3. Neuropsychological Test Performance of Patient 3

Variable	Test 1	Test 2	Test 3	1–2 Diff.[a]	1–3 Diff.
WAIS-R Verbal IQ	87	73	73	−14[b]	−14[b]
WAIS-R Performance IQ	81	62	77	−19[b]	−4[b]
WAIS-R Full Scale IQ	83	66	73	−17[b]	−10[b]
Information	5	6	6	+1	+1
Digit Span	6	3	5	−3[b]	−1
Vocabulary	10	8	6	−2	−4[b]
Arithmetic	6	7	4	+1	−2
Comprehension	9	4	4	−5[b]	−5[b]
Similarities	12	3	6	−9[b]	−6[b]
Picture Completion	5	3	3	−2[b]	−2[b]
Picture Arrangement	4	4	4	0	0
Block Design	8	4	9	−4[b]	+1
Object Assembly	10	4	8	−6[b]	−2
Digit Symbol	9	2	8	−7[b]	−1
Category Test (errors)	90	128	99	−38[b]	−9[b]
Trail Making Test A (sec.)	30	65	39	−35[b]	−9
Trail Making Test B (sec.)	94	153	244	−59[b]	−150[b]
TPT Dominant (min.)	6	14	12	−8[b]	−6[b]
TPT Nondominant (min.)	3	9	10	−6[b]	−7[b]
TPT Both (min.)	2	6	10	−4[b]	−8[b]
TPT Memory	3	5	6	+2	+3[b]
TPT Location	1	4	6	+3	+5[b]
Speech Sounds (errors)	32	25	23	+7[b]	+9[b]
Seashore Rhythm Test (correct)	15	10	18	−5[b]	+3
Aphasia Screening Test (errors)	4	3	2	+1	+2
Spatial Relations (errors)	2	2	2	0	0
Dynamometer–dom. (Kgs.)	44	38	40	−6	−4
Dynamometer–nondom. (Kgs.)	35	31	27	−4	−8
Finger Tapping–dominant	30	39	47	+9[b]	+17[b]
Finger Tapping–nondom.	30	37	43	+7[b]	+13[b]
Grooved Pegboard–dom. (sec.)	119	100	135	+19[b]	−16[b]
Grooved Pegboard–nondom. (sec.)	119	102	100	+17[b]	+19[b]
Sensory–Right (total errors)	9	3	9	+6[b]	0
Sensory–Left (total errors)	14	6	13	+8[b]	+1
Tactile Form Recog.–dom. (sec.)	9	15	4	−6[b]	+5[b]
Tactile Form Recog.–nondom. (sec.)	5	11	6	−6[b]	−1

[a] A positive sign indicates improved performance, whereas a negative sign indicates worse performance on the later evaluation.
[b] indicates significant change in score beyond the range seen in 95% of 126 control subjects.

at the time of the accident and subsequently developed numerous somatic complaints, reporting concentration difficulties and difficulties with other aspects of mental functioning. Magnetic Resonance Imaging (MRI) studies were unremarkable. Five months after his injury, the patient underwent the first of three neuropsychological evaluations (Table 9.3).

The results of the first evaluation reflect a variety of deficits suggestive of significant, diffuse cerebral dysfunction. Again, the level of impairment was worse than would be expected from the apparent nature of the injury and from the results of neurological evaluations. A few of the findings (on Speech Sounds Perception and Seashore Rhythm) were remarkably bad, even if one assumed a severe brain injury. However, an organic basis for the deficits certainly could not be ruled out on the basis of this pattern of findings in a single evaluation.

Approximately 2 years later, a second evaluation was conducted. This time the patient's scores on 16 of the 33 individual test measures demonstrated a marked decline, whereas those on 7 measures showed a significant improvement. On the third evaluation, approximately 1 year later, the patient demonstrated improvements on some measures since the first two evaluations, but his performance worsened on others (Trail Making Test B, Tactual Performance Test). On the first and third evaluations the patient demonstrated markedly different performances on approximately 50% of the measures. Overall, the pattern is one of significant variability, with the percentage of tests showing change (and especially worsening performance) being well beyond the expected level. In the third evaluation, the patient also was administered the California Verbal Learning Test (CVLT). The pattern of learning was uneven across trials, with inconsistent use of semantic encoding techniques. Delayed recall was poor, but recognition performance was worse, and approximately at a chance level. In comparison with previous memory studies, these results would be suggestive of a general and rather dramatic decline. As no new neurological events occurred between tests 1, 2 and 3, the variability in performances is not likely to be neurologically based.

SUMMARY

There is a strong need for additional neuropsychological studies of somatoform disorders and malingering. The few existing studies of somatization and conversion disorders suggest that neuropsychological deficits can be associated with these disorders, although further studies are needed to delineate more clearly the prevalence of these impairments and their similarities (and differences) from those manifested by nonexaggerating brain-damaged patients and malingerers. In the area of malingering, the existing research suggests that feigned deficits on a single clinical neuropsychological evaluation may be difficult to detect. However, clinical experience and existing studies provide some evidence to suggest that qualitative aspects of fakers' performances may be useful in identifying feigned results. With respect to standard comprehensive neuropsychological batteries (as frequently used in the forensic arena), more information is needed regarding patterns of performance that suggest faking. Additional factors that might be in-corporated in future investigations include the provision of data regarding behavioral observations during testing, more detailed histories that are "typical" of suspected malingerers, information regarding the nature of the suspected injury, inclusion of more clinical psychological data (e.g., MMPI results), and the incorporation of experimental neuropsychological methods into standard clinical batteries.

The three cases discussed in the previous section illustrate a previously unstudied method for detecting invalid test results. All three of the cases demonstrate highly variable neuropsychological performances over two or more evaluations. The percentage of test scores that showed marked changes between evaluations were all in the range beyond that seen in normal individuals, and beyond that which we have observed in neurologically stable patients who have undergone repeated testing (and who had no known reason to exaggerate or feign deficits). Also, the changes do not reflect a consistent pattern of improvement or deterioration in functioning. As noted, especially in the absence of new neurological events between evaluations, such marked changes in scores are likely to reflect unreliable performances. We are not suggesting that repeat evaluations should result in identical scores, because all tests are subject to measurement error and many are known to be susceptible to practice effects. However, neuro-psychologsits should become familiar with those changes in scores that depart markedly from what is normally seen in a test–retest situation. Examination of performance reliability across testings may be a powerful means by which the neuropsychologist can detect patients who are not consistently putting forth adequate effort on the examination. Careful consideration of the reported nature and severity of injury in light of neuropsychological findings is also useful in evaluating the likelihood of acquired cerebral dysfunction. Further research is necessary to refine the operational definition of "inconsistent results" on multiple testings, and to document its sensitivity to known malingering.

Finally, longitudinal studies are essential to define the natural history and long-term outcome of symptoms thought to reflect a psychogenic etiology. An excellent example of the importance of follow-up is Slater's (1965) work, reviewed earlier. That study indicated that the diagnosis of conversion need not convey a benign prognosis—almost a third of the patients developed medical disease, and many others were diagnosed as having major psychiatric disorders 9 years later. We do not have such outcome data on putative psychogenic neuropsychological impairment, but one should not exclude the possibility that a proportion of these individuals also might be at increased risk for medical or psychiatric disease.

REFERENCES

American Psychiatric Association (1987). *Diagnostic and statistical manual & mental disorders* (3rd ed., rev.). Washington, DC: American Psychiatric Association.

Benton, A. L. (1955). *The revised visual retention test: Clinical and experimental applications.* New York: Psychological Corporation.

Benton, A. L., & Spreen, O. (1961). Visual memory test: The simulation of mental incompetence. *Archives of General Psychiatry, 4,* 79–83.

Bernard, L. C. (1990). Prospects for faking believable memory deficits on neuropsychological tests and the use of incentives in simulation research. *Journal of Clinical and Experimental Neuropsychology, 12,* 715–728.

Binder, L. M. (1990). Malingering following minor head trauma. *Journal of Clinical and Experimental Neuropsychology, 4,* 25–36.

Binder, L. M., & Pankratz, L. (1987). Neuropsychological evidence of a factitious memory complaint. *Journal of Clinical and Experimental Neuropsychology, 9,* 167–171.

Binder, L. M., & Willis, S. C. (in press). Assessment of motivation after financially compensable minor head trauma. *Psychological Assessment: A Journal of Consulting and Clinical Psychology.*

Brandt, J. (1988). Malingered amnesia. In R. Rogers (Ed.), *Clinical assessment of malingering and deception* (pp. 65–83). New York: Guilford Press.

Brandt, J., Rubinsky, E. W., & Lassen, G. (1985). Uncovering malingered amnesia. *Annals of the New York Academy of Sciences, 44,* 502–503.

Bruhn, A. R., & Reed, M. R. (1975). Simulation of brain damage on the Bender-Gestalt Test by college students. *Journal of Personality Assessment, 39,* 244–255.

Butters, N., & Miliotis, P. (1985). Amnesic disorders. In K. Heilman & E. Valenstein (Eds.), *Clinical neuropsychology,* (2nd ed.; 403–451). New York: Oxford University Press.

Carter, A. B. (1949). The prognosis of certain hysterical symptoms. *British Medical Journal, 1,* 1076–1079.

Cloninger, C. R., Reich, T., & Guze, S. (1975). The multifactorial model of disease transmission: III. Familial relationship between sociopathy and hysteria (Briquet's syndrome). *British Journal of Psychiatry, 127,* 23–32.

Cullum, C. M., & Bigler, E. D. (1988). Short-form MMPI findings in patients with predominantly lateralized cerebral dysfunction: Neuropsychological and Computerized Axial Tomography–derived parameters. *Journal of Nervous and Mental Disease, 176,* 332–342.

Faust, D., Hart, K., & Guilmette, T. J. (1988). Pediatric malingering: The capacity of children to fake believable deficits on neuropsychological testing. *Journal of Consulting and Clinical Psychology, 56,* 578–582.

Faust, D., Hart, K., Guilmette, T. J., & Arkes, H. R. (1988). Neuropsychologists' capacity to detect malingerers. *Professional Psychology: Research and Practice, 14*, 508–545.

Flor-Henry, P., Fromm-Auch, D., Tapper, M., & Schopflocher, D. (1981). A neuropsychological study of the stable syndrome of hysteria. *Biological Psychiatry, 16*, 601–626.

Franzen, M. D., Iverson, G. L., & McCracken, L. M. (1990). The detection of malingering in neuropsychological assessment. *Neuropsychology Review, 1*, 247–279.

Goebel, R. A. (1983). Detection of faking on the Halstead-Reitan Neuropsychological Test Battery. *Journal of Clinical Psychology, 39*, 731–742.

Gough, H. G. (1954). Some common misconceptions about neuroticism. *Journal of Consulting Psychology, 18*, 287–292.

Graham, J. R. (1987). *The MMPI: A practical guide* (2nd ed.). New York: Oxford University Press.

Greene, R. L. (1979). Response consistency on the MMPI: The TR index. *Journal of Personality Assessment, 43*, 69–71.

Guze, S. B., Woodruff, R. A., Clayton, P. A. (1971). A study of conversion symptoms in psychiatric outpatients. *American Journal of Psychiatry, 128*, 643–646.

Hathaway, S. R., & Meehl, P. E. (1951). *An atlas for the clinical use of the MMPI.* Minneapolis: University of Minnesota Press.

Heaton, R. K., Smith, H. H., Lehman, R. A. W., & Vogt, A. T. (1978). Prospects for faking believable deficits on neuropsychological testing. *Journal of Consulting & Clinical Psychology, 46*, 892–900.

Hiscock, M., & Hiscock, C. K. (1989). Refining the forced-choice method for the detection of malingering. *Journal of Clinical and Experimental Neuropsychology, 11*, 967–974.

Lee, G. P., Loring, D. W., & Martin, R. C. (1991). *Rey's 15-item visual memory test for the detection of malingering: Normative observations on patients with neurological disorders.* Paper presented at the 19th annual meeting of the International Neuropsychological Society, San Antonio, Texas.

Levy, R. S., & Jankovic, J. (1983). Placebo-induced conversion reaction: A neurobehavioral and EEG study of hysterical aphasia, seizure, and coma. *Journal of Abnormal Psychology, 92*, 243–249.

Lezak, M. D. (1983). *Neuropsychological assessment* (2nd ed.). New York: Oxford University Press.

Ljungberg, L. (1957). Hysteria: A clinical prognostic, and genetic study. *Acta Psychiatrica Scandanavica, 32*(Suppl. 112).

Matarazzo, J. D., & Herman, D. O. (1984). Base rate data for the WAIS-R: Test–retest stability and VIQ-PIQ differences. *Journal of Consulting and Clinical Psychology, 6*, 351–366.

Matthews, C. G., Shaw, D. J., & Klove, H. (1966). Psychological test performances in neurologic and "pseudo-neurologic" subjects. *Cortex, 2*, 244–253.

Pankratz, L. (1983). A new technique for the assessment and modification of feigned memory deficit. *Perceptual and Motor Skills, 57*, 376–372.

Pankratz, L. (1988). Malingering on intellectual and neuropsychological measures. In R. Rogers (Ed.), *Clinical assessment of malingering and deception* (pp. 169–192). New York: Guilford Press.

Pankratz, L., Fausti, S. A., & Peed, S. (1975). A forced-choice technique to evaluate deafness in the hysterical or malingering patient. *Journal of Consulting & Clinical Psychology, 43*, 421–422.

Perley, M. J., & Guze, S. B. (1962). Hysteria—the stability and usefulness of clinical criteria. A quantitative study based on a follow-up of six to eight years in 39 patients. *New England Journal of Medicine, 266*, 421–426.

Pincus, J. H., & Tucker, G. J. (1985). *Behavioral neurology* (3rd ed.). New York: Oxford University Press.

Rawling, P., & Brooks, D. N. (1991). *The simulation index: A technique for detecting factitious mental impairment.* Paper presented at the 19th annual meeting of the International Neuropsychological Society, San Antonio, Texas.

Rogers, R. (Ed.), (1988). *Clinical assessment of malingering and deception.* New York: Guilford Press.

Schacter, D. L. (1986a). Feeling-of-knowing ratings distinguish between genuine and simulated forgetting. *Journal of Experimental Psychology: Learning, Memory, & Cognition, 12*, 30–41.

Schacter, D. L. (1986b). On the relation between genuine and simulated amnesia. *Behavioral Sciences and the Law, 4*, 47–64.

Slater, E. (1965). Diagnosis of "hysteria." *British Medical Journal, 1*, 1395–1399.

Spreen, O., & Benton, A. (1963). Simulation of mental deficiency on a visual memory test. *American Journal of Mental Deficiency, 67*, 909–913.

Squire, L. R., & Butters, N. (Eds.). (1984). *The neuropsychology of memory.* New York: Guilford Press.

Thompson, L. L., & Cullum, C. M. (1991). *Pattern of performance on neuropsychological tests in relation to effort in mild head injury patients.* Paper presented at the 1991 meeting of the National Academy of Neuropsychology, Reno, Nevada.

Trankell, A. (1972). *Reliability of evidence.* Stockholm: Beckmans.

Wiener, D. N. (1948). Subtle and obvious keys for the MMPI. *Journal of Consulting Psychology, 12*, 164–170.

Wiggins, E. C., & Brandt, J. (1988). The detection of simulated amnesia. *Law & Human Behavior, 12*, 57–78.

PART IV

Prognosis, Remediation, and Cost

chapter 10

Traumatic Brain Injury in Adults:
Recovery and Rehabilitation

DAVID   J.   FORDYCE

There was a marked change in the nature of brain injury rehabilitation in the 1980s. It can be characterized as a broadening of scope, an increase in intensity and duration, the substitution of new and innovative rehabilitation strategies for more traditional techniques, and an increase in rehabilitation costs and resources. These changes have been driven by clinical, social, and economic factors. The incidence of individuals surviving severe brain injury remains high. As shown below, a substantial number of these survivors live many years with significant disabilities in spite of contemporary medical practice and more traditional rehabilitation efforts. Interest in brain injury rehabilitation was kindled when new, innovative programs began to publish their methods and, to a lesser extent, preliminary results in the late 1970s and early 1980s. In addition, clearinghouse and advocacy organizations, such as the National Head Injury Foundation, have united professionals, families, and those suffering brain injury to promote better care for brain-injured patients and their families. Existing rehabilitation facilities and health care systems, and newly formed companies, developed innovative brain injury programs in response to these forces as well as their perceived profitability.

Ironically, the majority of patients surviving severe brain injury are unable to enter these programs. New rehabilitation services are typically not covered by conventional health insurance plans or government-funded systems such as Medicaid or Medicare and are often extremely costly. This state of affairs is contributing to the growing involvement of rehabilitation professionals in legal and political activities. In personal injury lawsuits rehabilitation specialists testify as to the likely long-term sequelae of a particular brain injury in a specific individual, as well as delineate the nature of appropriate rehabilitation activities, their cost, and their likely effects. This chapter attempts to summarize a small part of the literature and to discuss a few of the important issues relevant to this very difficult enterprise. As the greatest interest in brain injury rehabilitation is currently focused on head trauma, this clinical entity will be emphasized.

RECOVERY FROM BRAIN INJURY

Studies of recovery from brain injury vary along important dimensions affecting the potential validity, reliability, or generalizability of the findings. Discussions of these methodological issues are readily available (Dikmen, Reitan, & Temkin, 1983; Levin, Benton, & Grossman, 1982; Meier, Benton, & Diller, 1987; Parsons & Prigatano, 1978) and will not be discussed in detail. However, we must review certain variables that have tremendous importance.

Subject Variables

Analyses of deficit patterns and recovery characteristics are dependent on the particular population examined. In addition to demographic factors dictated by cultural or geographical region and the nature of the clinical setting in which the investigation takes place, studies will vary with respect to more explicitly defined variables such as age, sex, premorbid health, or severity and nature of the injury. The potential neuropsychological consequences of these factors suggest caution in generalizing the results from one study to a clinical population as a whole. In addition, the operation of noninjury-relevant subject variables demands the use of appropriate control groups, a feature sadly lacking in most analyses of brain injury recovery and rehabilitation. As preinjury data on the instruments utilized in assessing postinjury impairment are typically not available, a clear understanding of the nature of residual deficits from brain injury requires comparison to a similar uninjured, or differently injured, control group.

Method Variables

The specific assessment procedures employed will determine the nature of the impairments or dysfunction obtained. The relevant data, or lack thereof, have obvious implications for interpreting individual protocols as well as relevant research in the courtroom (Matarazzo, 1987). Researchers and clinicians choose a subset of the universe of measures and techniques available depending upon their specific interests, biases, and experience. Interpretations about the nature or magnitude of residual impairment and the effects of rehabilitation depend totally on the particular measures used in a study. Perhaps of greatest relevance for the issues addressed in this book are the timing of evaluations. The closer to the time of injury, the more obvious (and detectable) will be changes in behavior or psychometric performance. As chronicity lengthens, some deficits resolve, some become so subtle as to exceed our sensitivity to detect them reliably (they may or may not be clinically important), learning and adaptation occur (some negative and some positive), the potential for the patient's test performance to improve because of previous experience with a particular instrument increases, and the general long-term picture becomes more crystallized (although not fixed permanently). In addition, the traditional methods of performing psychological research center on the analysis of an abstraction of real life—average group performance. Significant results indicate that the average group performance overrides error variability or unique individual trends. Forensically, we are most concerned about an individual—not a group.

GENERAL OUTCOME FOLLOWING TRAUMATIC HEAD INJURY

The general outcome following traumatic head injury is often described in terms of broad, categorical ratings of disability or employment status. The Glasgow Outcome Scale (GOS) is the most frequently used instrument (Jennett & Bond, 1975). It divides general outcome from head injury into five categories, including death and persistent vegetative state. Of the remaining categories, severe disability is defined as a dependency on others to meet daily needs because of mental or physical handicaps, or both. Those with moderate disability are able to travel by public transportation, are capable of working within sheltered environments, and are independent in basic activities of daily living, in spite of significant functional impairments. Good recovery on the GOS reflects a resumption of "normal life" regardless of the presence of physical or neuropsychological deficits.

Although reliability statistics are seldom reported, the main criticisms of the GOS are its insensitivity to the more subtle, but quite important, posttraumatic sequelae (Brooks, Hosie, Bond, Jennett, & Aughton, 1986). Others have developed expanded ratings of dysfunction and outcome following head trauma (e.g., Livingston & Livingston, 1985; Rappaport, Hall, Hopkins, Belleza, & Cope, 1982), which do appear more sensitive to changes in function during recovery than the GOS (Hall, Cope, & Rappaport, 1985). An additional problem evident in GOS studies are the relatively brief follow-up periods employed, usually 6 months.

A significant proportion of those incurring severe head injury die in the early period of hospitalization (Table 10.1). As many deaths from severe traumatic head injury occur at the accident site (Frankowski, 1986),

TABLE 10.1. Glasgow Outcome Scale Results Following Traumatic Head Injury

Author	% of total sample					% of nonvegetative survivors		
	Dead	Vegetative	Severe disability	Moderate disability	Good recovery	Severe disability	Moderate disability	Good recovery
Bowers & Marshal, 1980[a]	36	4	8	10	42	13.3	16.7	70
Brakman et al., 1980[b]	48	2	7	16	27	14	32	54
Miller et al., 1981[c]	34	3	7	11	45	11.1	17.5	71.4
Jennett et al., 1979[d]	48	2	10	18	23	20	35	45
Jennett et al., 1979[e]	50	2	7	15	26	14.6	31.3	54.1
Jennett et al., 1979[f]	50	5	14	19	12	31	42	27
Lyle et al., 1986[g]	51	1	6	23	19	14	48	38
Teasdale & Jennett, 1976[h]	—	34	13	27	26	20	41	39
Teasdale & Jennett, 1976[i]	—	25	11	31	33	15	41	44
Teasdale & Jennett, 1976[j]	—	80	12	8	0	60	40	0
Teasdale & Jennett, 1976[k]	—	88	12	0	0	100	0	0
Levin et al., 1979[l]	—	—	—	—	—	19	44	37
Rimel et al., 1982[m]	3	0	10	49	38	11	50	39
Rimel et al., 1982[n]	0	0	0	22	78	0	22	78

[a] n = 200, chronicity = ?, Glasgow Coma Scale (GCS) ≤ 7 for ≥ 6 hours.
[b] n = 305, chronicity = 6 months, GCS ≤ 8 for ≥ 6 hours.
[c] n = 225, chronicity ≅ 1 year, GCS ≤ 8 for ≥ 6 hours.
[d] n = 593, chronicity = 6 months, GCS ≤ 8 for ≥ 6 hours.
[e] n = 239, chronicity = 6 months, GCS ≤ 8 for ≥ 6 hours.
[f] n = 168, chronicity = 6 months, GCS ≤ 8 for ≥ 6 hours.
[g] n = 159, chronicity = 2 years, GCS 7 for ≥ 6 hours.
[h] n = 172, chronicity = 3 months, best GCS: 5–7 2 to 3 days after injury. Dead & Vegetative outcomes combined.
[i] n = 80, chronicity = 3 months, best GCS: 5–7 2 to 3 days after injury. Dead & Vegetative outcomes combined.
[j] n = 36, chronicity = 3 months, best GCS: ≤ 4 2 to 3 days after injury. Dead & Vegetative outcomes combined.
[k] n = 17, chronicity = 3 months, best GCS: ≤ 4 2 to 3 days after injury. Dead & Vegetative outcomes combined.
[l] n = 27, chronicity = ≅ 1 year, admission GCS ≤ 8 patients screened for premorbid death. Nonvegetative survivors only.
[m] n = 170, chronicity = 3 months, GCS: 9–12 at admission.
[n] n = 424, chronicity = 3 months, GCS ≥ 13 at admission.

the figures in Table 10.1 underestimate the total early mortality. A very small percentage of patients remain in a persistent, vegetative state over the follow-up periods observed (maximum of 1 year). Other authors have confirmed in-hospital death rates of 35% to 50% following severe traumatic head injury (Carlsson, von Essen, & Löfgren, 1968; Fahy, Irving, & Millac, 1967; Lundholm, Jepsen, & Thornval, 1975; Lyle et al., 1986; Murray, Barlow, Teasdale, & Jennett, 1986; Overgaard et al., 1973).

Several studies have reviewed variables that tend to predict hospital death after traumatic head injury. Those most clearly associated are advancing age and measures of injury severity. Most reports indicate a general increase in the probability of posttraumatic death as age increases (Jennett et al., 1979; Miller et al., 1981; Murray et al., 1986; Teasdale & Jennett, 1976). The Glasgow Coma Scale (GCS) score at or shortly after admission is the most frequently used measure of initial severity. It ranges from 3 (deepest coma) to 15 (no coma). Although there can be considerable variability in GCS scores initially (Braakman, Gelpke, Habbema, Maas, & Minderhoud, 1980; Jennett et al., 1979), there remains a clear relationship between initial GCS scores and mortality (Bowers & Marshall, 1980; Braakman et al., 1980; Jennett et al., 1979; Miller et al., 1981; Teasdale & Jennett, 1976).

As many early clinical variables are interdependent, studies have combined these factors statistically in attempts to produce more parsimonious models for predicting mortality (Jennett et al., 1979; Lyle et al., 1986). Similar combinations of variables have been used to predict general outcome using the GOS. Murray et al. (1986) present a statistical model predicting 3-point GOS outcome (dead combined with vegetative state, moderate disability combined with good recovery). They report an overall 6-month successful classification rate of 70% based upon clinical information available 24 hours after injury. Braakman et al. (1980) describe a model predicting all five GCS categories at 6 months. The interdependence among the various predictors was highlighted by the small number chosen. The complete model included the variables of the GCS (early verbal, motor, and pupil responses), sex, and age. Again, an inaccurate GOS category was predicted 30% of the time.

Early, long-term forecasting of general outcome following traumatic head injury appears extremely difficult. In general, a measure of initial coma severity as reflected by the GCS score and/or the length of deep coma, coupled with age and perhaps the presence of other neurological signs of brainstem impairment, seem adequate indicators of injury severity. There remains tremendous variability, however, in patient outcomes for those who appear to have suffered injuries of similar severity. Lyle et al. (1986) demonstrate, for example, a full range of outcomes in patients with more than 14 days of coma, with a tendency for better outcomes in patients with less than 7 days of coma. Even a percentage of patients generating GCS scores of only 3 or 4 at 24 hours after admission purportedly made good recovery at 6 months (Bowers & Marshall, 1980; Miller et al., 1981). In all likelihood, the capacity of an individual to obtain a particular outcome on the GOS reflects many factors, only some of which relate to measures of injury severity.

Examination of Table 10.1 suggests that a large number of nonvegatative survivors of severe head trauma obtain a "good recovery." Eliminating those studies with an evaluation chronicity of only 3 months, an average of 50% (range 27% to 71.4%) of the patients reported were able to resume a "normal life." These data suggest that severe head injury does not consistently yield poor psychosocial outcome, even though all studies but one (Levin, Grossman, Rose, & Teasdale, 1979) included patients with potentially important negative prognostic features such as previous psychiatric or neurological disease, or alcoholism. Some patients achieving a "good recovery" may well have residual impairments they find distressing, and that may affect their lives in ways not captured by the GOS (i.e., cognitive impairment, emotional dysfunction, loss of friends, reduced employment status, etc.). Clearly, other measures of outcome must be obtained. Table 10.1 suggests that approximately 18% of those surviving severe traumatic head injury (11.1% to 31%) are severely impaired and totally dependent. Another 33% (16.7% to 44%) are listed as moderately disabled. Thus, approximately half show significantly reduced independence and major negative changes in life-style, presumably related to their injuries. With the exception of the Lyle et al. (1986) study, the follow-up periods are typically relatively brief, and researchers suspect that these figures may change with time. The direction of change is not entirely clear, however.

RETURN TO WORK AFTER TRAUMATIC HEAD INJURY

Vocational status is a complex measure of outcome given that many factors unrelated to brain injury can contribute to unemployment. Employment, nonetheless, remains an important index of the patient's status in society following brain injury. The literature on recovery from head injury is international. Return-to-work rates may vary as a result of cultural belief concerning work, disability and vocational rehabilitation systems, and general economic trends. The nature of the job and the degree of employer support also seem to greatly affect the potential for successful work following significant brain injury. Only studies looking at a wide range of severity levels can adequately comment on the relationship between correlates of injury severity and return-to-work potential. However, few studies delineate how many subjects were working prior to their injuries or whether premorbid personality or postinjury economic factors may have affected employment rates. Research also does not adequately address the quality of an individual's work behavior for those who are employed.

Head injury victims are often young males who may not be well established in their vocational careers. Although head injury can affect anyone, individuals from lower socioeconomic strata and unskilled laborers may be overrepresented in studied populations (e.g., Rimel, Giordani, Barth, Boll, & Jane, 1981). Minderhoud, Boelens, Huizenga, and Saan (1980) demonstrated a positive relationship between the physical demands of a job and posttraumatic vocational disability among minor head-injured patients. Rimel et al. (1981) reported a direct relationship between occupation level and return to work in mild head injury. Executives and business managers were 100% employed at 3 months in contrast to only 50% reemployment for unskilled laborers. Only a few discussions of vocational position and probability of vocational success following more severe head injuries are available (Fraser, Dikmen, McClean, Miller, & Temkin, 1988). Wrightson and Gronwall (1981) found no differences in reemployment rates for various occupational levels following mild head injury. Logically, it would seem that the more intellectually or socially demanding a particular position, the less likely a successful vocational outcome, especially after more severe injuries. Those in higher vocational positions may receive some more personal and favorable treatment by their employers, however.

The length of unemployment following injury is of obvious importance. For more mildly injured patients, the period of vocational disability can frequently last 3 months or more. Gronwall's studies (Gronwall, 1977; Gronwall & Wrightson, 1974; Wrightson & Gronwall, 1981) imply 100% vocational success at approximately 60 days for a group of mildly injured patients screened for relatively healthy premorbid histories, with the vast majority beginning work within 1 week. Rimel et al. (1981), on the other hand, demonstrated continuing unemployment of 34% at 90 days in an unselected patient population. Although Dikmen, McClean, & Temkin (1986) reported 20% full-time and 20% part-time employment rates at 1 month after mild head injury in patients with healthy premorbid histories, these figures improved to 75% and 10%, respectively, at 1 year. The authors further noted that in only one or two patients could unemployment at 1 year be attributed to head injury. Clinically, some individuals remain significantly disabled and unemployed after apparently mild head injuries. It should also be pointed out that as many as 60% will note continuing symptoms after initially returning to work (Wrightson & Gronwall, 1981).

Long-term unemployment is common a number of years after moderate to severe head injury (Table 10.2). In addition, a sizable percentage of patients are working in restricted or part-time capacities. Steadman and

TABLE 10.2. Employment Following Traumatic Head Injury

Author	Severity	n^a	Premorbid screening[b]	Chronicity[c]	% working[d]	% working with modification[d]
Minderhoud et al., 1980	mild	725	no	90 days	92	—
Rimel et al., 1981	mild	310[e]	no	90 days	66	—
Gronwall & Wrightson, 1974	mild	100	yes	≤ 60 days	100	—
Follow up				≤ 35 days	"most"	—
Gronwall, 1977	mild	320	yes	≤ 60 days	100	—
Dikmen et al., 1986	mild	20	yes	30 days	20	20
Follow up				1 year	75	10
Edna, 1987	mild	361	no	3–5 years	76	—
McLean et al., 1983	mild/mod.	20	yes	30 days	55	—
Rimel et al., 1982	mod.	113[e]	no	90 days	31	—
Merskey & Woodforde, 1972	mild/mod.	27	no	5 years	59	22
Klonoff, Snow, & Costa, 1986	wide	83	yes	2–4 years	—	78.3
Steadman & Graham, 1970	wide	415	no	30 days	51	—
Follow up				90 days	74	—
Follow up				5 years	99	—
Fraser et al., 1988	wide	48[5]	yes	1 year	—	73
Thienprasit, Fisher, & Akorn, 1985	mod./severe	68	no	1 year	35	40
Overgaard et al., 1973	mod./severe	129	no	2–3 years	52	16

Study	Severity	n[a]	Yes[b]	Time[c]	[d]		
Van Zomeren & Van Den Burg, 1985	mod./severe	57	no	2 years	58		18
Bruckner & Randle, 1972	mod./severe	88	no	5 years	40		24
Miller & Stern, 1965	mod./severe	92	no	11 years	51		38
Dye et al., 1981	mod./severe	48	yes	1–36 months	69		—
Gilchrist & Wilkerson, 1979	severe	72	no	1–15 years	39[f]		15.3[f]
Thomsen, 1974	severe	50	no	1–5 years	8		12
Weddell et al., 1980	severe	44	yes	2 years	18		36
Oddy et al., 1985	severe	43	yes	7 years	32		14
Fahy et al., 1967	severe	23[c]	no	6 years	52		30
Levin et al., 1979	severe	27	yes	1 year	—	22	—
Rusk, Block, & Lowman, 1969	severe	102	no	5–15 years	30		13
Prigatano et al., 1984	severe	18	no	2 years	—	50[g]	—
Prigatano et al., 1984	severe	17	no	1½ years	—	36[h]	—

[a] n = patients alive and nonvegetative.
[b] Yes = any exclusion of patients with premorbid psychological or neurological problems.
[c] Maximum or average time corresponding to employment data.
[d] Estimated from text and figures and including return to school and/or return to work within the home when clearly reported. "Working with modification" denotes any special circumstances such as part time, sheltered, or volunteer work. Dashes indicate data on modifications either not presented or combined with full-time employment data.
[e] All patients employed prior to injury.
[f] Unclear whether students or housewives excluded.
[g] Patients working both full and part time after rehabilitation.
[h] Patients working both full and part time.

Graham (1970) reported return-to-work (primarily previous job) rates of 51% at 30 days, 74% at 90 days, and 97% at 5 years in a large group of head trauma patients of widely varying severity. A serial study of 44 severely injured head trauma patients 2 years and 7 years postinjury indicated those employed at 2 years remained so at 7 years, whereas those initially unemployed stayed unemployed (Oddy, Coughlan, Tyerman, & Jenkins, 1985; Weddell, Oddy, & Jenkins, 1980). For those working, some upgrading did occur with 20% resuming their previous occupational status at 7 years compared to 11% at 2 years. Bruckner and Randle (1972) reported an average return-to-work time of 15 months, but with great variability (3–84 months) for those patients who were eventually employed within a follow-up period of 5 years.

The factors that contribute to unemployment following traumatic brain injury are not clearly delineated. In addition to noninjury variables, neurological, physical, cognitive, and behavioral impairments have all been linked to vocational failure (Bond, 1975; Bruckner & Randle, 1972; Gilchrist & Wilkinson, 1979; Gronwall, 1977; Levin et al., 1979; Najenson et al., 1974; Prigatano et al., 1984; Weddell et al., 1980). The importance of specific residual impairments will likely depend upon the nature of the job. Cognitive and behavioral deficits appear to have the most pervasive effect on vocational success (Bruckner & Randle, 1972; Fahy et al., 1967). Unfortunately, few studies have specifically and directly examined the causes of unemployment or vocational failure following traumatic brain injury. Levels of neuropsychological impairment correlate with unemployment rates (Fraser et al., 1988; Levin et al., 1979; Weddell et al., 1980) as do ratings of cognitive deficit (Bruckner & Randle, 1972; Gilchrist & Wilkinson, 1979). Similarly, ratings of personality change or dysfunction correlate with vocational outcome (Bond, 1975; Bruckner & Randle, 1972; Gilchrist & Wilkinson, 1979; Weddell et al., 1980). Heaton, Chelune, and Lehman (1978) have also shown significant correlations between both the degree of neuropsychological impairment (Wechsler Adult Intelligence Scale [WAIS] and Halstead-Reitan Neuropsychological Test battery) and emotional impairment (MMPI), and employment status in a large heterogeneous group of neurologically impaired patients. Experience suggests that selective severe deficits in the speed of thinking, memory functions, or behavioral control can be particularly damaging in the workplace, especially when coupled with poor personal insight. The likelihood of any or all of these problems occurring increases, of course, with the severity of injury.

Noninjury factors also likely influence return-to-work rates following head injury. These appear to be of particular importance in understanding vocational disability following milder head injuries. Age has been correlated with return-to-work rates. Although one study noted increased employment associated with greater age (Rimel et al., 1981), most have shown more unemployment with advancing age (e.g., Edna, 1987; Wrightson & Gronwall, 1981). This relationship may reflect, in part, reduced information processing associated with aging. Increasing levels of education are associated with less vocational disability (Edna, 1987; Rimel et al., 1981). Dresser et al. (1973) have demonstrated a positive relationship between tested premorbid intelligence and employability among soldiers suffering head injuries (primarily penetrating) of widespread severity. Some have felt that all disability after mild head injury is related to psychogenic factors secondary to compensation claims (Miller, 1961a, 1961b). Few studies have looked systematically at this issue, although it is clear that many who file claims or pursue litigation also return to work prior to completion of their action (e.g., Kelly, 1975). Some have found an association between legal claims and the amount of time one is absent from work following concussion (Cook, 1972). The presence of alcohol at the time of injury has also been associated with increased vocational disability (Wrightson & Gronwall, 1981).

NEUROPSYCHOLOGICAL IMPAIRMENT AFTER TRAUMATIC HEAD INJURY

Mild Head Injury

Research on recovery from mild head injury (e.g., GCS greater than 12, length of posttraumatic amnesia less than 24 hours, absence of positive neurological signs) has historically been controversial. This confusion has been substantially reduced with the recent publication of a series of methodologically improved studies. Within a few days of injury, uncontrolled studies have suggested the presence of information-processing deficits on objective neuropsychological tests for unselected mildly head injured patients (e.g., Ruesch, 1944; Ruesch & Bowman, 1945) and for those screened to eliminate premorbid neuropsychiatric dysfunction (e.g., Gronwall & Wrightson, 1974, 1975). Of more importance, fairly consistent early deficits on formal testing have been demonstrated when comparing mild head-injured patients with matched orthopedic patients (McMillan & Glucksman, 1987), nonhead-injured trauma patients (Gronwall, 1977), normal peers or relatives (Dikmen et al., 1986a, 1986b; Gentilini et al., 1985; McLean, Temkin, Dikmen, & Wyler, 1983), and normal subjects from the general population (Levin, Mattis, et al., 1987). In all these studies difficult measures of sustained attention and concentration, speed of thinking, and new learning seem most consistently affected.

A question of great importance and controversy is whether there are long-term residual neuropsychological deficits as a consequence of mild head injury. Often-cited studies reported overall very mild impairments relative to Halstead-Reitan battery clinical norms in a group of 70 mildly head injured patients seen 3 months after injury (Barth et al., 1983; Rimel et al., 1981). Not unexpectedly, there was considerable variability, with some patients showing fairly significant neuropsychological deficits and others showing none at all. The absence of an appropriate control group makes it difficult to attribute neuropsychological deficits to the recent head injury, especially given the unscreened nature of the population (e.g., 31% hospitalized for previous head injury) and the correlations between age, education, and level of neuropsychological impairment.

It now appears that the vast majority of patients without preexisting neurological or psychiatric problems will not show neuropsychological impairment when tested at least 2 months from the time of injury. In the study by Gronwall and Wrightson (1974), 85 of 90 concussed patients tested initially while in the hospital demonstrated normal auditory attention on the difficult Paced Auditory Serial Addition Task (PASAT) by 35 days. A group of ten patients who had failed an initial attempt to return to work generated normal PASAT performance no later than 54 days post-traumatically. Gronwall (1977) tested 320 patients between the ages of 14 and 55 with mild head injury. Patients whose PASAT scores improved slowly got additional cognitively oriented occupational therapy. Seventy percent of the therapy patients and 90% of the nontherapy patients generated normal PASAT performances in 2 weeks and were thus able to return to work. By 60 days, all were at work, implying normal PASAT scores, although 20% still complained of problems.

McMillan and Glucksman (1987) compared the neuropsychological test performances of 24 generally mildly injured patients at 1 week with a group of otherwise similar orthopedic patients. Those with previous psychiatric histories or who were significantly intoxicated at the time of their accidents were excluded. Of the several tests administered, only the more difficult portions of the PASAT distinguished the concussed group from orthopedic controls. Gentilini et al. (1985) tested 50 consecutive mild head-injured patients 1 month postinjury and compared their neuropsychological test performances to those of 50 peer- or relative-matched controls. Again, gross neuropsychological impairment was not demonstrated. There was a trend on four of six measures for the head-injured group to perform at lower levels than controls, but only on a visual cancellation task did this prove to be statistically significant.

McLean et al. (1983) saw premorbidly healthy patients at 3 days and 1 month from injury. Some of these patients had early neurological dysfunction and periods of posttraumatic amnesia extending beyond 3 days. Three days after injury, patients demonstrated deficits in visual-processing speed and selective attention (Stroop Test) and verbal learning (Selective

Reminding Test) relative to a matched peer control group. These deficits seemed to be evident primarily in patients who experienced a period of posttraumatic amnesia of more than 24 hours. At 1 month, the head-injured patients, on average, tended to do slightly worse than controls on these two tests, but no statistically significant differences were obtained. Dikmen et al. (1986b) tested 20 consecutive premorbidly healthy patients with mild head injury on the Selective Reminding Test and the Halstead-Reitan Neuropsychological Test Battery. One month after injury, head-injured patients tended to do less well on most neuropsychological measures relative to peer-matched controls, but statistically significant differences were obtained only for a test of auditory attention (Seashore Rhythm Test) and a measure of delayed recall from the Selective Reminding Test. In addition, scores for the head-injured population at 1 month were well within normal clinical limits. At 1 year there were no significant differences, nor apparently any general trends, between median Halstead-Reitan Neuropsychological Test Battery scores for mildly head injured patients and the peer-matched control group. The results of Levin, Mattis, et al. (1987) paralleled closely those noted above with a normalizing of neuropsychological test performance at 3 months after mild head injury in premorbidly healthy individuals.

Dencker and Löfving (1958) reported a long-term follow-up of 31 monozygotic twin pairs with one twin having suffered an apparently mild head injury at least 3 years previously (average of 10 years). The injuries are meagerly described, but appear generally mild. There was a trend for the probands to be slightly less efficient on formal neuropsychological testing relative to their partners, but only 4 of 25 measures (tests of mirror drawing, categorical sorting, prolonged concentration, and tachistocopic figure-ground discrimination) separated the twin pairs statistically. Proband and partner scores overlapped considerably, even on those measures that statistically discriminated the two groups. Extreme scores were more correlated with general intelligence than the history of injury, but the intertest correlation matrices did suggest some change in neuropsychological functioning related to the history of mild head injury. In discussing these subtle deficits, Dencker (1958) felt that they were largely inconsequential with respect to long-term living issues present some 10 years posttraumatically.

Recent comprehensive reviews of the long-term effects of mild head injury quite accurately underline the great uncertainty that remains in this literature (Binder, 1986; Levin, Eisenberg, & Benton, 1989). The study that tended to show more significant deficits at an intermediate point of time (3 months) examined an unselected population without reference to controls (Barth et al., 1983; Rimel et al., 1981). At 1 year, one study found no neuropsychological deficits apparent (Dikmen et al., 1986a), whereas at 10 years another found nonsignificant trends and a few significant differences on very difficult information-processing activities (Dencker & Löfving, 1958). Dencker and Löfving (1958) may have studied slightly more impaired patients and did not exclude patients with preceding or ensuing neurological or psychological disease. Clearly, simply having a mild head injury does not automatically yield residual neuropsychological impairment. For example, otherwise healthy, active amateur and professional boxers (with careers as long as 13 years) have demonstrated no major evidence for neuropsychological impairment (Brooks, Kupshik, Wilson, Galbraith, & Ward, 1987; Levin, Lippold, et al., 1987).

The studies reviewed above are group analyses that may obscure individual trends and outcomes. The neuropsychological consequences of any particular injury reflect, of course, the nature and severity of that injury. There may be some diminution of capacity following mild head trauma that cannot be detected neuropsychologically. Gronwall and Wrightson (1975) demonstrated lower PASAT scores among mildly concussed patients (posttraumatic amnesia less than 1 hour) who had incurred previous head injury relative to patients without such a history. Ewing, McCarthy, Gronwall, and Wrightson (1980) suggested that high-altitude hypoxia can lead to deficits in attentional skill performance in previously concussed patients relative to a matched-control group of patients without such a history. Gronwall (1989) also notes slowed recovery of PASAT performance with increasing age. Gronwall and Wrightson (1975) hypothesize that the PASAT measures information-processing capacity. They suggest that a concussion can have a temporary effect on performance as well as a more permanent effect on information-processing reserves. They imply that repeated insults may accumulate, or interact with age, yielding potentially longer PASAT recovery times and pershaps an increased probability of more permanent performance deficits. One is still faced with explaining the lack of consistent neuropsychological impairment in many active, experienced boxers. Other noninjury experiences or characteristics may put individuals at risk for prolonged postconcussive symptoms after mild head injury. Adams and Grant (1986), for example, have shown that evidence of even one medical "risk factor" (i.e., prematurity, previous mild head injury, general illness, learning disability, etc.) in alcoholic populations screened for major neurological or psychiatric disease negatively influences neuropsychological test performance in recently abstinent drinkers but not in long-term abstinent alcoholics.

Severe Head Injury

One study of 32 moderately head injured patients (admission GCS 9–12) has been reported (Rimel, Giordani, Barth, & Jane, 1982). The authors indicated that their head-injured patients generated average Wechsler IQ values, but that there was a tendency for approximately half of these patients to fall below the cutoff points on several of the Halstead-Reitan subtests 3 months after injury. Studies including severely impaired patients tend to show both more consistent and pervasive neuropsychological deficits on testing, but there remains considerable individual variability in outcomes.

Significant deficits have been observed on the WAIS with early testing (Bond & Brooks, 1976; Mandleberg, 1975, 1976; Mandleberg & Brooks, 1975), on most measures from the Halstead-Reitan battery (Dikmen et al., 1983, 1986b; Dye, Saxon, & Milby, 1981), and on other broad-based neuropsychological evaluations (Brooks & Aughton, 1979; Lundholm et al., 1975). In contrast to the case of mild head injury, tests of more complex functions such as abstraction, concept formation, memory, and psychomotor skills may show relatively more deficit than simple attentional and motor functions on early testing (Dikmen et al., 1983, 1986b).

Overlearned skills, such as those making up the WAIS Verbal IQ, may improve more rapidly than functions requiring more immediate problem-solving capacity such as performance IQ (Mandleberg & Brooks, 1975). There appears to be a strong early relationship between measures of injury severity and neuropsychological performance (Dikmen et al., 1986a), which weakens some as time passes (Mandleberg, 1975, 1976; Stuss et al., 1985). Although WAIS scores often normalize by 3 years (Mandleberg, 1976; Mandleberg & Brooks, 1975), examination of recovery curves suggests more permanent deficits in those with the most severe injuries (e.g., posttraumatic amnesia $\geq$ 8 weeks). Long-term studies employing broad-based neuropsychological exams show evidence of lingering neuropsychological impairment relative to controls (Norman & Svahn, 1961), even in populations screened to eliminate those with premorbid problems (Dikmen et al., 1983; Stuss et al., 1985). Levin et al. (1979) studied 27 severely injured patients (GCS < 8) screened to eliminate those with significant preexisting neurological and psychiatric problems. The patients were tested with the Selective Reminding Test and the Benton Multilingual Aphasia examination. Although the authors attempted to determine the "best possible" neuropsychological recovery after severe head injury, the inclusion of some patients with short chronicities (6 months) suggests that the neuropsychological results may not be fixed. The variability in neuropsychological outcome was noteworthy. Over the entire sample, WAIS verbal IQs ranged from 41 to 124, and performance IQs ranged from 39 to 115. Similarly, Selective Reminding Test performance ranged from severely impaired to excellent. Various neurological indices of severity were related to neuropsychological outcome, especially the presence of acute oculovestibular deficit.

Dikmen et al. (1983) provided a comprehensive analysis of the improvement in neuropsychological test scores by traumatic head-injured patients of wide-ranging severity screened for healthy neurological and psychological histories. Forty-five patients were tested with the Halstead-Reitan battery as soon as they were capable, and 27 patients remained available for follow-up testings at 12 and 18 months posttrauma. In contrast to 35 peer-matched controls, more complex cognitive operations such as abstraction, concept formation, and psychomotor skills tended to be most consistently impaired early after injury. In addition, both simple and complex functions tended to improve with time. Most important, the degree of recovery and 18-month outcome depended upon the amount of initial impairment. A "deficit-proportional" statistical model best explained changes in neuropsychological test scores. Those patients with greater initial impairment recovered relatively more of this over time but also left greater residual deficit, compared to those with better initial neuropsychological functioning.

In summary, studies including more severely injured patients typically do show continued deficits on some neuropsychological test measures compared to controls several years postinjury. Yet there appears to be tremendous individual variability in the neuropsychological outcome from even a relatively homogeneous group of severely head injured patients (Levin et al., 1979). This variability certainly relates to specific differences in neuropathological changes (Meier, Strauman, & Thompson, 1987), influenced by variables related to the person, the environment, and the particular instrument used. For example, Brooks and Aughton (1979) demonstrated that steady improvement on three spaced consecutive administrations of a neuropsychological test occurred for only 35% of their population. Fifty-two percent showed some deterioration in a later testing compared to performance on an earlier exam. In general, most improvement tends to take place during the first several months of injury. However, others have noted tremendous between- and within-individual variation in the recovery of specific neuropsychological functions (Hiorns & Newcombe, 1979). None of the studies reviewed looked at noninjury factors (age, sex, education) as predictors of neuropsychological outcome following traumatic head injury.

A few published case studies have demonstrated some changes in neuropsychological test performance well beyond the point that group studies have suggested. Brown (1975) presented a case study suggesting neuropsychological test improvement (including the WAIS and tests of memory) as long as 8 years postinjury in a severely injured patient. Similarly, Thomsen (1981) tested a severely head injured patient 2 and 10 years after injury. Improvements on most measures of language function, immediate and delayed visual memory, and delayed recall for logical verbal material were demonstrated between the two evaluations. Although there was no real change in the patient's capacity to learn a difficult word list, performance IQ values also increased from 91 to 108 between the two testings. It is difficult to know when these changes occurred, but the patient's wife considered his recovery to have continued for up to 6 years posttrauma. Assuming that these changes reflect reliable improvement in underlying cognitive skill and not testing error, these data suggest the potential for some long-term neuropsychological recovery. There are, unfortunately, few longitudinal data on neuropsychological recovery extending beyond 2 years after injury.

There does appear to be some general relationship between indices of initial severity and later neuropsychological outcome. Patients who have longer periods of coma, longer periods of posttraumatic amnesia, or more serious acute neurological symptoms or radiographic findings tend to do worse neuropsychologically later on. The strength of the relationship between these indices of early severity and neuropsychological outcome appears to diminish some with time. This probably reflects the reduction of variability among patient scores as time passes (i.e., patients returning to premorbid levels) as well as the opportunity for nonneurological factors to begin to influence neuropsychological test performance. The degree of early neuropsychological deficit may be more predictive of the degree of later deficit than neurological or clinical variables. It appears that all patients have the potential for some neuropsychological recovery. For those with relatively mild injuries and who were healthy premorbidly, this recovery can very likely be nearly complete, although more permanent deficits are certainly possible. Premorbid factors may set the stage for prolonged problems in functioning after head injury. These noninjury variables may be of particular importance in understanding the nature of difficulties following mild injury. Those with more severe injuries will likely have some permanent information-processing deficit leading to significant psychosocial dysfunction. Clearly those patients with the most severe kinds of injuries (loss of consciousness of several weeks) and the greatest early testing deficits will have the greatest probability of having clinically significant long-term neuropsychological impairment. Not surprisingly, the degree of cognitive impairment is negatively correlated with the level of functional independence (Levin et al., 1979; Lundholm et al., 1975).

PSYCHOSOCIAL RECOVERY FOLLOWING TRAUMATIC HEAD INJURY

Researchers have attempted to understand the consequences of brain injury by asking the patient and/or a relative to report changes in physical, cognitive, emotional, and psychosocial functioning. The complexities of the long-term consequences of brain injury are most evident in the case of the patient's own analysis. The issues regarding psychological symptomatology and recovery are necessarily subjective and ambiguous.

Methodological problems are again common, with patient groups often poorly defined and heterogeneous, assessment methodologies only briefly reported, and little concern for the degree of psychosocial dysfunction evident premorbidly. The very nature of asking patients to report on various symptoms may alter such symptomatology (Pennebaker, 1982). As time passes, the stage is set for further changes in behavior, self-perception, and attribution based on learning experiences (Fordyce, 1976). In addition, brain injury itself can change the attentional and perceptual processes underlying self-awareness and the physiological foundations of emotional feeling and expression (Heilman & Satz, 1983). We must remember that premorbid neurological and psychiatric disturbances are relatively common among those suffering head injury. Several studies have reported rates of preexisting social disturbance and/or neurological illness as high as 40% (e.g., Fahy et al., 1967; Gruvstad, Kebbon, & Gruvstad, 1958; Rimel et al., 1982), as well as evidence of poor academic performance (Haas, Cope, & Hall, 1987). These data again highlight the importance of including adequate control groups in studies of the psychological consequences of head trauma.

Mild Head Injury

Subjective complaints of dysfunction are present in many, but not all, patients shortly after mild head injury. These can be roughly broken down into physical (headache, insomnia, fatigue), emotional (anxiety, irritability, depression), and cognitive (diminished concentration, poor memory) domains. In one unselected group of mildly head injured patients interviewed 3 months after injury, 78% complained of persistent headaches, 59% of memory deficit, and 14% of difficulty in doing household chores (Rimel et al., 1981). Rutherford, Merrett, and McDonald (1977, 1979) evaluated 145 mildly head injured patients 6 weeks and 1 year after injury. At 6 weeks, 51% of their patients reported at least one symptom. At 1 year postinjury this had changed to 14.5%, with headache the most frequent symptom reported (8.4%). No patient symptom free at 6 weeks had a complaint at 1 year, whereas 38% of the patients who had three symptom complaints at 6 weeks tended to report symptoms at 1 year.

More recent studies have examined patients screened for major premorbid illness or dysfunction. In a multicenter study by Levin, Mattis, et al. (1987), 71% of the mildly head injured patients complained of headache, 60% of decreased energy, and 53% of dizziness within 7 days of injury. By 1 month, these figures diminished to 56%, 46%, and 35%, respectively.

At 3 months, 47% complained of headache, 22% of diminished energy, and 22% of dizziness. McLean et al. (1983) evaluated their mildly head injured patients and peer-matched controls with a symptom checklist, a rating of overall functioning, and ratings of discomfort on scales measuring pain, sleepiness, and anxiety. At 3 days after injury, head-injured patients reported more pain, discomfort, and sleepiness. On a symptom checklist, more head-injured patients indicated symptoms of headache, fatigue, dizziness, blurred vision, and memory problems relative to controls. At 1 month, head-injured patients did not rate more pain, sleepiness, or anxiety compared to controls. They continued to report problems of fatigue, blurred vision, difficulty concentrating, and memory problems, however. Head-injured patients rated their overall level of functioning at 1 month as significantly worse than controls.

Dikmen et al. (1986a) had their mildly head injured patients and peer-matched controls complete the Sickness Impact Profile (SIP) and a head-injury symptom checklist at 1 month and 1 year postinjury. The SIP generates a sickness-related impairment score over 12 functional areas (sleep and rest, emotional behavior, home management, communication, pastimes and recreation, work, etc). At 1 month, the head-injured patients, on average, reported significantly more dysfunction on the SIP relative to controls in almost every behavioral area assessed. At the end of 1 year, there had been a significant decline in all areas of dysfunction, with only the domain of alertness behavior statistically separating the head-injured population from controls. With respect to the symptom checklist, head-injured patients tended to report more symptoms compared to controls at 1 month (significant for noise sensitivity, insomnia, and memory difficulties), but at 1 year there were no significant differences between the two groups. It is important to note that the control group (screened for premorbid neurological and psychological dysfunction) tended also to endorse a number of complaints on the symptom checklist. This should not be surprising, as symptom complaints and related responses (i.e., use of aspirin) are relatively high in American culture (see Pennebaker, 1982).

The reduction in reports of postconcussive symptoms with time roughly parallels improved neuropsychological test performance. Yet it appears that complaints can continue beyond the point where test scores normalize (Dikmen et al., 1986a; Gronwall, 1977; Levin, Mattis, et al., 1987). Although some studies have suggested a relationship between measures of injury severity and subsequent postconcussive symptomatology (Minderhoud et al., 1980), others have found equivocal associations (Rutherford et al., 1979), and many have found no relationship at all (Dencker, 1958; Dikmen et al., 1986a; McLean et al., 1983). Many noninjury variables have been associated with symptom reporting in certain studies including age (Minderhoud et al., 1980; Rutherford et al., 1979), sex (Dencker,

1958; Rutherford et al., 1979), a history of previous concussion (Gronwall & Wrightson, 1975), and psychosocial factors such as socioeconomic status, education, compensation/insurance status, nature of employment, and the presence of preinjury stressors (Kelly, 1975; Minderhoud et al., 1980; Rimel et al., 1981; Rutherford et al., 1979). Although prolonged post-concussive features may relate exclusively to litigation or compensation issues (Miller, 1961a, 1961b), patients not involved in litigation also report posttraumatic symptomatology following mild head injury (Kelly, 1975; McMillan & Glucksman, 1987; Merskey & Woodforde, 1972). In studies specifically looking at the impact of compensation/litigation on symptom reporting, there does seem to be some positive relationship (McKinlay, Brooks, & Bond, 1983; Rutherford, 1989). Interestingly, although claim resolution may improve average symptom reporting, the changes may not be dramatic (Rutherford, 1989).

The reasons why some patients continue to evince complaints of dysfunction long after injury is not clear (Binder, 1986). Premorbid personality has been linked to the development of postconcussive symptomatology. The previous discussion on the neuropsychological sequelae of mild injury suggests that premorbid health (including neurological and psychological factors) may play a large role in overall recovery. Thus, some individuals may have a "selective vulnerability" to prolonged convalescence following concussion (Binder, 1986). As noted, early problems in sustaining attention and concentration appear to resolve in most patients. Initial information-processing deficits and early posttraumatic experiences may interact with personality characteristics to produce more durable complaints of dysfunction (Gronwall & Wrightson, 1974). The fact that people differ in their response to mild head injury based on their neurological or psychosocial histories would seem important in understanding the relative contribution of a single injury to prolonged problems in functioning. Of equal importance are recent studies suggesting that systematic intervention may reduce overall disability following mild head injury (Gronwall & Wrightson, 1974; Hinkle, Alves, Rimell, & Jane, 1986; Minderhoud et al., 1980). The study of the psychological consequences of more severe head injury yields further hypotheses about prolonged emotional sequelae.

Severe Head Injury

The magnitude of posttraumatic psychosocial dysfunction among injuries of wide-ranging severity varies with the particular domain assessed. Ratings of cognitive disturbance or associated dysfunction seem more clearly related to measures of injury severity compared to complaints of affective or psychiatric disturbance. Bond (1975) administered a structured interview to 56 patients with traumatic head injury who were 3 to 24 months postinjury. Subsequent analyses indicated that rated personality and psychiatric symptomatology did not correlate with injury severity (length of posttraumatic amnesia), whereas complaints of memory dysfunction did. Similarly, work and leisure capacity correlated with injury severity, whereas the degree of family distress and sexual dysfunction did not. Levin and Grossman (1978) administered the Brief Psychiatric Rating Scale (BPRS) to 50 head-injured patients under the age of 50 excluding those with premorbid histories of alcoholism, cerebral disease, or psychiatric illness. Severity of injury correlated with factor scores reflecting thinking disturbance as well as psychological withdrawal and retardation, but not to factors reflecting suspiciousness or anxiety/depression. Of importance is the observation that some of the more severely injured patients seem to have little appreciation of their residual deficits. Levin, High, et al. (1987) examined 101 previously healthy patients (ages 16–51) with a neurobehavioral rating scale based on the BPRS. Factors loading on cognitive impairment and withdrawal, diminished self-awareness and poor planning, and impaired language functioning were correlated with measures of injury severity. A factor loading on emotional distress and somatic concern did not show such a relationship. Analyses of individual items further underlined the dissociation between severity and certain emotional dimensions. Conceptual disorganization, inaccurate self-appraisal, and poor planning had a strong relationship to injury severity. In contrast, mildly head injured patients actually showed greater levels of anxiety and somatic concern than more severely injured patients. Twenty cases of differing severity were studied over time (average interval = 4½ months), and significant improvements were noted on all factors except emotional distress and somatic concern. With a few exceptions (Steadman & Graham, 1970), others have found no relationship between measures of severity and posttraumatic emotional and somatic complaints (Keshavan, Channabasavanna, & Reddy, 1981; Ruesch & Bowman, 1945).

Van Zomeren and Van Den Burg (1985) followed 57 patients and relatives 2 years after severe head injury with a questionnaire designed to indicate the presence of posttraumatic changes in functioning. Of the patients, 84% had some subjective complaint at 2 years with forgetfulness being the most common. Patient complaints of other cognitive dysfunction, emotional dysfunction, intolerance to environmental stimulation, and physical distress were also common. Again, indices of severity (length of posttraumatic amnesia and time to return to work) tended to correlate with symptoms of cognitive and physical dysfunction (complaints of slowness, forgetfulness, and inability to do two things simultaneously), but not to other complaints. Factor analyses yielded a "severity factor" loading on complaints of slowness, inability to do two things at the same time, forgetfulness, poor concentration, and the presence of depression. The second factor was labeled "having complaints," which reflected an intolerance to the outside world. This factor included such things as increased need to sleep, headache, intolerance to light and noise, indifference, dizziness, and irritability. Relatives' reports produced a similar "severity factor" but not a complaining factor. The authors felt that the more neuroticlike complaining symptoms may reflect failed attempts to cope with the effects of the head injury.

Several studies have utilized cohabitating relatives to rate psychosocial impairment following severe head injury. One study noted that 49% of the relatives interviewed reported major personality changes by 3 months, with 60% reporting such changes at 6 and 12 months (Brooks & McKinlay, 1983). Others have indicated that 70% of the relatives will report major personality change at 2 years (Weddell et al., 1980) and 84% at 2½ years (Thomsen, 1974). Although positive emotional changes are occasionally noted (Fahy et al., 1967), the vast majority of descriptors employed are negative. In addition to cognitive dysfunction, relatives will frequently report that their loved ones are exhibiting reduced emotional control, aspontaneity and listlessness, and a generally less mature response style (Brooks & McKinlay, 1983; Thomsen, 1974). Patients are also described as being socially isolated and lonely by relatives interviewed 2 to 2½ years after injury (Thomsen, 1974; Weddell et al., 1980), with 50% indicating continued isolation at 7 years (Oddy et al., 1985). Although patients appear less likely to acknowledge negative personality change compared to relatives (Fahy et al., 1967; Thomsen, 1974), they sometimes report social isolation (Oddy et al., 1985; Thomsen, 1974). The apparent increase in the number of relatives reporting negative personality change over time may reflect an exhaustion of their coping mechanisms (Brooks & McKinlay, 1983). However, it is also possible that the emotional condition of the head-injured patient may worsen as recovery continues.

Fordyce, Roueche, and Prigatano (1983) compared the emotional characteristics of patients injured at least 6 months prior to examination with more acutely injured patients. Although these two groups were generally equivalent with respect to level of neuropsychological impairment and measures of injury severity, the more chronically injured patients demonstrated more psychological dysfunction on the MMPI and, as completed by relatives, on the Katz Adjustment Scale. The authors suggested that some patients may demonstrate enhanced psychological dysfunction associated with increased general awareness, resolving neuropsychological impairment, and accumulated experiences as head-injured individuals. Dikmen and Reitan (1977) reported decreasing emotional distress on the MMPI in a longitudinal study of traumatic brain injury. Their data also indicated, however, that those with more severe neuropsychological impairment may show more durable negative emotional changes.

As in the case of mild head injury, several authors have postulated that premorbid personality dysfunction may predispose patients to problematic postinjury emotional adjustments following severe head injury (Bond, 1975; Brooks & McKinlay, 1983; Fordyce et al., 1983; Keshavan et al., 1981; Ruesch & Bowman, 1945). Although this notion is often likely to be true, it has proven difficult to clearly confirm (Gruvstad et al., 1958; Kozol, 1945, 1946). This most certainly relates to the difficulties in accurately defining and assessing personality, especially retroactively. Patients with premorbid "neurotic" traits may be more prone to posttraumatic emotional distress, but exceptions are not uncommon (Gruvstad et al., 1958; Kozol, 1946). Clinically, there often appears to be an accentuation of some premorbid characteristics following brain injury.

A single study looks at very early psychosocial functioning over a wide range of injury severities, with a peer-matched control group for comparison (McLean, Dikmen, Temkin, Wyler, & Gale, 1984). At 1 month, all 102 head-injured patients, on average, showed significant elevations on nearly all SIP scales compared to controls. On the symptom checklist, head-injured patients indicated more problems with headache, fatigue, dizziness, blurred vision, concentration problems, sensitivity to noise, memory problems, and insomnia compared to controls. As in previous studies, however, healthy controls indicated a significant number of these problems as well. Interestingly, there was a trend for total SIP dysfunction to increase with increasing levels of severity as measured by time to follow commands, whereas the number of so-called postconcussional symptoms and emotional distress tended to decrease with increasing levels of severity. Litigation seemed unrelated to the tendency to express complaints.

In summary, there appears to be no clear relationship between injury severity and the magnitude of posttraumatic emotional distress (Bond, 1975; Fordyce et al., 1983; Keshavan et al., 1981; Levin & Grossman, 1978; Levin, High, et al., 1987; Ruesch & Bowman, 1945; Van Zomeren & Van Den Burg, 1985). In fact, there is evidence that some more mildly injured patients may evidence more emotional dysfunction than more severely injured patients (Levin, High, et al., 1987; McLean et al., 1984; Ruesch & Bowman, 1945), although exceptions are also apparent (Dikmen & Reitan, 1977; Steadman & Graham, 1970). Some symptoms may be more correlated with injury severity (i.e., certain cognitive complaints), whereas levels of anxiety and depression may be more related to coping success based on current cognitive capacities and premorbid coping strengths (Fordyce et al., 1983; Van Zomeren & Van Den Burg, 1985). In more severely injured patients, emotional distress may generate more slowly after an initial buffer related to lack of awareness and environmental isolation. Those with permanent residual deficits in thinking (or physical functioning) related to severe brain injury will be at greater risk for long-term emotional dysfunction, especially if they are lacking in premorbid coping skills (Gruvstad et al., 1958; Keshavan et al., 1981; Kozol, 1946) and/or are experiencing postinjury adjustment failures.

REHABILITATION

Clearly, a substantial number of survivors of brain injury retain long-term deficits in spite of medical treatment and traditional rehabilitation efforts. Newer intervention techniques may augment the speed of recovery and level of ultimate outcome. Although many of these methods are being incorporated into neurosurgical and inpatient rehabilitation services, contemporary brain injury rehabilitation typically focuses on issues that extend well beyond the scope and time frames subsumed within more traditional hospital settings. Newer methods address cognitive, psychosocial, physical, and vocational problems months and often years after the point of injury. Few would argue that the concepts underlying these new rehabilitation activities are unreasonable. How and when they should be used, their general efficacy, and their cost effectiveness are less certain. The same questions also exist for many medical, traditional rehabilitation, and psychological treatments. As noted in the case of general recovery, rehabilitation studies based on groups may obscure important individual trends (Wilson, 1987). The question of whether rehabilitation is generally effective has been, and will be, difficult to answer. Perhaps of greater importance are issues of what activity should be prescribed when, for whom, and for how long.

Current knowledge about the effectiveness of brain injury rehabilitation is beyond the scope of this chapter, and is reviewed in several recent volumes (Meier, Benton, & Diller, 1987; Rosenthal, Griffith, Bond, & Miller, 1983). In the following pages, I review some of the important issues and provide examples to highlight major points.

Rehabilitation is guided learning. Virtually all organisms, humans in particular, have the capacity to exhibit regular changes in behavior on the basis of experience. We now know, for example, that even patients with severe amnestic disorders can learn certain skills and procedures at levels similar to perfectly normal individuals (Squire & Butters, 1984). Thus, all patients have the potential for benefiting from well-directed rehabilitation. The neuroanatomical and neurochemical changes that parallel early recovery following brain injury are slowly being clarified (Marshall, 1985). How these relate to specific functional or behavioral changes in humans remains largely a mystery, however. All behavior, in some sense, is physically reflected in brain structure or activity. Durable changes in behavior following brain injury, therefore, imply some underlying neurophysical change. There is, however, an upper limit to brain "plasticity," as permanent deficits are common. At some point, recovery becomes more or less similar to basic human learning, with capacities set by premorbid intellectual endowment and personality interacting with postinjury changes. Observable changes in behavior may thus not reflect neurological recovery, per se.

The distinction between impairments and disabilities seems to have great importance. According to Diller (1987), impairments reflect deficits in central mental or physical systems, often as measured through objective tests. Disabilities, on the other hand, are relatively durable failures or inefficiencies in behavior following brain injury. Impairments may underlie or contribute to certain disabilities. Talents, skill level, motivation, experiences, and other factors also contribute to the degree of disability generally manifested given certain impairments. The concepts of major life statuses and/or roles also seem important (Ben-Yishay & Diller, 1983). Although two patients may share similar impairments or disabilities following brain injury, their psychosocial position (employment status, parenting role) may be grossly different for reasons having to do with injury, person, or environment. Newer brain injury rehabilitation techniques are concerned with affecting impairments, disabilities, statuses, and roles (Table 10.3).

There is great interest in the set of brain injury rehabilitation activities most commonly labeled "cognitive retraining." In its broadest sense, cognitive retraining refers to the amelioration of disabilities resulting from cognitive impairments, including the development of substitute skills or compensation for such impairments. In a more narrow sense, cognitive remediation refers to attempts to improve actual cognitive impairments through systematic rehabilitation efforts. The concept of cognitive retraining is not new. Zangwill (1947), for example, noted that "reeducation" of psychological skills following brain injury reflects operations of "compensation and substitution" and "retraining." Compensation and substitution reflected a partial restoration of function by adjustment or reorganization of the manner in which goal-directed behavior was undertaken. Retraining was the direct stimulation of inefficient functions. Zangwill felt that compensation and substitution took place naturally but could be facilitated through rehabilitation efforts.

When examining cognitive retraining research or general rehabilitation outcome research, certain questions seem particularly important (Gordon, 1987):

1. Does retraining improve performance over that explained by spontaneous recovery?
2. Does cognitive retraining affect essential cognitive skills or simply improve performance on a specific set of tasks? Stated differntly,

do improvements realized on cognitive retraining tasks, which often bear little resemblance to real-life situations (Ben-Yishay & Diller, 1983), carry over to improve function in daily behaviors that depend upon the trained skills?
3. Are the effects of cognitive retraining durable?

Unfortunately, studies of cognitive retraining efficacy seldom employ untreated or alternatively treated patients, or utilize appropriate single case study methods. In addition, treatment efficacy is often determined by performance on instruments similar or identical to those used in training, without appropriate functional assessment or long-term follow-up.

Given these limitations, there is currently little evidence that core neurologically based impairments in thinking (Ben-Yishay & Diller, 1983;

TABLE 10.3. Targets of Comprehensive Brain Injury Rehabilitation

Impairments	Disabilities
Neuropsychological (deficits in)	ADL functions
Attention	Dressing
Visual–perceptual function	Grooming
Language function	Cooking
Memory/learning	Budgeting
Problem solving/judgment	Time management
Awareness	Mobility
Physical	Walking
Paresis	Changing position
Sensory Loss	Driving
Dysarthria	Public transportation
Incontinence	Running
Imbalance	Climbing
Incoordination	Communication
Emotional/energy	Expression
Inappropriate affect	Comprehension
Emotional lability	Social interaction
Reduced arousal	Appropriateness
Reduced stamina	Social awareness
Statuses/role	Capacity to show affection
Level of employment	Timeliness
Level of independence	Emotional
Role as a parent	Depression
Role as a child	Anxiety
Role as a spouse	Anger
Role as a friend	Denial
Criminal behavior	
Substance abuse	

Diller, 1987) can be consistently improved by rehabilitation activities. The absence of positive data may reflect, in part, the infancy of cognitive rehabilitation research. Some elaborate systems of cognitive retraining are well grounded in theory (Ben-Yishay & Diller, 1983; Sohlberg & Mateer, 1989). These systems, coupled with improved research design and methodology, offer more promising conditions for determining the circumstances of effective cognitive retraining. There is no question that even severely brain injured patients can be taught to improve their skills on a variety of cognitive tasks. However, we don't know whether these positive changes reflect durable improvements in particular cognitive functions, or enhanced performance on a particular set of activities.

The complexities of cognitive rehabilitation efficacy are exemplified in group outcome studies of speech and language therapy for residual language dysfunction following brain injury, usually stroke (Basso, 1987). Such dysfunction is based in part upon core linguistic impairments that reflect damage usually to the left cerebral hemisphere. Therapy includes direct attempts to remediate these deficits. Well-controlled studies have shown more patients with improved performance on language tests (following several months of intensive therapy) than untreated controls (e.g., Basso, Capitani, & Vignolo, 1979). Other equally intensive and methodologically sound studies have not demonstrated such differential treatment efficacy (Lincoln et al., 1984; Sarno, Silverman, & Sands, 1970). Still others have failed to demonstrate differences in measures of communication outcome between patients treated by trained speech therapists and those seeing volunteers for communication-related activities (Meikle et al., 1979), or general stimulation and interaction (David, Enderby, & Bainton, 1982). In all these studies, some patients in all groups tended to show some improvement, and those initially more impaired remained so regardless of the kind of treatment (Basso et al., 1979; David et al., 1982; Sarno & Levita, 1981).

Positive changes in language or communication skills are not isomorphic with social readjustment following stroke (Basso et al., 1979). Sarno and Levita (1981) found more impressive changes in nonverbal communication skills, alertness, and self-awareness than in basic language skills for seven severely impaired aphasic patients treated for nearly 1 year. The benefits of extended therapy may be in the development of compensations and adaptation, rather than in improved linguistic processing, per se. The common absence of statistically significant group treatment effects in the speech and language literature does not imply that specific benefits are not accruing to some treated patients. We can't define at this time who these treatable patients might be, however.

Recent efforts at improving nonaphasic neuropsychological impairments have employed well-specified and theoretically grounded techniques. These treatments are usually a component of a much broader set of general rehabilitation activities. Within this context, there is now clear evidence that performance on tests of certain psychological functions can be modified as a result of systematic intervention. The processes of attention and concentration are perhaps receiving the greatest study. Much of the best work in this area has originated from New York University Medical Center. Weinberg et al. (1977, 1979) have shown that systematic remediation activities designed to assist right hemisphere stroke patients scan visually to the left, and improve internal and external spatial awareness, significantly improved performance in a variety of spatial psychometric and neurological tasks compared to controls. Some controls also demonstrated improvement on these tests. Both experimental and control patients received the same traditional rehabilitation activities, whereas the experimental patients received 20 hours of visually based remediation work. Interestingly, the authors noted that those with more severe initial deficits seemed to show the greatest improvements relative to controls. It appears that as the testing task became more dissimilar to the training task, the magnitude of experimental effects diminished. The authors did not undertake analyses of change in functional activities with a visual-attention component.

Researchers used a different set of attentional training techniques in a large group of survivors of traumatic head injury. Instead of spatial scanning, training involved systematic practice on a hierarchy of five tasks of general visual and auditory attention (Ben-Yishay, Piasetsky, & Rattok, 1987; Rattok et al., 1982). Forty patients surviving 2–4 years after severe traumatic head injury underwent systematic attention training as part of a comprehensive outpatient brain injury rehabilitation program. All patients showed significant improvement on the five training tasks, and their final performance was usually within the normal range. In addition, they demonstrated enhanced performance on other psychometric instruments dependent upon attentional processes at the end of treatment. Five subjects were followed for 6 months, and treatment effects were maintained. The fact that sequential mastery of each of the five training tasks did not affect performance on any of the remaining tasks raises questions as to whether generalized improvement in attentional processes was occurring. The degree of general improvement and carryover to other functions and activities for each patient was highly variable. A case study is presented (Ben-Yishay et al., 1987) that suggests positive general changes in behavior accompanying these attention remediation techniques. Sohlberg and Mateer (1989) also note changes in attentional performance in four subjects studied with single-case design techniques.

One study has compared more general outcome among patients receiving systematic cognitive remediation activities relative to similar untreated patients (Fryer & Haffey, 1987). Eighteen brain-injured patients were treated with 30 sessions of outpatient cognitive retraining focused on auditory and visual attention, perceptual discrimination, and problem solving. The treated patients showed greater improvement in disability ratings compared to a group of nine similar patients who were not treated. These changes appeared to be durable up to 1 year of follow-up. This study is particularly interesting because it suggests that for some individuals with less severe impairment cognitive retraining may yield enhanced functioning in more general adaptive skills not directly practiced. Replication of these results with a control group treated with alternative methods and blind ratings of outcome would help isolate the specific benefits of cognitive retraining activities.

With respect to other cognitive functions, rehabilitation data are even more meager. To date there is little, if any, evidence that core memory skills for those with significant memory impairment can be improved through cognitive retraining activities. Popular memory-enhancing techniques are usually not effective for those with significant brain injury, or have such limited practical application as to be of little functional use. Recent data have suggested the ability to remember to do things in the future may be modifiable with systematic intervention (Sohlberg & Mateer, 1989).

Most contemporary brain injury rehabilitation efforts are broad in scope. As with cognitive remediation, however, the parameters governing the use of these more comprehensive strategies have not been identified. They do appear to offer great potential in assisting some brain-injured individuals to maximize independence and productivity given permanent residual deficits. As noted earlier, a significant portion of those surviving severe brain injury fail at returning to productive life because of residual problems in cognition, interpersonal functioning, or physical functioning. Comprehensive rehabilitation programs help some patients and relatives (a) to become more aware of the nature of altered skills and behaviors, (b) to accept and adjust to these changes, (c) to improve dysfunction or to develop new skills to circumvent, as much as possible, the psychosocial disability associated with residual impairments, and (d) to make environmental modifications (temporary or permanent) that allow for maximal independence and success.

Comprehensive brain injury rehabilitation programs acknowledge that residual cognitive problems are "barriers" not only to returning to "normal life" but to rehabilitation, per se (Ben-Yishay & Diller, 1983). Given deficits in areas of attention, memory, and generalization, the newer rehabilitation programs are generally intensive with considerable repetition. Multidisciplinary services are offered in an integrated fashion for multiple areas of functioning both in treatment facilities and out in the community. Unfortunately, accompanying this increase in scope and intensity are the associated costs of treatment. For those who are helped to return to work or live more independently, such costs may be recoverable (Aronow, 1987). Otherwise, social/political attitudes and policies must determine whether the potential enhancement of quality of life is sufficient to warrant treatment.

Different approaches are used for differing severities of injury and stage of recovery. Within and across these various approaches, it appears that greater initial injury severity (Aronow, 1987; Fryer & Haffey, 1987; Timmons et al., 1987), initial ratings of functional impairment (Fryer & Haffey, 1987; Timmons, Gasquoine, & Scibak, 1987) or initial psychosocial impairment (Prigatano et al., 1984) negatively correlated with outcome from rehabilitation. Although the more severely involved patient may do less well in rehabilitation, the positive changes that do occur may generate particularly significant economic and psychosocial benefits.

Only two papers examine the outcome effectiveness of comprehensive brain injury rehabilitation activities, in comparing treated patients to adequate control groups (Aronow, 1987; Prigatano et al., 1984). Prigatano et al. (1984) treated 18 traumatically head injured patients, well past the point of injury, for 6 months in an intensive outpatient rehabilitation program. Rehabilitation emphasized improved self-awareness and acceptance, social skill training, intensive cognitive retraining, and the development of compensatory skills to enhance psychosocial adjustment. Patients tested on measures of cognitive and psychosocial functioning were compared to a group of 17 matched controls who did not receive such treatment. The treated patients showed greater improvements on neuropsychological tests measuring thinking speed, attention, and memory. Scherzer (1986) showed similar changes in his patients who also completed intensive rehabilitation. In the Prigatano et al. (1984) study, 50% of those patients who graduated from the program were engaged in productive activities (work or school related) 75% of the time following discharge (follow-up period 8 months to 3 years) compared to 36% of the controls. None of the patients or controls had been employed prior to the first assessment. There was a suggestion of improved emotional functioning in some of the rehabilitated patients compared to controls when assessed by cohabitating relatives. Missing data points and the absence of more specific measures of psychosocial outcome create some problems in interpreting the results.

Aronow (1987) found significantly better overall outcome (as defined by the sum of several rated outcome variables) among 68 severe head trauma patients who received intensive inpatient rehabilitation services, compared to 61 controls from a different geographical area without access to such treatment. Although initial differences in severity were controlled for statistically, group differences unrelated to treatment may have an impact on overall outcome. The author does not describe outcome data in detail, but does present an interesting analysis of the potential economic benefits of intensive rehabilitation.

SUMMARY

The burdens shared by experts who help manage and guide the often contradictory forces focusing on the evaluation and long-term treatment of brain-injured individuals will increase with time. In the current atmosphere of government fiscal austerity and tightening health care financial resources, ever-increasing demands will be placed on professionals to dispense advice and services responsibly. In addition, brain injury specialists must respond to the devastating individual, family, and social consequences of these all-too-often permanent injuries. Accurate predictions of recovery and/or the nature of long-term residual deficits in an individual suffering brain injury are more possible now than in years past, but the uncertainties remain enormous. The capacity to predict potential benefits of newer rehabilitation services will depend on the expansion of the current data base by those who are offering such services. The following points seem reasonable given our current state of knowledge:

1. Those suffering from severe head injury (length of posttraumatic amnesia or coma measured in weeks) will typically demonstrate significant deficits and disability. Long-term dependency, social maladjustment, and unemployment will be common.
2. Those suffering less severe head trauma will evidence a range of impairments and levels of disability that, in the long run, are often poorly associated with indices of injury severity.
3. Improvement in neuropsychological impairments occurs over months. In general, changes slow with time. The more severe the injury, the longer detectable changes may occur. Those individuals showing greater levels of early neuropsychological deficit may recover relatively more of this but have greater levels of long-term impairment compared to those with more mild levels of early cognitive dysfunction.
4. Premorbid neurological history, intellectual endowment, personality characteristics, constitutional factors, and educational, vocational, and social histories all interact with injury variables and posttraumatic experiences to determine the nature and level of impairments realized and the degree of disability present. These factors are further affected by the particular psychosocial environments of the brain-injured person.

5. In general, the less severe the traumatic brain injury, the more unlikely long-term deficits will be present, and the more likely variables not directly related to the recent trauma will be contributing significantly to any long-term disability.
6. Emotional and behavioral symptomatology are poorly related to measures of injury severity or levels of neuropsychological impairment.
7. It is not yet clear whether core cognitive impairments can be improved through rehabilitation.
8. Nearly every brain-injured individual has the capacity to improve overall functioning through systematic intervention.
9. Given the pervasive problems in functioning that accompany serious brain injury, intervention must be intensive, comprehensive, and well organized. The specific degree of disability reduction from comprehensive rehabilitation is difficult to predict without attempting treatment.
10. Although comprehensive rehabilitation may assist some individuals in functioning more effectively after brain injury, it cannot eliminate underlying core deficits.
11. Those individuals who suffer brain injury and who have significant preexisting problems will seldom function better after injury, nor will rehabilitation improve their level of functioning above what was present prior to injury.

REFERENCES

Adams, K., & Grant, I. (1986). Influence of premorbid risk factors on neuropsychological performance in alcoholics. *Journal of Clinical & Experimental Neuropsychology*, *8*, 362–370.

Aronow, H. U. (1987). Rehabilitation effectiveness with severe brain injury: Translating research into policy. *Journal of Head Trauma Rehabilitation*, *2*, 24–36.

Barth, J. T., Macciocchi, S. N., Giordani, B., Rimel, R., Jane, J. A., & Boll, T. J. (1983). Neuropsychological sequelae of minor head injury. *Neurosurgery*, *13*, 529–533.

Basso, A. (1987). Approaches to neuropsychological rehabilitation: Language disorders. In M. Meier, A. Benton, & L. Diller (Eds.), *Neuropsychological rehabilitation* (pp. 294–314). New York: Guilford Press.

Basso, A., Capitani, E., & Vignolo, L. (1979). Influence of rehabilitation on language skills in aphasic patients. *Archives of Neurology*, *36*, 190–196.

Ben-Yishay, Y., & Diller, L. (1983). Cognitive deficits. In M. Rosenthal, E. Griffith, M. Bond, & J. Miller (Eds.), *Rehabilitation of the head-injured adult* (pp. 167–184). Philadelphia: Davis.

Ben-Yishay, Y., Piasetsky, E., & Rattok, J. (1987). A systematic method for ameliorating disorders in basic attention. In M. Meier, A. Benton, & L. Diller (Eds.), *Neuropsychological rehabilitation* (pp. 165–181). New York: Guilford Press.

Binder, L. (1986). Persisting symptoms after mild head injury: A review of the postconcussive syndrome. *Journal of Clinical & Experimental Neuropsychology, 8*, 323–346.

Bond, M. (1975). Assessment of the psychosocial outcome after severe head injury. *CIBA Foundation Symposium, 34*, 141–153.

Bond, M., & Brooks, D. (1976). Understanding the process of recovery as a basis for the investigation of rehabilitation for the brain injured. *Scandinavian Journal of Rehabilitation Medicine, 8*, 127–133.

Bowers, S., & Marshall, F. (1980). Outcome in two hundred consecutive cases of severe head injury treated in San Diego County: A perspective analysis. *Neurosurgery, 6*, 237–242.

Braakman, R., Gelpke, G., Habbema, J., Maas, A., & Minderhoud, J. (1980). Systematic selection of prognostic features in patients with severe head injury. *Neurosurgery, 6*, 362–370.

Brooks, D., & Aughton, M. (1979). Cognitive recovery during the first year after severe blunt head injury. *International Rehabilitation Medicine, 1*, 166–172.

Brooks, D., Hosie, J., Bond, M., Jennett, B., & Aughton, M. (1986). Cognitive sequelae of severe head injury in relation to the Glasgow Outcome Scale. *Journal of Neurology, Neurosurgery & Psychiatry, 49*, 549–553.

Brooks, M., Kupshik, G., Wilson, L., Galbraith, S., & Ward, R. (1987). Neuropsychological study of active amateur boxers. *Journal of Neurology, Neurosurgery & Psychiatry, 50*, 997–1000.

Brooks, M., & McKinlay, W. (1983). Personality and behavior change after severe blunt head injury—A relative's view. *Journal of Neurology, Neurosurgery & Psychiatry, 46*, 336–344.

Brown, J. (1975). Late recovery from head injury: Case report and review. *Psychological Medicine, 5*, 239–248.

Bruckner, F., & Randle, A. (1972). Return to work after severe head injuries. *Rheumatology & Physical Medicine, 11*, 344–348.

Carlsson, C., von Essen, C., & Löfgren, J. (1968). Factors affecting the clinical course of patients with severe injuries. *Journal of Neurosurgery, 29*, 242–251.

Cook, J. (1972). The post-concussional syndrome and factors influencing after minor head injury admitted to hospital. *Scandinavian Journal of Rehabilitation Medicine, 4*, 27–30.

David, R., Enderby, P., & Bainton, D. (1982). Treatment of acquired aphasia: Speech therapists and volunteers compared. *Journal of Neurology, Neurosurgery & Psychiatry, 45*, 957–961.

Dencker, S. (1958). A follow-up study of 128 closed head injuries in twins using co-twins as controls. *Acta Psychiatrica et Neurologica Scandinavica, 33*(Suppl. 123).

Dencker, S., & Löfving, B. (1958). A psychometric study of identical twins discordant for closed head injury. *Acta Psychiatrica et Neurologica Scandinavica, 33*(Suppl. 122).

Dikmen, S., McLean, A., & Temkin, N. (1986a). Neuropsychological and psychosocial consequences of minor head injury. *Journal of Neurology, Neurosurgery & Psychiatry, 49*, 1227–1232.

Dikmen, S., McLean, A., Temkin, N., & Wyler, A. (1986b). Neuropsychologic outcome at one month postinjury. *Archives of Physical Medicine & Rehabilitation, 67*, 507–513.

Dikmen, S., & Reitan, R. (1977). Emotional sequelae of head injury. *Annals of Neurology, 2*, 492–494.

Dikmen, S., Reitan, R., & Temkin, N. (1983). Neuropsychological recovery in head injury. *Archives of Neurology, 40*, 333–338.

Diller, L. (1987). Neuropsychological rehabilitation. In M. Meier, A. Benton, & L. Diller (Eds.), *Neuropsychological rehabilitation* (pp. 3–17). New York: Guilford Press.

Dresser, C., Meirowski, A., Weiss, G., McNeel, M., Simon, G., & Caveness, W. (1973). Gainful employment following head injury. *Archives of Neurology, 29*, 111–116.

Dye, O., Saxon, S., & Milby, J. (1981). Long-term neuropsychological deficits after traumatic head injury with comatosis. *Journal of Clinical Psychology, 37*, 472–477.

Edna, T. (1987). Disability 3–5 years after minor head injury. *Journal of Oslo City Hospital, 37*, 41–48.

Ewing, R., McCarthy, D., Gronwall, D., & Wrightson, P. (1980). Persisting effects of minor head injury observable during hypoxic stress. *Journal of Clinical Neuropsychology, 2*, 147–155.

Fahy, T., Irving, M., & Millac, P. (1967). Severe head injuries: A six-year follow-up. *Lancet, 2*, 475–479.

Fordyce, D., Roueche, J., & Prigatano, G. (1983). Enhanced emotional reactions in chronic head trauma patients. *Journal of Neurology, Neurosurgery & Psychiatry, 46*, 620–624.

Fordyce, W. E. (1976). *Behavioral methods in chronic pain and illness*. St. Louis: Mosby.

Frankowski, R. (1986). Descriptive epidemiologic studies of head injury in the United States: 1974–1984. *Advances in Psychosomatic Medicine, 16*, 153–172.

Fraser, R., Dikmen, S., McLean, A., Miller, B., & Temkin, N. (1988). Employability of head injury survivors: First year post-injury. *Rehabilitation Counseling Bulletin, 31*, 276–288.

Fryer, L., & Haffey, W. (1987). Cognitive rehabilitation and community readaptation: Outcomes from two program models. *Journal of Head Trauma Rehabilitation, 2*, 51–63.

Gentilini, M., Nichelli, P., Schoenhuber, R., Bortolotti, P., Tonelli, L., Falasca, A., & Merli, G. (1985). Neuropsychological evaluation of mild head injury. *Journal of Neurology, Neurosurgery, and Psychiatry, 48*, 137–140.

Gilchrist, E., & Wilkinson, M. (1979). Some factors determining prognosis in young people with severe head injuries. *Archives of Neurology, 36*, 355–359.

Gordon, W. (1987). Methodological considerations in cognitive remediation. In M. Meier, A. Benton, & L. Diller (Eds.), *Neuropsychological rehabilitation* (pp. 111–131). New York: Guilford Press.

Gronwall, D. (1977). Paced Auditory Serial Addition Task: A measure of recovery from concussion. *Perceptual & Motor Skills, 44,* 367–373.

Gronwall, D. (1989). Cumulative and persisting effects of concussion on attention and concentration. In H. Levin, H. Eisenberg, & A. Benton (Eds)., *Mild head injury* (pp. 153–162). New York: Oxford University Press.

Gronwall, D., & Wrightson, P. (1974). Delayed recovery of intellectual function after minor head injury. *Lancet, 2,* 605–609.

Gronwall, D., & Wrightson, P. (1975). Cumulative effect of concussion. *Lancet, 2,* 995–997.

Gruvstad, M., Kebbon, L., & Gruvstad, S. (1958). Social and psychiatric aspects of pretraumatic personality and post-traumatic insufficiency reactions in traumatic head injuries. *Acta Societatis Medicorum Upsaliensis, 63,* 101–113.

Haas, J., Cope, D., & Hall, K. (1987). Premorbid prevalance of poor academic performance in severe head injury. *Journal of Neurology, Neurosurgery & Psychiatry, 50,* 52–56.

Hall, K., Cope, D., & Rappaport, M. (1985). Glasgow Outcome Scale and Disability Rating Scale: Comparative usefulness in following recovery in traumatic head injury. *Archives of Physical Medicine & Rehabilitation, 66,* 35–37.

Heaton, R., Chelune, G., & Lehman, R. (1978). Using neuropsychological and personality tests to assess the likelihood of patient employment. *Journal of Nervous & Mental Disease, 166,* 408–416.

Heilman, K., & Satz, P. (1983). *Neuropsychology of human emotion.* New York: Guilford Press.

Hinkle, J., Alves, W., Rimell, R., & Jane, J. (1986). Restoring social competence in minor head injury patients. *Journal of Neuroscience Nursing, 18,* 268–271.

Hiorns, R., & Newcombe, F. (1979). Recovery curves: Uses and limitations. *International Rehabilitation Medicine, 1,* 173–176.

Jennett, B., & Bond, M. (1975). Assessment of outcome after severe brain damage: A practical scale. *Lancet,* Vol. 1, 480–484.

Jennett, B., Teasdale, G., Braakman, R., Minderhoud, J., Heiden, J., & Kurze, T. (1979). Prognosis of patients with severe head injury. *Neurosurgery, 4,* 283–289.

Kelly, R. (1975). The post-traumatic syndrome: An iatrogenic disease. *Forensic Science, 6,* 17–24.

Keshavan, M. S., Channabasavanna, S. M., & Reddy, G. N. (1981). Post-traumatic psychiatric disturbances: Patterns and predictors of outcome. *British Journal of Psychiatry, 138,* 157–160.

Klonoff, P. S., Snow, W. G., & Costa, L. D. (1986). Quality of life in patients 2 to 4 years after closed head injury. *Neurosurgery, 19,* 735–743.

Kozol, H. (1945). Pretraumatic personality and psychiatric sequelae of head injury, I. *Archives of Neurology & Psychiatry, 53,* 358–364.

Kozol, H. (1946). Pretraumatic personality and psychiatric sequelae of head injury, II. *Archives of Neurology & Psychiatry, 56,* 245–275.

Levin, H., Benton, A., & Grossman, R. (1982). *Neurobehavioral consequences of closed head injury.* New York: Oxford University Press.

Levin, H., Eisenberg, H., & Benton, A. (Eds). (1989). *Mild head injury.* New York: Oxford University Press.

Levin, H., & Grossman, R. (1978). Behavioral sequelae of closed head injury. *Archives of Neurology, 35,* 720–727.

Levin, H., Grossman, R., Rose, J., & Teasdale, G. (1979). Long-term neuropsychological outcome of closed head injury. *Journal of Neurosurgery, 50,* 412–422.

Levin, H., High, W., Goethe, K., Sisson, R., Overall, J., Rhoades, H., Eisenberg, H., Kalisky, Z., & Gary, H. (1987). The neurobehavioral rating scale: Assessment of the behavioral sequelae of head injury by the clinician. *Journal of Neurology, Neurosurgery & Psychiatry, 50,* 183–193.

Levin, H., Lippold, S., Goldman, A., Handel, S., High, W., Eisenberg, H., & Zelitt, D. (1987). Neurobehavioral functioning and magnetic resonance imaging findings in young boxers. *Journal of Neurosurgery, 67,* 657–667.

Levin, H., Mattis, S., Ruff, R. M., Eisenberg, H. M., Marshall, L. F., Tabaddor, K., High, W., & Frankowski, R. (1987). Neurobehavioral outcome following minor head injury: A three-center study. *Journal of Neurosurgery, 66,* 234–243.

Lincoln, N., McGuirk, E., Mulley, G., Lendrem, W., Jones, A., & Mitchell, J. (1984). Effectiveness of speech therapy for aphasic stroke patients: A randomized controlled trial. *Lancet, 2,* 1197–1200.

Livingston, M., Livingston, H. (1985). The Glasgow Assessment Schedule: Clinical and research assessment of head injury outcome. *International Rehabilitation Medicine, 7,* 145–149.

Lundholm J., Jepsen, B., & Thornval, G. (1975). The late neurological, psychological, and social aspects of severe traumatic coma. *Scandinavian Journal of Rehabilitation Medicine, 7,* 97–100.

Lyle, D., Pierce, J., Freeman, E., Bartrop, R., Dorsch, N., Fearnside, M., Rushworth, R., & Grant, J. (1986). Clinical course in outcome of severe head injury in Australia. *Journal of Neurosurgery, 65,* 15–18.

Mandleberg, I. (1975). Cognitive recovery after severe head injury 2. Wechsler Adult Intelligence Scale during post-traumatic amnesia. *Journal of Neurology, Neurosurgery & Psychiatry, 38,* 1127–1132.

Mandleberg, I. (1976). Cognitive recovery after severe head injury 3. WAIS verbal and performance IQs as a function of post-traumatic amnesia duration and time from injury. *Journal of Neurology, Neurosurgery & Psychiatry, 39,* 1001–1007.

Mandleberg, I., & Brooks, D. (1975). Cognitive recovery after severe head injury 1. Serial testing on the Wechsler Adult Intelligence Scale. *Journal of Neurology, Neurosurgery & Psychiatry, 38,* 1121–1126.

Marshall, J. (1985). Neuroplasticity in recovery of function after brain injury. *International Review of Neurobiology, 26,* 201–247.

Matarazzo, J. (1987). Validity of psychological assessment: From the clinic to the courtroom. *Clinical Neuropsychologist, 1,* 307–314.

McKinlay, W., Brooks, D., & Bond, M. (1983). Post-concussional symptoms, financial compensation, and outcome of severe blunt head injury. *Journal of Neurology, Neurosurgery & Psychiatry, 46,* 1084–1091.

McLean, A., Dikmen, S., Temkin, N., Wyler, A., & Gale, J. (1984). Psychosocial functioning at one month after head injury. *Neurosurgery, 14,* 393–399.

McLean, A., Temkin, N., Dikmen, S., & Wyler, A. (1983). The behavioral sequelae of head injury. *Journal of Clinical Neuropsychology, 5,* 361–376.

McMillan, T., & Glucksman, E. (1987). The neuropsychology of moderate head injury. *Journal of Neurology, Neurosurgery & Psychiatry, 50,* 393–397.

Meier, M., Benton, A., & Diller, L. (Eds.). (1987). *Neuropsychological rehabilitation.* New York: Guilford Press.

Meier, M., Strauman, S., & Thompson, G. (1987). Individual differences in neuropsychological recovery: An overview. In M. Meier, A. Benton, & L. Diller (Eds)., *Neuropsychological rehabilitation* (pp. 71–110). New York: Guilford Press.

Meikle, M., Wechsler, E., Tupper, A., Benenson, M., Butler, J., Mulhall, D., & Stern, G. (1979). Comparative trial of volunteer and professional treatments of dysphasia after stroke. *British Medical Journal, 2,* 87–89.

Merskey, H., & Woodforde, J. (1972). Psychiatric sequelae of minor head injury. *Brain, 95,* 521–528.

Miller, H. (1961a). Accident neurosis: Lecture 1. *British Medical Journal,* Vol. 1, 919–925.

Miller, H. (1961b). Accident neurosis: Lecture 2. *British Medical Journal,* Vol. 1, 992–998.

Miller, J., Butterworth, J., Gudeman, S., Faulkner, E., Choi, S., Selhorst, J., Harbison, J., Lutz, H., Young, H., & Becker, D. (1981). Further experience in the management of severe head injury. *Journal of Neurosurgery, 54,* 289–299.

Miller, H., & Stern, G. (1965). The long-term prognosis of severe head injury. *Lancet, 1,* 225–229.

Minderhoud, J., Boelens, M., Huizenga, J., & Saan, R. (1980). Treatment of minor head injuries. *Clinical Neurology & Neurosurgery, 82,* 127–140.

Murray, G., Murray, L., Barlow, P., Teasdale, G., & Jennett, W. (1986). Assessing the performance and clinical impact of a computerized prognostic system in severe head injury. *Journal of Statistics & Medicine, 5,* 403–410.

Najenson, T., Mendelson, L., Schechter, I., David, C., Mintz, N., & Groswasser, Z. (1974). Rehabilitation after severe head injury. *Scandinavian Journal of Rehabilitation Medicine, 6,* 5–14.

Norman, B., & Svahn, K. (1961). A follow-up study of severe brain injuries. *Acta Psychiatrica et Neurologica Scandinavica, 37,* 236–264.

Oddy, M., Coughlan, T., Tyerman, A., & Jenkins, D. (1985). Social adjustment after closed head injury: A further follow-up 7 years after injury. *Journal of Neurology, Neurosurgery & Psychiatry, 48,* 564–568.

Overgaard, J., Christensen, S., Hvid-Hansen, O., Haase, J., Land, A., Hein, O., Pedersen, K., & Tweed, W. (1973). Prognosis after head injury based on early clinical examination. *Lancet,* Vol. 2, 631–635.

Parsons, O., & Prigatano, G. (1978). Methodological considerations in clinical neuropsychological research. *Journal of Consulting & Clinical Psychology, 46,* 608–619.

Pennebaker, J. (1982). *The psychology of physical symptoms.* New York: Springer-Verlag.

Prigatano, G., Fordyce, D., Zeiner, H., Roueche, J., Pepping, M., & Wood, B. (1984). Neuropsychological rehabilitation after closed head injury in young adults. *Journal of Neurology, Neurosurgery & Psychiatry, 47*, 505–513.

Rappaport, M., Hall, K., Hopkins, K., Belleza, T., & Cope, D. (1982). Disability rating scale for severe head trauma: Coma to community. *Archives of Physical Medicine & Rehabilitation, 63*, 118–123.

Rattok, J., Ben-Yishay, Y., Ross, B., Lakin, P., Silver, S., Thomas, L., & Diller, L. (1982). A diagnostic remedial system for basic attentional disorders in head trauma patients undergoing rehabilitation: A preliminary report. In Y. Ben-Yishay (Ed.), *Working approaches to remediation of cognitive deficits in brain-damaged persons* (pp. 177–187). NYU Medical Center, Rehabilitation Monograph #64.

Rimel, R., Giordani, B., Barth, J., Boll, T., & Jane, J. (1981). Disability caused by minor head injury. *Neurosurgery, 9*, 221–228.

Rimel, R., Giordani, B., Barth, J., & Jane, J. (1982). Moderate head injury: Completing the clinical spectrum of brain trauma. *Neurosurgery, 11*, 344–351.

Rosenthal, M., Griffith, E., Bond, M., & Miller, J. (1983). *Rehabilitation of the head injured adult*. Philadelphia: Davis.

Ruesch, J. (1944). Intellectual impairment in head injuries. *American Journal of Psychiatry, 100*, 480–496.

Ruesch, J., & Bowman, K. (1945). Prolonged post-traumatic syndromes following head injury. *American Journal of Psychiatry, 102*, 143–163.

Rusk, H., Block, J., & Lowman, E. (1969). Rehabilitation following traumatic brain damage. *Medical Clinics of North America, 53*, 677–684.

Rutherford, W. (1989). Postconcussion symptoms: Relationship to acute neurological indices, individual differences, and circumstances of injury. In H. Levin, H. Eisenberg, & A. Benton (Eds.), *Mild head injury* (pp. 21–228). New York: Oxford University Press.

Rutherford, W., Merrett, J., & McDonald, J. (1977). The sequelae of concussion caused by minor head injuries. *Lancet, 1*, 1–4.

Rutherford, W., Merrett, J., & McDonald, J. (1979). Symptoms at one year following concussion from minor head injuries. *Journal Injury, 10*, 225–230.

Sarno, M., & Levita, E. (1981). Some observations on the nature of recovery and global aphasia after stroke. *Brain & Language, 13*, 1–12.

Sarno, M., Silverman, M., & Sands, E. (1970). Speech therapy and language recovery in severe aphasia. *Journal of Speech & Hearing Research, 13*, 607–623.

Scherzer, B. (1986). Rehabilitation following severe head trauma: Results of a three year program. *Archives of Physical Medicine & Rehabilitation, 67*, 366–374.

Squire, L., & Butters, N. (Eds.). (1984). *Neuropsychology of memory*. New York: Guilford Press.

Sohlberg, M., & Mateer, C. (1989). *Introduction to cognitive rehabilitation: Theory & practice*. New York: Guilford Press.

Steadman, J., & Graham, J. (1970). Rehabilitation of the brain injured. *Proceedings of the Royal Society of Medicine, 63*, 23–32.

Stuss, D., Ely, P., Hugenholtz, H., Richard, M., LaRochelle, S., Poirier, C., & Bell, I. (1985). Subtle neuropsychological deficits in patients with good recovery after closed head injury. *Neurosurgery, 17*, 41–47.

Teasdale, G., & Jennett, B. (1976). Assessment and prognosis of coma after head injury. *Acta Neurochirurgica, 34*, 45–55.

Thienprasit, P., Fisher, S. V., & Alcorn, M. H. (1985). Long-term outcome of closed head injury. *Minnesota Medicine, 68*, 559–561.

Thomsen, I. (1974). The patient with severe head injury and his family. *Scandinavian Journal of Rehabilitation Medicine, 6*, 180–183.

Thomsen, I. (1981). Neuropsychological treatment and long-term time follow-up in an aphasic patient with very severe head trauma. *Journal of Clinical Neuropsychology, 3*, 43–51.

Timmons, M., Gasquoine, L., & Scibak, J. (1987). Functional changes with re-habilitation in very severe traumatic brain injury survivors. *Journal of Head Trauma & Rehabilitation, 2*, 64–73.

Van Zomeren, A., & Van Den Burg, W. (1985). Residual complaints of patients 2 years after severe head injury. *Journal of Neurology, Neurosurgery & Psychiatry, 48*, 21–28.

Weddell, R., Oddy, M., & Jenkins, D. (1980). Social adjustment after rehabilitation: A two-year follow-up of patients with severe head injury. *Psychological Medicine, 10*, 257–263.

Weinberg, J., Diller, L., Gordon, W., Gerstman, L., Lieberman, A., Lakin, P., Hodges, G., & Ezrachi, O. (1977). Visual scanning training effect on reading-related tasks in acquired right brain damage. *Archives of Physical Medicine & Rehabilitation, 58*, 479–486.

Weinberg, J., Diller, L., Gordon, W., Gerstman, L., Lieberman, A., Lakin, P., Hodges, G., & Ezrachi, O. (1979). Training sensory awareness and spatial organization in people with right brain damage. *Archives of Physical Medicine & Rehabilitation, 60*, 491–496.

Wilson, B. (1987). Single-case experimental designs in neuropsychological reha-bilitation. *Journal of Clinical & Experimental Neuropsychology, 9*, 527–544.

Wrightson, P., & Gronwall, D. (1981). Time off work and symptoms after minor head injury. *Injury, 12*, 445–454.

Zangwill, O. (1947). Psychological aspects of rehabilitation in cases of brain injury. *British Journal of Psychology, 37*, 60–69.

chapter 11

Estimating Cost of Care and Economic Loss in Brain Injury

M A R G A R E T A. W E S T
and D A V I D R. K N O W L E S

Many recent technological advances have improved the survival rate for persons who have sustained traumatic injuries. An estimated 7 million head injuries per year in the United States result in 500,000 hospital admissions (Rosenthal, Griffith, Bond, & Miller, 1983). The National Head Injury Foundation estimates that 50,000 to 70,000 people per year survive head injuries but continue to show significant cognitive and psychosocial deficits that interfere with independent living and employment.

Technological advances have resulted in a proliferation of new treatments and services for those who have sustained acute head injuries. However, determining the most beneficial kinds of treatment and the most appropriate length of time for treatment has become complicated and costly.

In this chapter, we describe a process for determining care and treatment needs for persons with brain injuries. We also provide analytic procedures for deriving the present value of the cost of care and of economic loss in order to determine special damages in personal injury litigation. The determination of general damages (i.e., pain and suffering) is beyond the scope of this chapter. In addition, the actual costs associated with specific individual needs vary greatly from one situation to another, and from one period of time to another.

The process of determining care and service needs for individuals who have sustained brain injury requires careful attention to the interrelationship between individually assessed present and future needs, as well as the resources and treatments available in the community. Appropriate decisions for treatment and rehabilitation depend upon understanding the various phases of treatment for brain injury, accurately identifying the status of the individual patient, selecting the most suitable treatments and services, and providing for their costs.

When determining service and treatment needs for purposes of legal settlement, one must consider several additional factors. Because persons who have sustained brain injury may have premorbid conditions that also require treatment, one must distinguish the treatment needs for these preexisting conditions from those required for the brain injury itself. This is often difficult and may not be possible, as the need for treatment as well as the premorbid condition may have been exacerbated by the injury.

In addition, we should regard some costs incurred by people with brain injuries as normal costs of living, expenses that we can reasonably expect an adult individual or family to incur. Loss of earnings and costs of medical care and treatment are separate categories in the determination of special damages. It is therefore important to distinguish the costs of treatment and services specifically associated with the brain injury from anticipated living costs. Costs of living (housing, food, maintenance, utilities, transportation, recreation, and education) are compensated in terms of loss of earnings rather than as costs of medical care and treatment. Expenses related to basic living costs, however, should be included in the medical care and treatment costs when they exceed normally anticipated costs of living.

PHASES OF TREATMENT

Each phase of treatment for brain injury is associated with a different menu of services provided by different facilities and agencies. Burr (1981) has described six stages of head injury management: (a) early management (acute care); (b) assessment of the patient's pre- and postmorbid life-style and personal social support resources including intelligence, communication, perception, and motivation; (c) goal setting by professionals, family, and the patient; (d) retraining—much of which will take place outside of "treatment times" and will involve the family; (e) return to the community; (f) review—after return to the community and periodically for an extended period of time.

These activities may be divided into four phases of treatment: acute care, active treatment, rehabilitative/remediation, and habilitation (see Table 11.1).

The goal of each phase of treatment is to return the individual to his or her "normal" functional levels. It is difficult to determine whether and if spontaneous recovery or restoration to normal functioning has occurred, especially for individuals whose brain injuries occur between the ages of

TABLE 11.1. Treatment Phases

Phases of treatment	Goal
Acute care	Spontaneous recovery/return to premorbid functional level or active treatment
Active treatment	Return to premorbid functional level or rehabilitate
Rehabilitative/remediation	Specialized training or community reintegration
Habilitation	Return to community

16 and 25. These individuals have not attained mature adult functioning prior to injury, making it difficult to best predict what their future potential will be. Predictors include premorbid functioning and accomplishments of the individual. This information is available from family history, school records, previous medical history, and documentation of participation in extracurricular or community activities. In addition, family patterns of ability and achievement may be helpful in predicting family outcomes for brain-injured patients in this age group.

Due to the complexities and time involved in the legal processes for resolving personal injury cases, in most instances of forensic neuropsychology the client will be in the rehabilitative/remediation or habilitation phases of treatment. This generally means that the individual is medically stable and has returned to the community.

Rehabilitation, according to Stedman's Medical Dictionary (1972), is "restoration, following disease, illness or injury, of ability to function in a normal or near normal manner." However, many persons with brain injury may not realistically regard "return to normal or near normal" as a goal of rehabilitation (Goldstein & Ruthoen, 1983; Rosenthal et al., 1983).

> As the rehabilitation of a head injured adult proceeds from the first few hours of devoted lifesaving intervention to attempts to remediate the deficits created by the neurologic insult, management techniques become less based on controlled scientific research and more determined by clinical experience and intuition. (Rosenthal et al., 1983) Hall has defined the purpose of rehabilitation for head-injured persons as "re-establishment of the maximum physical, intellectual, and emotional independence and dignity that is possible for that person in their particular environment" (Hall, Johnson, & Middleton, 1990).

DETERMINING THE STATUS OF THE INDIVIDUAL

Current information about a brain-injured person and his or her family is essential for determining appropriate care and treatment. A team approach is often used for assessment and rehabilitation (Gloog, 1985; Hall et al., 1990). The team typically includes a physician; nurse; occupational, physical, and recreational therapist; speech and language pathologist; vocational counselor; academic specialist; psychologist; and social worker (Warner & Vaugh, 1986). The team must maintain contact throughout the rehabilitation process (Finger & Stein, 1982), especially for the large number of persons between 16 and 25 years of age who have many normal developmental issues demanding attention as well as those specifically related to their injuries. In addition to recommending treatment and care, the team must make difficult decisions about terminating treatment for the injured person (Warner & Vaugh, 1986).

Goal setting for treatment includes (a) establishing and communicating reasonable and explicit goals based on the physical limitations imposed by the patient's neurological condition and (b) adjusting functional goals from return to normal status to probable levels of ability identified by research (Goldstein & Ruthoen, 1983).

IDENTIFYING AND LOCATING APPROPRIATE TREATMENT AND CARE

To identify treatment and locate services for a brain-injured person, we must consider the patient's expected level of recovery. Once care and treatment have been determined, the patient and family must be notified or consulted and assisted when necessary in obtaining services.

Goldstein and Ruthoen (1983) identified three major clinical problems in head injury rehabilitation: (a) Patients may have untreatable problems; (b) patients may be so physically and/or mentally debilitated that only supportive physical care is appropriate; (c) patients with a profound physical or neurological deficit may not readjust.

Treatment and rehabilitation of head-injured adults generally result from addressing one of three goals: (a) resolving the individual's remaining deficits, (b) improving coping ability, and (c) modifying the environment (Goldstein & Ruthoen, 1983). To best meet these goals, we must consider the above-mentioned major clinical problems, become familiar with the range of services available in the community, and understand the capacity of these services to meet the needs of the individual. The National Head Injury Foundation has provided informational assistance to many families of brain-injured patients and has summarized "what to look for when selecting a rehabilitation facility" in a checklist for families, which covers overall program, program structure, family involvement, rehabilitation process, cognitive aspects, behavioral aspects, vocational aspects of rehabilitation, discharge planning, and financial accountability of the program.

In the United States, the current philosophy of treatment and care for persons with disabilities mandates that these individuals should have as "normalized" a life as possible in a mainstreamed or least restrictive living environment (Rosenthal et al., 1983). In planning for care and treatment, these two ideals have complex and different meanings when applied to different situations. What is "most normalized" and "least restrictive" for one person may be "least normalized" and "most restrictive" for another. In general, however, this philosophy has enabled individuals to return as quickly as possible to community settings with as much restoration of normal daily activity as possible.

NEEDS AND OUTCOMES

Because each person who has sustained a brain injury is uniquely affected, the plan for treatment and services must be designed to meet the specific needs of the individual patient and the goals that can be reasonably established for him or her.

In forensic neuropsychology, the overall determination of care and treatment needs calls for both knowledge of an individual's current status and needs, and projections of future needs based on probable outcome of current treatment, probable next steps in treatment, and the most likely results. This process requires distinguishing among desired, possible, and probable outcomes.

Desired outcomes are those the patient, family, or care providers hold as ideal (e.g., return to normal functioning), but that, according to research findings and clinical practice, may have little or no probability or possibility of occurring. Possible outcomes are those having a small chance of occurring, according to research findings or clinical practice experience with persons having similar problems. Probable outcomes are those that according to similar research findings and clinical experience are more likely to occur than not.

Forensic practice most often deals in the realm of possible and probable outcomes of treatment and services. In designating items to be included in care and treatment, we must distinguish between possible and probable projections of future prognosis and need. The calculation of special damages in forensic neuropsychology will usually focus on the probable future outcome and treatment needs of the individual.

For example, in the state of Washington, official jury instructions define special damages in the following manner (terms in brackets refer to specific cases):

WPI 30.07: Measure of Damages—Elements of Damages—Medical Expense— Past and Future. The reasonable value of necessary medical care, treatment, and services received [and those [reasonably certain] [with reasonable probability] to be required in the future].

WPI 30.08: Measure of Damages—Elements of Damages—Loss of Earnings— Past and Future—Adult Plaintiff, Emancipated Minor Whose Parent Has Waived Waged Claim. The reasonable value of [time] [earnings] [earning capacity] [salaries] lost and the present cash value of the [time] [earnings] [earning capacity] [salaries] [reasonably certain] [with reasonable probability] to be lost in the future.

WPI 30.17: Aggravation of Preexisting Condition. If you find that before this occurrence the [plaintiff] [defendant] had a preexisting bodily condition which was causing pain or disability, and further find that because of this occurrence the condition or the pain or the disability was aggravated, then [if your verdict is in favor of the [plaintiff] [defendant]], you should consider the aggravation of the condition or the pain or disability proximately due to such aggravation, but you should not consider any condition or disability which may have existed prior to the occurrence or from which [plaintiff] [defendant] may now be suffering which was not caused or contributed to by reason of the occurrence.

WPI 34.02: Damages Arising in the Future—Discount to Present Cash Value. [Damages for _____ must be discounted to present cash value.] Present cash value as used in these instructions means the sum of money needed now, which, when added to what that sum may reasonably be expected to earn in the future, will equal the amount of the loss at the time in the future when [the expenses must be paid] [or] [the earnings would have been received] [or] [the benefits would have been received.]

The rate of interest to be applied by you in making this determination should be that rate that in your judgment is reasonable under all the circumstances taking into consideration the prevailing rates of interest in the area that can reasonably be expected from safe investments that a person of ordinary prudence, but without particular financial experience or skill, can make in this locality.

[Damages for [pain and suffering] [disability] [impairment of earning capacity] [and] [disfigurement] are not reduced to present cash value.] (Washington Supreme Court Committee on Jury Instructions, 1980)

TREATMENT AND CARE

Treatment and care needed by individuals with brain injuries can be divided into the following categories: medical care and follow-up, supplies and medication, specialized therapies and training, case management/coordination and advocacy; adaptive equipment and technology, residential support services or living programs, environmental modifications, and guardianship. When designating specific care and treatment components, we must keep in mind that each individual will require a unique combination of services from these various areas.

Medical care and follow-up comprise all required inpatient and out-patient medical treatment, which may include a range of specialty services (as determined by the residual medical problems of the brain-injured person), as well as future surgeries and hospitalization.

Supplies and medications include medications prescribed by treating physicians for residual medical problems, for example, seizure or psychotropic medication, and respiratory, bowel, or bladder care supplies.

Specialized therapies form a broad cluster of services that could include various individual professional treatments provided by many different specialists. These therapies are generally aimed at remediating residual problems for which there has been no spontaneous recovery and for which medical treatment alone is insufficient. These therapies are goal directed, aimed at improving or maintaining optimum functioning, and generally limited in duration. Examples include occupational therapy, physical therapy, psychological testing and counseling, respiratory therapy, speech therapy, and vocational training.

Psychological counseling includes a broad range of treatments such as behavioral management for the brain-injured patient and individual or group therapy for the patient and/or his or her family. In addition to counseling, psychological services may also include neuropsychological testing or psychiatric evaluation. Vocational training might include the use of prescribed assisting devices and technology, on-the-job training and support, as well as specific job skill training.

Case management/coordination and advocacy will often have been an integral component of the multidisciplinary team process described earlier. After the patient's discharge from the rehabilitation program, professionals in a number of community service programs can provide assistance in case management and advocacy according to the needs of the individual. The state or local chapter of the National Head Injury Foundation can provide assistance in locating needed case management and advocacy services.

Adaptive equipment, functional assisting technology, and transportation adaptations may be required by individuals with brain injuries who continue to have physical and/or communicative impairments. These include mobility and positioning aids such as wheelchairs or guide dogs, medical equipment such as respirators, communication aids, equipment maintenance services, and transportation.

Residential care or services for personal assistance may be needed when independent living without supervision and/or physical assistance is impossible. These services include attendant care, domestic assistance, respite care, group home residence, or skilled nursing care.

Environmental modifications may allow some persons with brain injuries to live independently. These modifications are important for persons who continue to have severe physical impairments but are able to manage daily decision making by themselves. Modifications of the existing home environment might include the construction of ramps, bathroom and kitchen alterations, and environmental controls.

A plan for the long-term needs of individuals with brain injury may provide for limited guardianship, especially for those who have chronic, severe disabilities including a significant impaired cognitive capacity. A designated family member or a court-appointed guardian may fill this role. Guardianship is an especially important consideration in cases where the cognitively brain injured person is the recipient of financial compensation and does not have adequate social and/or family support to assist in managing these funds.

The process outlined in this chapter is most readily applicable for persons whose brain injury occurred during adolescence or adulthood. In applying the process to young brain-injured children, professionals must maintain a developmental perspective that focuses on the normal tasks for each stage of development. The rate and extent to which the brain-injured child makes developmental progress are important indictors of the need for specific care and treatment.

In determining the most appropriate treatment and care for persons with brain injuries, we must take into account desired, possible, and probable outcomes and treatment needs. Special damages are determined by applying predictors derived from research and clinical practice to the synthesis of unique individual characteristics obtained from functional assessments and biomedical information. Care providers select specific services for an individual from the categories of services outlined above. The current actual costs of these services, along with projected areas of need, will provide a basis for determining the nature and cost of comprehensive, lifetime treatment and care.

PROCEDURES FOR ESTIMATING THE PRESENT VALUE OF ECONOMIC LOSS TO BRAIN INJURED PATIENTS

In identifying the type of care commonly needed by brain-injured patients, we can readily ascertain the annualized costs for the necessary services. Long-term decision making, however, must focus on the issue of determining the amount of resources needed today to ensure yearly payments into the future. In the following sections, we discuss one method for identifying the present value of future care costs and the present value of future lost earnings.

The proper identification of annual care needs for the head-injured patient is necessary to develop an annual cost estimate for providing services. However, we will address the procedure for estimating how much money is needed now to meet the future annual care needs of the patient, that is, "the present value of the future total care costs."

CRITICAL ELEMENTS IN THE ESTIMATION PROCESS

The estimation of the present value of future care costs requires that the purchasing power of the patient be assured and maintained. Today's estimate of annual cost of care must therefore also include an estimate of future expected cost changes. Normally, a historical examination of past general price changes will provide the analysis with an appropriate inflation adjustment factor. If the future estimate requires a long-term prognosis (30 to 40 years), then the examination of past price changes should also include price changes incurred over a similar time period. Because of the possible wide variation in price changes among individual components of the consumer price index during any single time period, long-term analysis should reflect overall price changes rather than price changes for any single commodity or service. Recognition that individual components within the consumer price index will tend to change over time at the approximate rate of change of the overall index reduces the speculative nature of forecasting future price changes.

A key element in developing a present value estimate is deciding upon an appropriate future time period for care needs. For several key care elements, this may involve identifying only a 3- to 5-year time period. If, however, the patient requires long-term or even lifetime care, the proper estimation of the time necessary for cost reimbursement becomes critical. An incorrect time period designated for lifetime care needs will result in a totally useless estimate of the present value of future care costs.

DEVELOPING THE PRESENT VALUE ESTIMATE

Financial instruments are currently available for an appropriate identification of the present value of future care costs. These instruments allow for inflation adjustments, the timely reimbursement of care costs, and the exact replication of the appropriate time period for the future income stream.

The cost of single-premium annuities can be an appropriate estimate of the present value of the future cost of care. Single premium annuities are financial instruments that allow an individual to purchase a future stream of income by making a one-time initial investment. For instance, anyone may purchase an annuity that will pay an individual $1,000 a month for life. These annuities may be purchased from large insurance corporations in order to ensure the conservative nature of the investment. Care providers and recovering patients must identify the amount of money needed now to replace a future income stream—properly adjusted for expected inflation as well as for the appropriate period of time needed for care. Thus, if the price of the annuity is the cost associated with replacing lost income, then it is also equal to the present value of that income.

One can purchase annuities that will guarantee any monthly amount deemed necessary to pay for the costs of care. These payments can also increase according to some predetermined inflation adjustment per year for the duration of the annuity. Most importantly, the time period of the annuity may be fixed for a specific period of time or guaranteed for the lifetime of the individual. The ability of the annuity to guarantee payment for an individual's lifetime eliminates the need to attempt to accurately predict length of life—one of the most speculative elements in the present value estimation process.

Present value estimations that focus on one specific time period for estimating lifetime payments such as the normal life expectancy rates in actuarial tables are obviously subject to the validity of the time period selected. If the person lives longer than the time period selected, the present value estimate will underestimate the money needed now to replace a future income stream for life. Cost of care will not be reimbursed beyond the time period selected during the present value estimation process. If the individual dies earlier than predicted, the estimate will overstate the money necessary for care costs in present value terms.

The selection of an annuity that guarantees payment for life is thus the most appropriate way to ascertain the amount of money needed now to ensure or to replace a future income.

Annuities from large insurance corporations clearly represent safe investments. An annuity eliminates the need for the patient or guardian to continually reinvest funds over long periods of time. Obviously, the more often one makes investment decisions, the more likely that mistakes will occur to disrupt the cash flow process.[1]

THE PRESENT VALUE DETERMINATION OF LOST EARNINGS CAPACITY

Head-injured patients very commonly lose a significant portion of their earning capacity. In this section, we will describe a procedure for deriving a reliable estimate of the present value of lost earnings due to the disabilities resulting from head injuries.

Earning capacity for patients disabled prior to the development of any significant work history must be estimated using data that identify average tendencies for specific labor groups in the country. National statistics produced by the Department of Commerce and the Department of Labor's Bureau of Labor Statistics (BLS) provide the crucial framework for earnings capacity analysis.

The first component used to estimate earning capacity is the work life expectancy of an individual. The BLS published work and life expectancy tables that control for an individual's gender, age, and level of education (Bureau of Labor and Statistics, 1986). BLS tables on work life expectancy estimate the number of years an individual will spend in the work force (employed or seeking employment) during his or her expected lifetime. Available statistics allow the BLS to properly control for the probability of an individual's premature death or withdrawal from the labor market. Alternative approaches to estimating work life expectancy (such as subtracting chronological age from predicted age of retirement) are inappropriate.

Work life tables indicate that people will enjoy longer work life expectancies if they are currently in the labor force. In addition, the higher the education level, the longer the participation in the work force. The BLS also predicts that, on average, men will have longer work life expectancies than women. The BLS periodically updates work life expectancy tables to account for changes in the labor force over time.

Estimates of the normal variance of work life expectancy clearly indicate that earning capacity varies significantly when age, education, and gender are considered (Table 11.2). For instance, 22-year-old men with 15 years or more of formal education will participate in the labor force over 6 years more than 22-year-old men who quit high school. Among 22-year-old women, there is a 10-year difference in work life expectancy between those with 15 or more years of formal education and those who quit high school. Data are also available on the variances of work life expectancy by race.

TABLE 11.2. Variance in Work Life Expectancy by Age, Gender, and Education

	Years of education					
	Male			Female		
Age	< 12	12–14	≥ 15	< 12	12–14	≥ 15
18	34.5	39.5	—	21.9	29.6	—
22	32.0	36.6	38.9	20.2	27.2	30.7
35	22.0	25.4	27.7	14.8	19.2	21.7
50	9.6	12.8	14.6	8.3	10.3	10.9
60	4.9	5.9	7.4	2.3	5.4	5.4

Note. From *Worklife Estimates: Effects of Race and Education* (p. 14), 1986, U.S. Department of Labor, Bureau of Labor Statistics, Bulletin #2254.

After identifying the appropriate time period for estimating loss in earning capacity, one must calculate an average yearly earnings figure. Again, for individuals with no earnings history, one must obtain estimates from national averages published by the federal government. The Bureau of the Census publishes yearly earnings data controlled for gender, education, age, and status in the work force. The federal government has published these income figures since at least the mid-1950s.

Average yearly earnings throughout an individual's work life can be determined on the basis of education level. For example, year-round full-time male workers who have 1 to 3 years of college education and are between the ages of 25 and 29 earned $21,212 in 1984 (U.S. Department of Commerce, 1984). Women with identical characteristics earned $15,565 in the same year.

Obviously, for brain-injured patients who have extensive work histories, earnings capacity is determined on the basis of actual past earnings. Actual data on earning capacity, if available, are normally better for estimating future earnings.

Normal fringe benefits available to workers must also be included in the loss analysis. The U.S. Chamber of Commerce publishes employee benefit surveys on a yearly basis (U.S. Chamber of Commerce, 1985). Although there is a large array of potential benefits available to some employees, pension and medical insurance plans are most common. The percentage of total payroll attributed to fringe benefits has varied from year to year. Currently, the percentage is slightly over 12%.

ESTIMATING THE PRESENT VALUE OF LOST EARNINGS

Work life expectancy, average annual earnings, and the average fringe benefit percentage are the necessary components for estimating the present value of the entire future expected earnings stream. The present value computation must generate a figure equal to the total number of dollars necessary today to ensure a future income to replace the disabled worker's lost income. The computation must account for expected future salary increases so that the worker's real income is maintained.

The procedure for deriving the present value of lost earnings capacity is similar to the one discussed in the section on care costs. As an example, a 22-year-old male with 12 to 14 years of education will spend 36.6 years in the labor force (Table 11.2). The Department of Commerce document will allow us to estimate the average earnings he would receive during his work life. Accounting for the additional money necessary to cover expected fringe benefits generates the annual figure needed to replace the future earnings lost by the patient. The remaining component needed for the present value calculation is the expected future annual rate of change in earnings, generated by carefully examining the past annual rates of change.

Once we have this information, we can ascertain the present value of the future lost income stream by simply identifying the cost of an annuity that will pay out the correct yearly amount of compensation for the specified time period, and that will include an annual adjustment to compensate for expected future wage changes.

Annuity quotations for the replacement of specific future income streams are readily available on the market, which consists of numerous insurance corporations. To ensure the safety of the investment, the individuals should purchase the annuities from large corporations that are rated "A+" by the A. M. Best Report. Purchasing an annuity from a firm is tantamount to investing in that corporation. The price of the annuity includes the investment yield that one will receive from the firm. In essence, purchasing an annuity from a large insurance corporation allows the unsophisticated investor to tap into higher yields from the insurance corporation's relatively sophisticated portfolio.

SUMMARY

In this chapter, we have outlined a process for determining special damages for a person with a brain injury, a process that integrates clinical information and expertise into the development of a plan for present and future care and treatment as well as the determination of economic loss. In addition, we have described a procedure for providing adequate financial resources for meeting these needs over the lifetime of the individual.

A team of professionals representing various disciplines should work together to determine the most appropriate assessment, treatment, and rehabilitation of the brain-injured individual. The present costs of this treatment and care can then become the basis for determining the income needed to ensure provision of care and to compensate for economic loss associated with diminished earning capacity. The information in this chapter should be used as a guide for developing an overall long-range care plan to meet the needs and costs associated with the care and support of brain-injured individuals.

REFERENCES

Bureau of Labor & Statistics, U.S. Department of Labor. (1986). *Worklife estimates: Effects of race and education* (Bulletin #2252). Washington, DC: U.S. Government Printing Office.

Burr, M. (1981). The rehabilitation and long-term management of the adult patient with head injury. *Australian Family Physician, 101*, 14–18.

Finger, S., Stein, D. G. (1982). *Brain damaged and recovery, research and clinical perspectives.* New York: Academic Press.

Gloog, D. (1985). Rehabilitation after head injury: Behavior and emotional problems, long term needs, and the requirements for services. *British Medical Journal, 290*, 3–23.

Goldstein, G., & Ruthoen, L. (1983). *Rehabilitation of the brain damaged adult.* New York: Plenum Press.

Hall, D. M. B., Johnson, S. L. J., Middleton, J. (1990). Rehabilitation of head injured children, *Archives of Disease in Childhood, 65*(5), 553–556.

Rosenthal, M., Griffith, E. R., Bond, M. R., & Miller, J. D. (Eds.). (1983). *Rehabilitation of the head injured adult.* Philadelphia: Davis.

Stedman's Medical Dictionary (22nd ed.). (1972). Baltimore: Williams & Wilkens.

U.S. Chamber of Commerce. (1985). *Employee benefits, 1985.* Washington, DC: U.S. Government Printing Office.

U.S. Department of Commerce. (1984). *Bureau of current population reports, consumer income* (Series p-60, #157). Washington, DC: U.S. Government Printing Office.

Warner, S. V. (1986). The social worker's role in long term rehabilitation of head injury survivors: A new look at parent social work alliance. In *Improved care and treatment for the chronically ill child.* Washington, DC: National Center for Education in Maternal and Child Health.

Washington Supreme Court Committee on Jury Instructions (1980). *Washington pattern jury instructions, civil* (2nd ed.). St. Paul, MN: West Publishing Co.

NOTE

1. *Editors' note.* The reader must be aware that no investment is without risk. The continuity of periodic payouts such as annuities depends on the continuing fiscal solvency of the company issuing the annuity. Nothing in this chapter should be taken as specific financial advice. Such advice should be sought from reputable professional financial consultants.

Commonly Asked Questions in Testimony

A. Questions dealing with qualification to expert witness status and experience as expert.

What is your profession?
Do you practice?
Are you licensed?
What professional organizations are you a member of?

With regard to your membership in the professional societies you have testified to, what are the qualifications for its members?

Describe your educational background.
Describe the nature of your current professional work.
What is the source of your referrals?
Do you take direct referrals by patients?
What are the components of your practice?
How often do you see patients referred through attorneys?

Of these patients, what percentage was referred by plaintiffs' attorneys as opposed to defense attorneys?

Name texts and journals you refer to in your work as neuropsychologist.
What are the texts you consider authoritative in the area of neuropsychology? [Comment: Unless you agree completely with every detail in a text, do not accept it as "authoritative." Indicate specifically which statement you agree with if you use a text as a source.]

How many times have you (given depositions testified) in court? What are your billing rates as expert witness?

What do you charge for a (neuropsychological battery/clinical interview/ _____ test)?

How many times have you (given/interpreted) the _____ test/battery?

B. Questions relating to the nature of the relationship with the patient, employing agency or attorney, awareness of issues relating to the legal case, and rendering of opinions.

When were you first contacted in this case?
Who first contacted you in this case?
What were you asked to do?
What was sent to you to review?

Were there documents you reviewed in reaching your diagnosis other than what appears in your file?

Did you have conversations with the referring attorney about this case?
Do you know the circumstances of the accident?
How many hours have you spent on this case so far?

Does your report contain all your opinions in this case? [Comment: In your answer, do not exclude the possibility that you might offer other opinions when asked in the future. The report typically reflects what you anticipated might be important at the time, but other questions might come up on which you might have an expert opinion.]

Are these all the opinions you will present during testimony? [Comment: Unless you are absolutely sure all conceivable questions have been asked and answered, qualify your answer such as "to the best of my knowledge at this time."]

C. Questions dealing with definitions of neuropsychological terms and practice.

Is neuropsychology an art or a science?
Define neuropsychology.
Are there further subspecialty areas within neuropsychology?
How does neuropsychology differ from psychology?
What is the task of a neuropsychologist?
Is there a place in medicine for neuropsychology?

How would you distinguish a (neurologist/psychiatrist/physician) from a neuropsychologist?

From a neuropsychological point of view, how would you define brain damage?

How many neuropsychological tests exist in the literature?

What neuropsychological functions should be addressed by a comprehensive examination?

D. Questions dealing with the basic physiological and psychological knowledge base of neuropsychology.

Is the degree of impact, the amount of trauma to the skull, determinative of whether or not there would be brain damage?

Are there instances where there has been a history of impact with no positive EEGs (electroencephalogram), MRIs (magnetic resonance imaging) or CTs (computerized axial tomography), but evidence of significant deficits after the accident?

Can you have an X-ray, CT scan, and MRI, each of which does not demonstrate a lesion, and still have damage to neurons in the brain?

Is the brain the organ of behavior?
Define secondary gain.
Define malingering.

Do you agree that there are many ways to determine whether or not someone is malingering?

Define somatization.
Does age affect one's ability to cope with head injury? Is age at time of trauma a variable in outcome?
Do brain functions deteriorate with age?
Where does memory reside in the brain?
What is a postconcussive syndrome?
Can one be unconscious without a concussion?

Is there a higher incidence of alcohol or drug abuse in patients who had a head injury?

What is the difference between focal damage and diffuse damage?
What are the essential features of dementia?

Is it possible that multifactorial psychological overlay could be the cause of behavioral problems? How would this come about?

Is it common for a brain-damaged person to be depressed? Is this caused by organic or psychological factors?

What is an iatrogenic disease?
Define concussion.

Define contusion.

What is a "functional" disorder?

Is somebody who is brain damaged forever brain damaged?

Can the body grow new neurons after trauma?

Can chronic pain be found as a result of brain damage?

Is it possible that neurological signs don't show up immediately after trauma?

Does performance on neuropsychological tests depend on the patients's cooperation?

Describe the normal course of recovery after trauma.

Is the force of impact significant in determining the probability of the brain being
    bruised from hitting the skull?

What is the cause of shearing in trauma?

What are the major structures in the brain?

What is the function of the major structures of the brain?

Do the right and left hemispheres have different functions?

How much space is there between the brain and the skull?

Define (glial cells/neurons/axons/dendrites/synapse/grey matter/white matter).

Define coup and contrecoup in brain injury.

How does the brain present itself when taken outside the skull?

What keeps the brain structures intact in our head?

What is the function of the frontal lobes?

When you are referring to the central nervous system, are you referring to the
    brain?

How many neurons are contained in the average human brain?

What is the typical time course of recovery after injury?

**E. Questions relating to a specific assessment procedure, interpretation,
and psychometrics of tests employed.**

Do you personally remember this patient?

How much time did you spend with this patient?

Did anyone other than you interview or test the patient?

When a patient presents himself/herself to you, what procedure do you follow?

Do you give instructions to your assistant prior to him/her giving the tests?

What is the purpose of each test?

What does the (Wechsler Adult Intelligence Scale/Wechsler Memory Scale/etc.)
    consist of?

How long does the _____ take?

What is the patient asked to do on the _____ test?

Would you agree that patients who take the test respond to additional stress or coaxing?

Are there any tests or subtests that are more and those that are less sensitive to organic brain damage?

Is there a single test that you could give that would allow you to make a diagnosis of organic brain damage?

What is the incidence of people with no history of brain damage or illness who will fall below "cut-off" on tests?

Define false positives/false negatives.
Define (standard deviation/standard error of the mean/normal curve).

Is it important to use ("age-correlated"/gender-corrected/education corrected) norms?

Does cultural background have an impact on test performance?
Does a person's taking medication affect test performance?

F. Questions relating to areas of agreement/disagreement among experts.

You have read Dr. _____ 's (report/deposition). Do you agree or disagree with his/her conclusions? [Comment: Unless you agree or disagree with every detail of the document, do not give a generic yes or no but refer to specifics.]

Do you find Dr. _____ a reliable (neuropsychologist/neurologist/physician/etc.)? [Comment: Aside from information regarding basis credentials, e.g., license or certification, it is unlikely that an "expert opinion" can be offered. Most experts have not studied the career of other experts. In this case, a proper reply might be to acknowledge that the respondent is not "an expert on expert" and stick to the data base.]

In a perfect world, would two neuropsychologists who administer the same tests reach the same conclusions? [Comment: Even in a less-than-perfect world, scores on tests administered according to standard procedures to patients whose biopsychosocial circumstances remain unchanged should be very comparable on repeat testing (correcting for practice effects). The interpretation of the test results is a function of the experience and training of the neuropsychologist as well as the data base. In the perfect world, these factors would match; in the real world, they may not.]

Have you ever been wrong in a professional opinion?